A Kind of Homecoming

by E. R. BRAITHWAITE

A Kind of Homecoming is both an illuminating portrayal of contemporary Africa and an enthralling account of an experience universal in its appeal—the return to one's roots.

The author is a Negro, born in British Guiana in northeastern South America and educated in New York City and England, who had never seen Africa before visiting Ghana, Sierra Leone, Guinea and Liberia. The first three are newly-independent nations while the latter is the world's oldest Negro republic.

Braithwaite talked to government leaders, teachers, tribesmen, old-time colonials . . . Africans of every station and degree of development . . . as he made his way from the coastal cities to the remote hinterland. As a Negro he associated with the Africans as one of themselves, and yet as a non-African, he was able to view the current African scene objectively and report on it in incisive, human terms. Running through the whole narrative are the reactions of a sensitive, perceptive human being as he probes the lives of people who are shouldering new responsibilities.

Here is a close-up, intimate view of the African—groping, building, learning and experimenting—as he searches for a better kind of society and a better way of life in the future.

To Braithwaite, the new sights and sounds that he heard in the ancient lands of his ancestors seemed strangely familiar to him and his journey proved to be a special Kind of Homecoming.

By the Same Author

TO SIR, WITH LOVE

A
KIND   *E. R. Braithwaite*
OF
HOMECOMING

Prentice-Hall, Inc.

ENGLEWOOD CLIFFS, N. J.

Table of Contents

Part One	Guinea	1
Part Two	Sierra Leone	55
Part Three	Liberia	171
Part Four	Ghana	219

A
Kind
of
Homecoming

Part One
GUINEA

Today, February 17, 1961, I set foot on African soil for the first time. I had expected and anticipated a spiritual excitement, a kind of dramatic consciousness of identity with the spirits of ancestors long dead and unknown, and I wished very hard to feel something, anything truly different after the long hours in the airplane. But all that happened was the heat, which soon had my shirt sticking to my back in the short walk from the plane to the airport lounge. Airport guards with rifles, or with pistols holstered at their sides, yet wearing friendly smiles and saluting the travelers with friendly gestures of welcome. The sky blue and clear and limitlessly empty except for the large wry-necked carrion crows which circled lazily, patiently confident that sooner or later they would find a meal.

The long ride to the hotel in Conakry, capital of the former French colony of Guinea, along a narrow asphalt road fringed with trees suddenly and sweetly familiar, the trees of boyhood and hometown. Cocoanut palms curving sinuously upward, their tufted tops swaying in disdainful majesty above the green banana and papaya trees. Mango trees, so deeply green each leaf seemed to be in shadow, breadfruit and laden orange trees. Here and there a clump of the sweet cassava plant, or the blooming hibiscus and bougainvillea. And now it came to me in a tear-starting rush. I had seen it all before in the British Guiana of my boyhood, all of it: the crows and the trees, and the low huts straw-thatched, with walls and floors of packed clay. As the car sped along the road I caught glimpses of familiar faces long remembered and I had the feeling that if I leaned out and called out a name, someone would answer with pleased recognition.

As I approached the center of Conakry, the feeling of being in familiar surroundings decreased, probably because the buildings seemed so strange, square and shuttered. Ten-thirty in the morning and everywhere groups of people, sitting at doorways or outside the shops, or in the shade beside the road. Men, always the men sitting, dozing, or in friendly argument among themselves. Men

3

talking and laughing while women moved among them with bundles or large household vessels balanced casually on their heads, and tiny children strapped straddle-legged on their backs.

In front of the shops the innumerable tailors, each one pedaling industriously on his treadle-type sewing machine, undisturbed by the talk and laughter of the groups of men around them who had plenty of time to stand, stare and comment. And the others, those easily identifiable as strangers, always in groups of four or more, strong-featured men who reminded me of the drillers and survey-ors and oilmen of Maracaibo, but without their easy banter and ribaldry. Russians, Czechs, and Chinese, all looking serious and dedicated as if determined to prove that they were not tourists.

I called at the bank to change some travelers checks into the local currency, but finding it closed during the midday lunch period (not much lunch for the staff, I thought, for now is the time of Ramadan, the Moslem month of fasting), I wandered around and sat in the Bar St. Germain for a beer and sandwich. Nine Chinese, eight men and one woman, sat at a nearby table waiting to be served the lunch they ordered, meanwhile reading technical pamphlets and books, with hardly a single word exchanged between them. The waiter, a friendly little man originally from somewhere in the West Indies, noticed my interest in the Chinese group.

"We call them the miracle workers," he said. "They build well and very quickly. Have you seen the Exposition Building?"

I replied that I didn't know there was one.

"Nice," he said, "very nice. And they build it like that—" and he snapped finger and thumb to indicate high speed.

The men were lean, hard-looking and young; the woman slim and petite, her hair severely short, her face impassive and without make-up. When the food arrived, they kept their books open and read while they ate, as if the food held little interest for them and was merely a necessary interruption in the flow of more positive endeavors.

Other people dropped into the bar and my friend the waiter would say "Russian" or "American." One partly graying man approached my table, greeted me in French and sat down. He said he was a correspondent from Yugoslavia, in Guinea to cover the impending visit of Marshal Tito.

4

"Now I know why there are all the flags and street decorations," I said.

"Well, partly," he replied. "Most of them are left over from the visit of the Russian Premier, who was here a short while ago."

I returned to the bank in the afternoon. The staff was just arriving and was busy shaking hands with each other in the French manner. The bank is a large building, the offices at street level. With several other customers, white and black, I waited at the counter while the staff showered each other with courtesies. They were all very young, and when they were finally seated at their desks and had begun their various activities, they seemed very slow and inexperienced. Typewriters and adding machines were operated slowly and ponderously, and I had the feeling that they were all in training, if not completely new to the job. When finally a clerk approached me, he took what seemed to be an awfully long time to complete several forms. Then I was told to sit and wait, so I stood at a barred window and watched the movement in the street outside.

People spitting all over the place, so with some disgust I turned away.

"Awful, isn't it?"

A man was standing beside me. He too must have been watching the people.

"I mean the spitting," he went on. "But there's a reason for it. They're fasting, most of them, and what with the heat and the dust, it is very difficult to swallow the saliva, so they spit; same thing in all Moslem countries. Try fasting and you might feel yourself wanting to spit too."

He was tall and thin and very red, as if new to the heat and strong sunshine. He spoke in English, each word clearly and carefully enunciated, as is the case when one is using a foreign language. His thin, bony face had a sharp, intelligent look, but pleasant with curiosity and understanding.

"It must be difficult for them in this heat," I replied, not knowing what else to say.

"They're accustomed to it," he said. "It's one of the things that binds these people together, their religion, and helps to rally them for political action when necessary. Which part of Africa you from?"

"I'm from the West Indies," I answered, "and I am visiting Africa for the first time to take a look at things."

"I come from Prague," he told me. "I'm a teacher. I am here helping to train teachers."

So we talked about teaching. I mentioned that I had taught in schools in Britain, and referred to the kind of problems I had encountered there.

In Guinea, he said, there was never any problem of discipline because religious and other influences conditioned the child to respect his elders, and the educated person commanded a position of prestige. The main problem was how best to meet the acute shortage of schools, teaching staff and equipment, and at the same time keep pace with the hunger for education which was everywhere in evidence. As I spoke with him I realized that he had a real and simple belief in human dignity, and his work was important in that it was geared to a readiness to be sympathetic and helpful.

I noticed that while talking, the time had slipped away and we were still waiting for our money, so I approached the clerk who had attended me and asked if there was any reason for the delay.

"Everything is ready," he replied, "but the cashier has not yet returned from lunch."

He was very matter-of-fact about it, and I felt myself becoming impatient and irritable, especially as the clerk casually ignored me and went on laboriously adding figures on a machine.

The Czech teacher said, "This is not Paris or London, you know. After all, there's nowhere to go in a hurry, so don't be too impatient. These young people are trying to do a very complicated job without much experience. When the French left, they took every piece of equipment they could with them, together with the experienced staff, so these young men and women have to learn as they go, and banking is not the easiest of business transactions. Nevertheless, they are making it work, no matter how slow it seems. As they become more and more accustomed to the routine of the work and the techniques of international finance, the whole thing will speed up. And here's something else. When it is finally running smoothly, all these young people will have the satisfaction of knowing that they did it themselves—that's important, you know."

Soon afterward the cashier arrived, a good-looking, obviously pregnant young woman. She quickly checked through the forms, made some rapid calculations on a small adding machine and paid me the amount I required in Guinea currency. From the speed with which she worked in such contrast to her colleagues, it was clear that she was very experienced, and, pregnant though she was, very much needed.

Once out in the street the Czech teacher remarked, "That's a sign of the times. All the white faces were on the wrong side of the counter."

I understood his little joke.

When I left him I wandered away from the center of town through the narrow streets lined with the all-purpose shops of the Lebanese traders, past a high wall behind which could be heard the all-too-familiar sounds of children's voices. I followed the wall around to a wooden gateway and entered a small courtyard where about a hundred children sat in tight rows behind long, narrow, trestle-type desks and repeated the instructions of a teacher as he explained simple arithmetical tables with the assistance of a blackboard. I paused, but he noticed me and came over.

I apologized for interrupting his lesson but he seemed quite pleased to have a visitor, especially when I mentioned that I too had been a teacher. As soon as the children saw me they all stood up very quietly, a gesture of respect I had received previously only in the "public schools" of Britain, and it occurred to me that whatever the shortages in other fields, this new State was not ignoring the importance of social niceties. The class was mixed, boys and girls of about eleven years, all simply, sometimes poorly, dressed, without any attention to uniformity, but their black faces and lively eyes shone with their hunger for knowledge and information. The teacher wore khaki slacks and shirt, and simple sandals of broad strips of leather fastened to thick rubber soles which I suspected had been cut from old motorcar tires. On his brown, intelligent face he sported a sparse, scraggly beard which did nothing for him, nor took anything from him—it was simply there, that's all. His

7

French was beautifully articulated, and I later discovered that he had studied for eleven years in Dakar.

"Are you over here to help us, as a teacher?" he asked.

"Oh, no," I replied. "I'm merely wandering around Africa looking for things to write about. My first visit, you know."

"Welcome again," he said, and we shook hands again. "But it's a pity you're not a teacher. We desperately need all we can get. See for yourself. I need at least another teacher to help me here."

"Any likelihood of the situation improving?"

"Oh, we're getting help," he replied, "but not enough quickly enough. People are coming to help us from China and Czechoslavakia and Yugoslavia, and the West Indies. You know, Martinique and Guadaloupe, where they speak French. Sometimes it even becomes a bit complicated when some of the new teachers have to teach through interpreters until they can manage in French. Damned funny at times." His laugh was easy and pleasant.

"I suppose that limits the scope of the teaching you are able to do," I suggested.

"Not too much," he replied, "because we are adapting our educational plans to our needs, and right now we need artisans and agricultural workers more than we need clerks and potential bureaucrats. So we are concentrating on primary education to supply a broad general base, then in the secondary schools we are providing technical education planned to create an interest in the country and a willingness to contribute to its development. The child who gets an education must appreciate that the State needs his trained usefulness."

"You mentioned teachers from China, Czechoslavakia, etc.," I said. "Do not they present the possible danger of introducing communistic ideas into the minds of the youngsters?"

Immediately his face lost its pleasant, friendly mien; his eyes shone with controlled anger and he replied, "You Americans are all alike. Black or white, you're all the same."

In a hasty attempt at apology I said, "I'm sorry. I did not mean to offend you by asking that question. Incidentally, I'm not an American, I'm a West Indian. Please forgive me if my question annoyed you."

"I'm not annoyed," he said, carefully. "I'm merely sorry for

8

you, because you Americans have developed such a phobia about the word 'Communist' that you see nothing but Communists wherever you go. Here in Guinea we are desperately trying to transform independence from a political attainment into an economic reality. To do that we need help, and we are not too proud to accept help, but we will not accept any help if it means jeopardizing any part or aspect of that independence we sacrificed so much to achieve."

I looked at the children and noticed that they were watching somewhat anxiously. Something of the teacher's changed mood must have transmitted itself very quickly to them and they were in silent response to it. The teacher himself seemed suddenly aware of the children's interest, because he turned and rapidly wrote a few simple problems on the blackboard which he instructed them to copy and solve in their notebooks. When they were busy at this he turned once more to me.

"Maybe you Americans would like to help us, *if*," he emphasized that little word with hands and shoulders and eyes—it even had a strangely sibilant sound as he hissed it at me. "Maybe you would help us, but only on your terms, because you neither understand nor believe in African neutrality, and that is simply explained by the fact that, as yet, you do not believe or respect Africans." He paused and shrugged, a tired, patient gesture. "I am not a Communist; I'm merely a teacher trying to do my job as well as I am able. This is not a Communist country and I think I can safely say it never will be. The day you black Americans understand what personal independence really means, you will begin to understand how we feel about our country."

He was not angry. But I was becoming bored with being called an American and being blamed for their supposed sins of omission. I made one more try.

"I'm not an American, I'm from the West Indies."

"Oh, yes, so you said," he answered, smiling suddenly. "But you sound like an American. You ought to stay here awhile and become—what is the term?—'brain-washed'." He laughed at this and I joined him, and on that easier note I left him.

The afternoon sun was very warm and I made my way in the general direction back to my hotel, anticipating a refreshing shower and a change from my sweat-damp clothes. Here and there I saw

9

groups of workmen swarming over the skeleton of a new building, and it was with something of a shock that I realized that nowhere in sight was there a single piece of mechanical equipment—everything was being done by hand. Ladders were makeshift arrangements from roughly cut saplings, as were all other wooden supports in use; concrete was mixed by hand and passed by a chain of hands to the place desired. Here and there I saw a European directing operations, and I guessed from their Slavic features that they were Eastern European. But in spite of what the young Guinea teacher had just said, there was not much evidence of concentrated popular effort. In fact, Conakry was, to me, singularly depressing.

*

Back at the hotel I tried, without success, to obtain a newspaper: the desk-clerk informed me that there were no newspapers in Guinea nowadays. "We're putting first things first," he said, "and at the moment we cannot afford either the money or the time necessary to run a newspaper. Each day the Department of Information puts out a news bulletin, and we find that it is enough for our needs."

Later, however, I found a two-week-old copy of the *Manchester Guardian* in a drawer of the wardrobe. It was the first time I can remember reading a newspaper so thoroughly. After a shower and change of clothing, I sat in the lounge of the hotel drinking canned pineapple juice, looking out across the wide expanse of rocky, muddy beach, crudely exposed by the receding tide, and wondering how long it would be before I could get my face into some real, fresh, Afrcan, ripened-on-the-tree fruit as a change from the tinned variety which I was drinking.

Around six o'clock in the evening I decided to take another stroll around town, but this time I'd wear slacks and sports shirt, and be as much as possible like the local people. "After all," I thought, "I look as African as any of them, and it should not be too difficult for me to fade into the general background." So, suitably dressed, or so I thought, I set out, and was soon mingling with the groups which moved about the now-shady streets. But time

10

and again people would look at me, and smiling, greet me, *"Bon soir, Monsieur, ça va?"* and I would reply with, *"Bon soir, ça va bien."* There was no mistaking the fact that they knew I was a stranger.

I stopped outside a tiny wooden shop where some young men were industriously carving animal and human figures from ivory tusks, under the watchful eye of a bald ancient with the long neck and narrow head of a Mandingo tribesman. I was fascinated by their deft, sure application to their craft, now grossly commercialized to meet the increasing demands of tourists from many countries. Twin female figures delicately carved from small brown tusks caught my attention and I inquired of one of the young men, *"Combien?"*

Instead of answering my query, he asked, *"Americain?"*

"Non."

"Quel pays?"

"Guayanne Anglaise," I replied.

"O, le pays du Doctor Jagan, non?" he inquired. I looked in amazement at him. How come he knew of Cheddi Jagan and British Guiana when there were no newspapers and the news bulletin was primarily devoted to internal affairs.

"Oui, combien," I repeated.

The price he requested was very much in excess of what I could afford and I thanked him and wandered on, through a large, self-service store which reminded me of the Presunic stores in Paris, crowded with shoppers, mostly women with sleeping infants tied securely to their backs.

The streets in the center of Conakry were now alive with people, dogs, goats and taxicabs, yet for me the feeling of depression remained; there was little gaiety or that indefinable something which gives to any town or city or village its own special élan. I wandered on toward the administrative section of town, where the streets were wide and shaded with the ubiquitous large mango trees, all in blossom and hovering protectingly over the buildings which housed the various ministries.

I passed a group of women dressed in their national costume, with wide flaring skirts and an overmantle of embroidered gauze. On their heads they wore headkerchiefs of brightly patterned

11

cotton, tied to show wide points rising elegantly from each side like the wings of some exotic bird. Immediately the rusty wheels of my memory quickened into gear and I recalled seeing women similarly dressed long ago in my native British Guiana on market day in the countryside.

Yes, memory was clearer now. I could even remember seeing a photograph of my grandmother wearing that distinguishable headkerchief. I looked closely at the women, observing their finely shaped features, black and silky smooth. Did my origins lie somewhere here with these people? I could not understand a word they said, for they spoke an African dialect, but they smiled at me and I bowed as I passed. I was feeling something now and it was a good feeling. For the very first time in many years I was walking among people without being conscious that I was different from them; although a stranger to Africa, I felt sufficiently identified to be at ease, comfortable, to belong. Passers-by might readily recognize that I was a stranger to Guinea, but unless my speech gave me away, it would be assumed that I was African, from some other territory or State. A stranger but not strange, because I was by origin a fragment of the whole. Back in England, persons often asked me, "From which part of Africa are you?" because on first contact they immediately associated my black skin with Africa. Now, in an African town, among Africans, I felt at ease, and realized with something of a shock that the white faces looked strange to me.

A group of men standing outside the office of Air France chatted softly but earnestly about the Congo and Patrice Lumumba's death, for which they blamed the United Nations in general and the negligence of Ghana in particular. I sat nearby to listen, surprised at the amount of information they seemed to have. With them the Congo was a *cause célèbre,* and indcated the need to so order their own internal affairs that it would never be necessary for the United Nations or any other organization to intervene. From a passing taxi a radio blared forth the sound of children's voices in song, something in praise of President Sekou Touré, their voices too loud and evidently untrained, but undeniably enthusiastic. As the men spoke of the Congo it was clear that Lumumba's death, and in such strange circumstances, crystallized

12

in their minds the evils of all colonialists and their policies. One man made a reference to Tshombe and spat on the ground to show his disgust. From what they said I learned that the Guinean forces in the Congo had been recalled; some had already returned home. Now and then someone spoke of "We in Africa," or "We Africans," but I had the feeling that, for them, Africa meant Guinea, because there was little or no reference to any of the other African States. It was very exciting to watch them and notice that the language they used, their mannerisms and fondness for the philosophical turn of phrase were all very French indeed, but none of it detracted from their dignity or belief in the rightness of their opinions.

Back at the hotel I had an excellent dinner, and from my corner table observed the other diners, some of whom were guests at the hotel, others officials resident in the town and able to afford the exorbitant prices charged for the meals. Bits of conversation could be heard in Russian, Yugoslav, Czech, Chinese, German, French, Arabic, English and American. Eating was a long, drawnout affair, because after dinner there was nowhere to go and nothing to do for entertainment.

Having eaten I sat at the bar next to a tall, very black man, who, between sips from his glass, held it up to the light as if determined to discover how such a harmless-looking liquid could produce the kind of effect it was having on him. His hands, holding the glass fondly like a communicant, were large and powerful-looking, as were the shoulders and chest which bulged the thin, gaily colored shirt, and I was sure that when he stood up he'd be six feet tall or more. His thin face was dominated by a large aquiline nose and marked high on each cheek with three vertical incisions which made him look rather like a pirate in festive mood. I ordered beer and surreptitiously studied the antics of my companion as they were reflected in the mirror over the bar. He must have caught me at it, because he suddenly turned to me and asked, "Stranger?" He spoke in English.

"Yes," I replied.

"Ghana?"

"No, I'm West Indian."

He looked more closely at me as if to locate something in my

13

face. "You look like a Ghanaian, he said, tonelessly, and went back to his careful examination of his drink, turning the frosty glass slowly in his fingers. Then, "How do you like my country?" He shot the question at me without turning his head.

"I only arrived today," I replied. "I've been wandering around town taking a look."

"Are you a salesman, or with a mission or something?"

"No, I'm a writer, looking for copy. This is my first visit to Africa and I'm trying to record my impressions."

He pivoted around on his stool and very seriously extended a large hand. "Welcome to Africa," he said. His grip was strong, the fingers cool from contact with the glass. "This is my first food today," he continued, shaking the glass. "Been fasting, sunup to sunset. Ramadan, you know."

"I've read of it," I replied.

"Know anyone in town?"

"Not really, just nosing around."

"I could show you around tonight if you like," he offered.

His drink completed, we set out. He was even taller than I had guessed, about two inches over six feet, and walked with a slightly stooped posture as if accustomed to accommodating persons much shorter than himself. The night was cool from the soft sea breezes and from the forecourt of the hotel could be heard the soft murmur of the tide on the beach close by. Overhead the towering mango trees lost their tops against the darker sky, now crowded with stars which seemed brighter because of the dimly lit streets. We followed the road around from the hotel and he pointed out the stately garden-surrounded houses, once the residences of high-ranking French officials and now converted to service as ministries of one sort or another.

"When the previous occupants, the French, left," he remarked, "they literally gutted the houses. What they could not cart away they smashed—baths, toilet bowls, everything."

On into the town. By now the shops were closed and the streets were, for the most part, deserted except for an occasional group of two or three men chatting beside an open doorway. A general air of depression seemed to hover over the whole place, and

14

nowhere could I detect any sound of music or laughter. "God, what a place to be stuck in," I thought.

"What does one do for entertainment in this place?" I asked.

He stopped, with that curious habit of listening with his head cocked to one side.

"Entertainment?" he echoed. "Oh, I see what you mean. There are no night clubs or brothels here these days. The French took them with them when they departed so hastily. But we manage very well without them." He laughed. "Luckily we are a polygamous people, so we have ways of entertaining ourselves." Then in a serious vein, "We do know how to enjoy ourselves, believe me, but right now most people are observing Ramadan, and that is a very quiet period for us."

We walked in silence for a while, past the deserted market with its tiers of open stalls, through narrow streets lined with closely packed two-story buildings, dark behind their tight shutters and empty except for mongrel dogs foraging in the shadows, on past the high wall of the soldiers' cantonments until we reached some open ground beyond which the Chinese Exhibition Building rose in massive silhouette. Here we stopped.

"Very impressive," I offered, in an attempt to probe his thoughts.

"What?" he asked.

"The Exhibition Building, like a transplanted piece of New China."

"Oh sure," he replied, his thoughts elsewhere, "before long all the open land like this will either become development areas or be turned into parks and playgrounds for our children. But before that happens we have lots of lessons to learn and the chief one is to live without the things we cannot afford—things like night clubs and brothels." He turned and grinned at me, his teeth a flash of white in the dark gloom of his face.

"We Africans often talk glibly about independence," he continued after a while. "Before it is achieved the very word has a certain magic quality, and very often we expect that many of the problems which attend the winning of independence will solve themselves in some magical way. Here in Guinea we are learning that independence must be more than a political milestone—it

15

must become a spiritual quality, so that we can better apply ourselves to the grave tasks ahead of us.

"This quality of the spirit is not breathed in with the night air—" at this he waved his arms in the gesture of an orator—"it has to be learned and developed. We, the old ones, learned it through fighting and sacrifice, and we have to teach it to our children with everything else they learn; in that way all of us will understand and accept that each one of us has the responsibility for making this country great."

"Excuse me, please," I interrupted, "but are you a lawyer, or teacher perhaps?"

"No," he replied, "I'm a soldier." He began walking and I fell into stride with him.

"Have you been to the Congo?"

His answer was long in coming. "Yes," he finally replied. "And for me the most important lesson is this: that under no circumstances must we in Guinea allow our internal affairs ever to deteriorate to the point where any outside country or organization needs to intervene, or is asked to intervene. But fortunately, that is very unlikely."

We walked in silence for a while. All kinds of questions clamored within me, but I felt that he was in the mood to talk and needed no prompting from me.

"It was a saddening experience for me," he continued, "to see an organization like the United Nations forces, of which we were a part, become so completely ineffectual as an organ for peace and stability, through the vagueness of its mandate, the irresolution of its authority, and the proved inexperience of some of its top personnel, who, though tagged and uniformed as military personnel, had neither the tradition of military action nor the personal experience of situations of armed conflict to guide their decisions. Much of what happened in the Congo since July of 1960 must be laid at the doorstep of the United Nations, and it will long remain a matter of national and personal regret that we contributed, by association, to the whole unhappy situation.

"The Congo dilemma is a monument to human error. Everyone involved in it made mistakes, varying only in degree. Unfortunately in nearly every instance mistaken action was persisted in,

16

primarily to save somebody's face, or defended because no other course of action seemed effective. Stupidity is no respecter of persons, and many innocent people have died because of it. We in Guinea can avoid such fatal stupidity by teaching ourselves and our children to appreciate the disciplines and responsibilities of independence, and so to believe in this little country of ours that no hardship is too great and no contribution too small in helping its progress."

"Does the man in the street feel the same way as you do about the country's development and his involvement in it?" I asked.

"Yes, of course," he replied, "even though he might not be as articulate in exposing his feelings. While you're here, talk to them yourself, and if you have the time, get up into the country among the smaller towns and villages. Talk with the people. You might run into a few surprises."

We continued our walk, swinging right along the tarmac road which followed the twisting coastline. Overhead the palm fronds whispered softly as they touched each other, sly sounds vaguely heard against the wash of the tide and the heavier chorus of crickets, frogs and the sleepless nightjars. People passed us, talking softly together, the slap, slap of their sandaled feet audible long after they had faded into the distance.

"We need help to do the things we need to do here," he continued, "and we are getting help from certain quarters but we need more. The time must come when we shall resolve our differences with France without sacrifice to our national pride or integrity, and one fine day the Americans will think seriously enough of us and other African States to treat us with the dignity due to independent States and their inhabitants. We are sick of being badgered or maneuvered into situations of choice between East or West merely because the United States will not conceive that we are free people and intend to remain free from any kind of influence or control.

"Jesus Christ, the damn folly of it!" he exclaimed. "Do you know something? None of the Russians or Czechs or Yugoslavs or Chinese who come here ever ask about the United States and what we think of them. We have a few American teachers in our schools, but no one asks us if that means that we're becoming capitalists! Why the hell can't Americans recognize that to people like us freedom and independence are the most precious things we have?

"Anyway," he said more calmly, "it may all work toward our good. The hardships we experience now might prove to be the best possible thing that could have happened to us."

"Don't you think," I ventured, "that your political conduct, I mean your country's political conduct, must reflect a truly neutralist attitude if you expect to be believed?"

"That is not what is expected of us," he replied. "No one believes in African neutrality; we are expected to be either pro-West or pro-Communist, and if we refuse to enter bodily into one camp we are promptly branded with the label of the other. If I or one of my countrymen should visit Russia tomorrow, the word would go around that I am pro-Russian or pro-Communist and I'd have a hell of a time if after that I wanted to visit the United States. But take the other side of the coin: no Eastern European country would refuse me entry merely because I had previously visited the United States. What does that make you think? Who is it that has the growing up to do?"

We were now once more outside the Hotel de France.

"Well, here we are," he said. "Tell you what, if you like I could take you around tomorrow. We could take a run up into the country and let you see what's happening there. Conakry— brothels apart or the lack of them—is like any town anywhere which has felt the influence of a cosmopolitan population. Upcountry you might better see and understand the things I've been talking about."

"I'd like that fine," I replied, delighted to have so interesting and responsible a companion showing me around. This was indeed a lucky break.

"One thing you can do," he said, seeming in no hurry to leave. "When you write about us, let them know that what we need even more than their money or their machines is their respect. They've got to learn to respect us as equals. Much of the time they humor us. I've seen it with my own eyes so I know what I'm talking about. Nowadays wherever an African goes and speaks, he is listened to, and nobody ever attempts to be critical of him unless

18

they feel that his political complexion differs from theirs. They're never very much concerned with the man or the content of his talking, but merely with the kind of political alignment he represents or seems to represent. We command attention in the councils of the world primarily because we are Africans, and so we are wooed and solicited and pampered like clever performing monkeys. Because nobody is really taking the trouble to look behind the façade and understand the African.

"The first thing about our new independence is our desire to be seen and heard. Often we are unprepared to be seen and heard and our posture is merely an imitation of those who so recently controlled us, yet it is readily applauded and encouraged uncritically, just because we are Africans. However, when we are reported, I notice that our remarks are invariably qualified by reference to our use of English or French, as if that were the seal of cultural arrival. It is hardly ever noticed that every African who stands up in the world's councils speaks a language different from the one he learned at his mother's breast and is consciously or unconsciously making a concession to those who would otherwise find it nearly impossible to communicate with him.

"On the other hand we Africans do not seem to have finally made up our own minds about the grave responsibilities which lie ahead. We resent the old image which non-Africans entertain about us, but we have done little to present a new and clearer image of ourselves. Very often we behave as if we are shipwrecks struggling helplessly in the floodtide of independence, instead of capable marines managing our political affairs with judgment and discretion. We have a hell of a lot to learn, from each other and from non-African people with wider experience of government, industry and representation than ourselves, but we need the kind of constructive criticism and appraisal, free of political bias, which would stimulate us to increased responsibility of expression and action."

He laid a fatherly hand on my shoulder and said, "You must forgive me, my young friend, for preaching to you, but it is not every day that one has the opportunity to talk like this with an outsider. Too often you people are in a hurry to judge us out of hand, and naturally our first impulse is to resent your criticism

19

because you have shown very little inclination to understand and be, at least, patient with us. Try to balance everything you see and hear against the fact that we were suddenly thrown upon our own limited resources with the added handicap of the antipathy and distrust generated by the conduct of the French in the last days of their control. Remember that, in spite of our difficulties, we are a small country but a united one. Have a good night, and we'll start upcountry early in the morning. I'll call for you around eight o'clock."

I watched his tall figure swing easily down the path, onto the road, to move into the tree-crowded shadow of the still African night.

*

I breakfasted at 7 A.M. and, comfortable in cool khaki shirt and slacks, I waited for my friend, who arrived promptly on time in a large chauffeur-driven American car. He may have noticed my surprise because he said, laughing, "I wangled it on the argument that you were an important visitor. It's one of our official cars."

Outside the hotel, the air was damp and fresh with dew which still hung in misty patches over every ditch or narrow gully. The driver leaned heavily on his horn as we moved through the town streets, already crowded with people on their way to their various jobs or to the large market in the center of town. We slowed down as we passed the market, the air now heavy with the ripe odors of dried fish, fruit and a wide variety of unfamilar herbs and roots. People shouted at each other across the inches which separated them, in the age-old exercise of haggling over the price of an article, their arms flailing the air in wild gestures or their fingers fluttering in insistent illustration.

Every kind of merchandise seemed to be on sale, but most of it utilitarian and of cheap manufacture, brightly patterned cloth from Japan, cheek-by-jowl with gay enamel cooking utensils stamped with the legend "Sierra Leone Independence 1961"; large bunches of bananas and plantains, piles of local oranges, chickens lying on their sides with legs securely tied, their eyes half-

20

glazed with fear, the public letter-writer sitting at his little table ready to serve the illiterate for a price, and the ubiquitous tailor, the whir of his restless treadle lost in the general cacophony.

Beyond the market traffic was heavy and our car followed in slow procession behind some makeshift buses overloaded with workers, and many kinds of army vehicles carrying very youthful green-uniformed soldiers who seemed frighteningly inexperienced but purposeful. Near the edge of town several new building sites were swarming with workmen, their feet indistinct in the low-hanging mist of morning, as if they were melting away from the knees downward. Very quickly the town took on a new character as dilapidated thatch huts appeared, sometimes close to modern brick houses, as the buildings thinned out toward the edge of town. These huts seemed less out of place and shantylike, more picturesque, against the background of palm, papaya and mango trees. But only at a distance—too close a look revealed the piles of rubbish, the rusty discards from tinned food and the bits of bone from which the profligate mongrels had stripped every last shred of meat, and which were now covered with flies. More and more cultivated patches of ground appeared, given mostly to cassava or banana plants, with here and there a clump of sugar cane, covered by its own dried leaves.

Children and more children trudged along the road to school, each with one or more books casually balanced on his head, as if it was most important to keep both hands free, always. Few of them wore shoes, but this did not seem surprising or out of place. As we passed the airport and headed inland the country stretched out in gently undulating reaches of strong-looking grass through which the rusty brown earth showed in deep brown gashes. In the distance the slopes of the hills peeped blue-gray through the thin veil of mist, and presented a vague silhouette against the pale blue sky. Already it was becoming warm, but through the open windows the wind blew around us.

"This country is rich, very rich," my friend said. "Look at the color of the earth, we've not even begun to tap our resources of bauxite, or let's say we're only scratching the surface so far. Under that useless grass there's wealth waiting to be dug up, but it requires money, lots of it. Wish I knew a shortcut to Fort Knox,"

21

he laughed. Then as if struck by a sudden idea, he said, "Tell me something about President Kennedy's Peace Corps. What will it do and how does he plan to set about assembling it?"

"Why does everyone ask me questions about America as if I am an American or somehow responsible for what happens there. I seem to spend an awful lot of time explaining that British Guiana is not the U. S. A. All I know about it is what I have read or heard in France," I replied.

"Strange the way Americans see Africa," he murmured, more to himself than to me. "I wonder who it is that advises him about us in Africa? Peace Corps! Where would he send them and what will they do? And what is most important, how will he choose them? I read that they will be mostly young men. Will their expressed liberality be a qualification? Would they have to like black people before they become eligible? Or will they be taught how to be liberal after they are chosen? Would a man be barred because he is a Southerner? Even if they satisfy all of Mr. Kennedy's requirements, does that imply that we in Africa will believe in them? What guarantees have we that the men of the Peace Corps who come to be nice to us in Africa would be just as nice to black Americans in the U. S. A.? And when they come over here what will they do? Just tell us what nice people Americans are? We're not interested in Peace Corps; we're not interested in hearing how peace can best be preserved from young liberal Americans. We'd rather have some of the practical symbols of peace out there." He pointed at the blur of landscape flitting by. "You know, bulldozers and tractors. And we'd welcome young peaceful Americans who could teach us how to turn this brown, grassy promise into a productive certainty, so that our people might taste the fruits of peace before they grow too old to care.

"Peace Corps," he whispered, "that is the kind of charity which should begin at home and be firmly restrained from leaving it." His lips tightened into a thin, bitter line. "Or perhaps he intends sending black Americans to teach us about peace. They are not much better than the white ones. I hear that they want to identify with us Africans, and that they've started all kinds of organizations which claim to reflect their African heritage. Very good, provided they maintain the distance between America and Africa,

22

and are sensible enough to understand that a black skin does not make everyone an African. I've seen them here and in other places in Africa, and been rather sorry for some of them when I observed their disillusionment with us. From thousands of miles away tom-toms and grass huts and polygamy seem very attractive and picturesque, and freedom for Africa is an exciting battle-cry; but close at hand the heat and the dirt and disease and shortages play havoc with lofty resolutions."

I suddenly felt somewhat out of accord with him. Maybe this was aimed obliquely at me, because I too felt a sense of identity with Africa's political destiny.

"Surely," I interrupted, "the expressions of solidarity from black Americans is all of a piece with African progress, even though they come from people several generations removed from the African scene."

"I'm concerned with positive values, " he replied sagely, "not with questionable postures. The best contribution any outsider can make is to be as active and positive as possible in the fight against indignity and inhumanity. Americans are Americans, and the black ones should concentrate all their efforts in fighting the many forces of indignity which beset them in America. That is the kind of contribution we need here—the encouragement of knowing that on all fronts the fight for social equality and political freedom is firmly joined. Do you know," and once again his face relaxed in a smile, "quite often I meet black Americans in Africa, and, by God, they're so American in everything they do and say, that they don't seem to realize it, and we Africans find it most irritating because of the common factor—our black skins."

"Seems pretty hopeless, does it?" I asked.

"Not altogether," he assured me, laughing. "Maybe one day we Africans will become as familiar with air-conditioning and labor-saving devices and department stores so that we'll develop a few more factors in common with our American cousins."

The rugged grassland now gave way to thinly forested slopes deeply scored by dry gullies in which large boulders lay in fierce threatening repose. "Come the rains, I thought, and those will be really rugged."

Our driver kept the car humming along the smooth macadam

23

road which followed the basal curves of the hills very much as if it were really the modern improvement of a footpass descried by the feet of centuries of travelers. Here and there the trees thickened to form a leafy canopy over the black ribbon of road which now shimmered in the heat as the sun swung slowly upward in the sky and the reluctant mists faded away.

We rushed across a bridge below which the narrow stream flowed thinly between boulders and rotting vegetation, past orange groves heavy with spotted yellow fruit, climbing upward toward the interior and the cooler mountain air. We were quiet, my friend seemed lost in his own thoughts, and so far the driver had said nothing. All I could see of him was the back of his neck and the peaked official khaki cap he wore, though now and again I caught a quick glimpse of his broad intelligent face in the driving mirror. The road was clear of traffic except for an occasional car or heavy truck laden with building material or market produce. Trees flashed by, familiar as yesterday, and I found myself saying their names aloud: mango, breadfruit, guava, banana, cassava—"we call it 'manioc'," he intervened—and the flowering plants, hibiscus, frangipani, bougainvillea. . . .

"Over there," he pointed to some tall, stately trees with pale trunks, silvery in the early sunlight. "Those are curare trees, deadly poisonous." It was the first time I had seen these trees, although I knew that the Aborigines of British Guiana's hinterland had long practiced the technique of extracting the poison and using it for hunting and fishing. An arrow tipped with a film of curara produces quick paralysis. The trees looked so harmless and blended beautifully with the surrounding profuse growth. They were deadly but not evil, having their place in the scheme of things.

My mind kept reverting to my companion's recent remarks, and I felt obliged to throw in my "tuppence worth." "What do you really expect from us—in America or the West Indies or anywhere else—those of us who claim African heritage?"

Again that tilting of his head to one side, the eyes closed, the large hawklike nose in strong profile, as if he were for a moment listening to some other voice, something attuned beyond the limits of my hearing. "My young friend, I expect no more from you and others like you wherever they are than I expect from white men

24

wherever they are—and no less. If you really wish to help us in Africa, you must begin by being the best kind of American or West Indian you can possibly be, so that we can support each other in our drives toward the highest standards in every possible field of enterprise. I have an idea you're not very pleased with my references to black Americans. Try to see the matter from our point of view. Over here we never hear anything about black Americans unless it is related to interracial conflict, and we know that throughout the whole of America the black ones are treated as second-class persons, the treatment varying only in degree. This suggests that black Americans have a huge task ahead of them to fight against everything in their country which stigmatizes them, not merely as black persons, but as persons. We in Africa are not interested in back-to-Africa schemes directed from the United States, because such schemes would not improve or uplift us here. Liberia is a historical lesson very much to that point."

He leaned forward to whisper to the driver, who nodded. "We in Africa need you people outside to stimulate us much more than to emulate us. Too often you entertain fanciful ideas about us and what is happening here in Africa; you seem to imagine that the movements toward political freedom and economic development are spontaneous phenomena like the swarming of locusts. In fact, all such movements owe their origins to people like Dr. Azikwe, Nkrumah, Kenyatta, and others, all of whom lived for a time outside of Africa and were thus better able to view their countries' disabilities and potential, before returning determined to stimulate change for the better. As I hear it, you take pride in current African political achievement, and would like to be part of it, so you adopt pseudo-African gestures and postures."

Now his voice took on a sharper note. "We are not flattered by them. We would prefer to hear and see signs that you, all of you, are really fighting, as Americans, to rid yourselves of the stigma of second-class citizenship."

There it was again, this thing about America which included me. Observing his face I realized that there was no anger, rather a kind of compulsive resolve to set the record straight as he saw it.

The car slowed and coasted to a smooth stop before a collection of small houses and huts half-hidden by a cluster of dwarf cocoanut palms heavy with green fruit. Several small, naked children played about the smooth yard of packed earth in front of the largest house. The boys were naked, the little girls all wore a brief, tight, bikini-type garment.

They came rushing up to the car, but stopped a few feet away, looking at us, their faces alight with shy, wide-eyed expectancy. My friend alighted and spoke to them in dialect, at which they capered around him happily and preceded him toward the houses, out of which several persons, men and women, now emerged. The men greeted him with a double handshake, while the women each held his hand and genuflected low, a graceful, fluid movement. "He must be a very important person," I thought, and made a quick mental re-evaluation of our relationship to reassure myself that I had at no point been guilty of any indiscretion through ignorance of his status.

I noticed that, after greeting him, the women stood slightly apart, looking pleased and rather proud of the man. After a while he beckoned to me to join him, and on my approach, he introduced me to the men, each of whom gave the same handshake, in which my right hand was gripped in both of theirs; then I was introduced to the women: first to a tall, handsome young woman, his wife, and then to the others. All the women greeted me with the same charming curtsey they had made to him, and I realized that it was a customary form of address practiced among them.

After the introduction, his wife went into one of the buildings and returned with a sleeping infant in her arms, holding it up for my friend's inspection. He made a few pleasant remarks at which she laughed shyly, evidently delighted with whatever it was he had said to her. Meanwhile the men had brought chairs and stools from the houses and were seated in a circular group. My friend invited me to join them. The women called the children away and left us.

My friend spoke to the men rapidly, in dialect, then explained to me that he had told them I was a visitor from Europe making my very first trip to Africa. From the look of pleasure and surprise on their faces at this information I realized that this was a novel situation for them, as it were: an African who was not an African. Now the questioning began, with my friend acting as interpreter.

They wanted to know what it felt like for me to live in Europe,

26

and I told them truthfully the kind of experiences the non-European was likely to encounter, the differences in attitude one would discover in London and Paris, for example. I explained that I was born in British Guiana, and their interest seemed to quicken. Was that the country of Dr. Jagan? When was British Guiana going to become independent? When last had I been there? And a host of others, all of which indicated that they were somehow informed and interested in matters beyond local limits. I answered as best I could, often having to confess that my own information was based on such newspapers and hearsay I was able to get in Europe. Though I had met Dr. Jagan, Mr. Burnham and other leading British Guianese at various times in London, events were sufficiently volatile to produce rapid change about which I would be quite unaware. Then it was my turn and I asked them about themselves.

I learned that we were on the edge of a large village, and several of the men present were officials of one sort or another. What did independence mean to them, at the village level? No less than at any other level, one of them replied proudly. It was a challenge to them to prove that they could run their affairs at least as efficiently as had been the case under the French; more than that, they were really doing things themselves instead of waiting for things to be done for them. As an example he mentioned the case of their children's education. Apparently for some time village children had to travel some distance each day to school because the only school available was in a larger village. His people had met, discussed the matter and decided to do something about it. They selected a site in their own village, and on week-ends and all other available times, every able-bodied man and woman worked on building their own schoolhouse, and making rather rough but utilitarian school furniture. When everything was completed, including painting, they requested the local authority to provide a teacher, and soon had the satisfaction of having their children taught in their own village.

"That's how personal our independence is to us," he added somewhat proudly.

I asked about local government, their crops, marketing, health problems, and, through my interpreter friend, discovered that village life in Guinea was not awfully different from village life in, say, Essex, England, except for certain niceties resulting from heavy

27

industrialization. It was explained that, politically, they belonged to the Parti Démocratique de Guinée, the only political party in Guinea, and led by President Sékou Touré himself. There were several study groups and councils which met regularly in the village.

Presently some of the women returned, set up a table and laid out bottles of whisky and freshly picked green cocoanuts, so that I was simultaneously refreshed and stimulated. One of the men, who seemed to be something of a wit, made some reference to the way I was drinking the cocoanut milk with obvious relish, and his colleagues roared with laughter; even the women smiled shyly, turning their faces away as if to avoid embarrassing me. My friend, translating, explained that green cocoanuts were supposed to be the repast of amorous males, and the wit had told the women that, from the way I was enjoying the fruit, they had better watch out.

It was pleasant sitting there with them, enjoying the naturalness of their acceptance. The women, handsome, gracious creatures, attended their tasks quietly; now and again a few of them would be seized with giggling, or break out into hearty laughter. My friend did not share in the refreshments; both he and the driver, now soundly asleep in the car, which had been parked in the shade, were strict Muslims and observed their fast from sunup to sunset. I particularly observed the relationship between my friend and the rest of the group, two of whom were quite old, almost patriarchal. They all treated him with deference, and his whole bearing was of such authority that I suspected he exerted considerable political influence among them.

As we prepared to leave, the wit spoke rapidly to my friend, explaining that they were surprised I had asked no questions about communism. I replied that their political leanings were their own affair, but if they wanted to talk about communism I was quite willing to listen. There followed some discussion among them, which, translated, affirmed that they were Africans, not Frenchmen nor Russians nor anything else from outside; the political structure obtaining was necessary to bring about the fullest involvement by everyone at all levels so that their country would benefit by everyone's contribution.

As I followed his translation it occurred to me that they were hypersensitive about themselves and anything which they believed

28

to be critical of themselves, evidence that they had a lot of growing up to do politically. They had raised the matter of communism because, for all their apparent familiarity with current affairs, they seemed to divide black people into two groups—Africans and Americans. I was admittedly not an African, so I must be American, and their attitude to Americans was, if not distrustful, at least very reserved. I was learning very quickly that my best line was to say as little as possible and ask questions only when the information was not spontaneously forthcoming. They were hospitable and kind, but evidently proud and very sensitive.

The women appeared for our goodbyes, and we left them, a tight group bound together as much by blood relationships as by the deeper ties which seemed to spring from the earth itself.

En route my friend explained that he was born in a neighboring village but knew most of the people of the district and arranged to visit them and attend their councils or study groups whenever the opportunity presented itself. The road continued upward, and in the distance, across the valleys, the green hills of Sierra Leone demarked the territorial boundary; for a while the vegetation became sparse, then gave way to flat parkland with low shrubs. Farther on the road bisected a banana plantation, which, my friend explained, was one of the government experimental stations, geared to the improvement and extension of banana crops. We made two stops along the road at villages where he wished to call briefly on friends or relatives before reaching Kindia, a large town and regional headquarters.

It was pleasant to stretch one's legs through the shady streets, the crowded shopping center and the market place, where most of the vendors were women—robust, well-muscled creatures who kept up a flow of cross-chatter with each other. Their produce was heaped in pyramidal piles: yams, cassava, eddoes, tannias, bananas and plaintains, together with bundles of lettuce (over which they occasionally sprinkled water to keep them freshly crisp) and huge piles of oranges and grapefruit, and I wondered what chance there was of all this stuff being sold before it spoiled and rotted in the oppressive heat. I saw groups of Europeans, Czechs, Germans and a few Yugoslavs, and learned that they were busy on various agricultural or construction projects.

After a quick lunch at a local restaurant (I felt uncomfortable eating while my companion would not even take water) we drove to the Pasteur Research Institute at Kindia. The director, a Frenchman, received us and took us on a tour of the extensive grounds, where several species of monkey were housed in large wire cages. Some of these animals were used at the Institute for experimental purposes, while others were held pending transfer to hospitals or other research institutes throughout the world. As we passed one cage of large howler monkeys, some of them scooped up handfuls of their droppings and flung them at us. I exclaimed, "How beastly," and immediately realized that I had applied human standards to the animals. After all, they were beasts, and their behavior should be beastly. My friend had overheard me, however, and said kindly, "They're only likely to behave like that when they are caged."

A special piece of ground was reserved for a family of chimpanzees. It was a large outcropping of rock which contained a natural cave, surrounded in its entirety by a deep dry ditch of reinforced concrete, steeply smooth to defeat any attempts by larger members to climb out. The family consisted of a large male, two females and four young animals. Our guide said that the youngest could scale the wall of the ditch and raid the fruit trees, prompted by their parents, but if they dared return empty-handed they were promptly spanked and sent back to fetch fruit.

We were shown the special enclosure, where several varieties of venomous snakes were kept, including mambas, cobras, rattlesnakes and many less-familiar ones, most of them beautifully patterned in colors of green, copper and black.

The director, a vigorous but kindly man with short-cropped gray hair and smooth, florid, youthful face, was courteous and informative, and seemed quite happy and content among his dangerous charges.

The afternoon was now well advanced, and on the way back to Conakry my friend dozed and I watched the countryside, the richness of green growth, and the sheer beauty of wild, natural color. How long would it remain like this? In the wake of the restless quest toward education and educational development must come the bulldozers, and new roads and railheads would cut their way through to bring better communication, health and more improved standards of living. Maybe the planners for Guinea's progress would give some thought to retaining as much as possible of this natural beauty.

The sun was sliding away behind the hills, reddening the undersides of the fleecy clouds till they glowed in several shades of coppery gold against the blue-green of the outline of hills; the trees bordering the road cast long shadows, and the air was full of the lively chirping of birds. We stopped by the roadside to relieve ourselves, and from some village hidden by the trees I heard a loud, mournful wail, repeated at regular intervals. It started always on a high, sustained note, then broke away in a series of indistinguishable sounds. My companion answered my unspoken query:

"A Muezzin," he explained. "He is telling everyone within earshot that it will soon be time for prayer. We'll have to hurry a bit, as I like to break my fast with my family at home."

As we drove along I thought of that one. I had met one wife; now we were returning to Conakry and his family. He said it so naturally that it seemed to me that polygamy imposed no strain on him. In Europe I often read of bigamists, and it seemed that they were in a constant state of anxiety lest their activities be found out. Yet here was a man who took the fact of more than one wife easily in stride. I wondered how the wives felt about it.

Twilight was a short interlude of blue-gray half light, with indistinct silhouettes, before night supervened with silky blackness through which the car's headlights pierced long probing fingers. As we passed villages I noticed groups of people standing or kneeling in attitudes of prayer; sometimes a single person would be kneeling on a prayer mat beside a lighted lantern. My friend, awake, must have noticed my interest.

"Most of us in Guinea are Muslims," he said, "in spite of Christian missionaries of one kind or another. Having a common religion was another advantage in our struggle for political freedom, because it was one of the bases for unity. Churches operate freely in our country, but you will notice that as Muslims, our faith is part of our daily lives instead of the occasional observances characteristic of Christian churches. No Muslim needs to be exhorted to attend

31

the mosque, to fast or to pray; some are less strict than others but they fulfill the general pattern of religious duty."

As we neared the capitol the praying groups became larger, the long-robed figures seeming taller in the flickering lamplight. On the edge of town, near the Department of Radio and Information, we passed a church in which I could see about half a dozen persons singing to the accompaniment of barely audible organ music.

We approached a group of neat, freshly painted bungalows and my friend signaled the driver to stop.

"Sorry to rush like this," he apologized, "but I must be with the family for prayers. After I've broken my fast and cleaned up a bit I'll drop by your hotel for a drink or so, as I'll be very busy tomorrow and we might not be able to get together after this."

He hurried indoors and the driver took me on to my hotel. On the way I tried to engage him in conversation but he replied only in monosyllables. I suppose he was tired or hungry, or both.

The hotel was agog with activity: a fashion show of some kind was being staged that night and members of the staff were hurrying to and fro. In a tiny alcove, looking as cool as the potted plants beside them, was a group of four or five European girls, probably between eighteen and twenty-three years old, dressed in sloppy sweaters and skin-tight jeans. Some little distance away from them sat several African girls, younger-looking and shy in spite of their attractive, brightly patterned national dress. Near the bar was a large, hastily designed poster advertising the fashion show and describing each of the European girls as the most beautiful in her country, and recent contestant for the Miss World title. The African girls were to present a series of national dances.

"Not bad," I thought. So once again I had jumped the gun. Things did happen in this place, after all.

I had a leisurely shower, shaved and dressed for dinner. The main dining hall had been commandeered for the evening's per-formance, so dinner was served in a small annex, the overflow accommodated in the lounge. During dinner there was more than the usual buzz of conversation; even the waiters seemed to have thrown off their usual air of indifference and were caught up in the general excitement. This sort of thing did not happen every night. After dinner I remained at my table sipping a cold beer; it was now about 8:30 P.M., and the night's entertainment was not scheduled to begin until nine-thirty.

At about nine my friend arrived, looking very refreshed and elegant in a cream linen suit and dark tie. Now he could have a drink with me, so we settled ourselves like a couple of old friends, exchanging quips about this and that. There was a question which had been on my mind all day. Now that he seemed relaxed and affable, I decided to plunge in.

"About your President," I began.

"Well, what about him?"

"So far you have said nothing about him. In European newspapers I have seen him referred to as 'dictator,' 'pro-Communist,' 'strong man,' and 'demagogue.' So far you have been very frank and outspoken in your observations about the outsiders; would you be just as frank in telling me about Guinea's leadership after two years as an independent State?"

Again the familiar head-on-one-side pause, but this time the beginnings of a smile tickled the side of his mouth and ran along the big arched nose.

"The things you read were mainly true, but the people who wrote them did not understand the truth they were writing; they did not even know they were writing the truth because they do not know the man." Easy, relaxed, patient, even fatherly; now he'd be generous and explain it carefully for me. "Two things they do not understand: the African's background and the meaning of African nationalism. In Africa we have always been accustomed to authoritarian rule; it has been the basis of our social structure long before any European ever set foot on African soil, and it still survives in the heart of every African, no matter how 'Europeanized' he might seem to be. In Africa we respect strength, and we honor it when it is allied to personal courage and skillful leadership.

"Our President has these qualities and he is an African in the fullest sense. He is well informed although he never attended university either here or abroad, and when he speaks, he speaks the language of our people in the way our people understand. We trust him and we follow him. 'Dictator,' 'demagogue,' those are European terms, they have no meaning in the context of Africa. Nor has the term 'democracy.' In Guinea we are, for the most part of our three

33

million people, illiterate; democracy presupposes a literate majority of the population. What we need, what we must have, is strong, forceful leadership toward achievable targets, designed to involve everyone, irrespective of educational or other considerations."

He sipped his drink before continuing. "As for the other thing, it seems impossible for the outsider to get into the skin of the African, to understand the terrible but wonderful spirit which has recently been released within and among us. You blind yourselves with label and name tags and refuse to look behind them to apprehend the facts. If an African reads Marx or Engels you brand him Communist; if he visits Prague or Moscow you brand him Communist. Would you consider him a capitalist if you caught him reading the *Financial Times*? The lesson you need to learn, all of you, both East and West, as you are fond of describing yourselves, is that we are, first and last, Africans. We are willing and ready to learn from you, all of you, but we have no wish or intention to be anything but Africans—free, independent Africans.

"Your newspapers expend a lot of time and energy criticizing our form of government. Let them note that we are all first-class, hundred per cent Africans; there are no second-class citizens among us. Let them also note that the one-party rule, which they find so difficult to swallow, is not restricted to Guinea, Liberia, Ghana, Tunisia, these are but a few where the same things exists. And Sierra Leone. Go there and take a look. Milton Margai has no opposition party to contend with. Then, there's Nigeria.

"Right now we have the job of feeding, housing and educating our people, and of building our economy so that we can continue to improve their food, housing and education, and we have a leader who is young, strong and vigorous enough to do just that.

"I suppose you have noticed that our shops have no luxury goods, and our women do not wear the latest Paris fashions; but what is important is the fact that although the French revoked their support of our budget we are not economically crippled; as a matter of fact we are stable and moving ahead. Later on we may give some attention to putting a little icing on the cake."

He laughed, and I felt an admiration for this man. If he truly expressed the general attitude of the people, then Guinea was well on the way to setting its mark on the whole continent of Africa.

34

This was undoubtedly a big night. People were arriving for the show, mostly Europeans, men and women dressed fashionably in light linens and silks, all looking enthusiastic, greeting each other somewhat loudly. Now and then my friend would indicate an ambassador or special envoy from Europe or another African State. A tall, distinguished-looking, fair-skinned Negro, immaculate in a white sharkskin suit, was identified as the United States ambassador. The tone of my friend's voice did not convey much enthusiasm.

"He may be leaving us soon," he remarked, as the gentleman passed us on his way to the main hall. I thought that the ambassador may have completed his tour of duty and was moving to some other theatre of operations.

"One must never underestimate the deep effects of conditioning," he said, seemingly talking more to himself than to me. "That is why we must use every means possible to keep reminding our people that every aspect of their daily lives must reflect their consciousness of freedom and independence. Treat a man unequally and after a time he will think or behave unequally; even if you subsequently place him in high office, he will occasionally betray some residual traits of inequality. We are a free and sovereign State and would prefer that representatives from other States at ambassadorial and other levels are chosen from among the best in their field, and at the moment we are inclined to doubt that black Americans have had sufficient opportunities at higher diplomatic level to provide them with the background and experience necessary to the efficient execution of the job of an ambassador. We cannot be expected to entertain the highest regard for a black ambassador when we know that in many parts of his own country he would be refused hotel accommodation and other facilities merely because of the color of his skin. And when he speaks to us on matters of importance, we cannot be sure that he speaks on behalf of all America. It therefore follows that America must quickly introduce changes to equate the status of her black citizens with that of her white citizens or keep the black ones out of international-representative office."

"May I ask you a rather frank question?" I interrupted.

"Why not? It's a free country," he grinned.

"You are bitter about America, aren't you? One might even say

35

you are positively anti-American. Aren't you guilty of the same kind of phobia which you so determinedly condemn in them?"

"It's strange," he replied, "but I feel no hatred. No, none whatsoever. Is that difficult for you to believe? Let's put it this way. I'm impatient to see some improvement in the relationships between other countries and ourselves, but I think it is necessary to speak one's mind. I've been speaking frankly with you because I hope that, in reporting me, you will present the truth and perhaps it might lead to some revision of attitudes. No, I'm not anti-American. I am merely pro-African, even if at the moment all Africa for me is concentrated in the word 'Guinea.' "

I suggested that we get seats for the fashion show and we inquired at the desk, but discovered that we were days too late; all available seats had been sold and there was not even standing room. It was no great disappointment because the long car trip, the heavy meal and the beer all conspired to produce a comfortable lassitude and we agreed that perhaps bed would be best. I said goodbye to my friend, as he would be busy from then on and would be unable to spend more time with me, and retired to my room to scribble down everything I could remember of our conversation. Later I could hear the sounds of music and cheering from downstairs; but soon these subsided into the dark peace of the African night.

*

I breakfasted late and determined to take it easy that day, my last in Guinea, as my air passage was booked for early the following morning. A few hundred yards from the hotel the beach was deeply indented to form a deep, pleasant cove, bordered along its perimeter by wild grape trees and a species of pine erratically reflected in the gray-green water. Under the trees the strange, soft mixture of sand and powdered seashell was pleasantly warm underfoot and I spent more than an hour alternately swimming and lying in the shade, enjoying the novelty of having that piece of paradise all to myself. Presently three figures approached from around the rocky promontory, which hid the curve of the beach, small figures in shorts and bright-colored shirts. Once near, I saw that they were

36

Chinese, two men and one woman, neat, smooth-muscled, compact persons. They smiled at me, bowed in greeting and moved some distance away to deposit their towels and cameras. Soon they were romping around, chasing each other in a game of tag or plunging into the water, their laughter erupting in silvery echoes around the cove. Like happy, carefree children; like people on a holiday and enjoying it; just like people released from the rigors of concentrated physical or intellectual effort. It pleased me to see and hear them in a mood so different from the tight isolation I had observed about them in the hotel and on the streets. I wondered what reaction there would be if I went over to talk to them; at least they would speak, so, acting on the thought I went toward them.

"Hello, there," I called.

"Good morning," one of the men replied in English.

"I've been sitting around by myself for some time," I said, "and wondered if I might join you."

"Of course," he replied, approaching and signaling to his companions to follow him. I introduced myself and he introduced his companions, all of them experts in various agricultural projects. They were associated with the exposition currently in Conakry. I told them that I was making my first visit to Africa, and Guinea was my first stop. We sat on the warm sand and talked and talked about nothing in particular. I tried in every way I could to extract from them some particular comment about China, but they simply suggested that I visit the country, assuring me of a welcome. I tried to discover their reactions to being in Africa, working with Africans, but they countered by extolling the continuous warmth, the wonderful variety of trees and fruit. Everything was wonderful—the people were wonderful. So I gave up, and merely relaxed and enjoyed being with them.

The men were small-boned, each about five feet six or seven inches, a few inches taller than the girl, who wore her hair in a short page-boy bob. There was something impersonal about her, in spite of her well-rounded figure. I did not discover her relationship to either or both of the men, but would not be surprised to learn that it was either platonic or that they were blood relatives; they seemed happy together without any indication or suggestion of special emotional overtones. Friendly people, nice people—but very

37

shy. We chatted for more than an hour, but all the time I knew that I was quite outside the tight harmony of their relationship, and I wondered whether they and others who, like them, were active in Africa, were ever able to let down the barriers behind which they seemed so securely ensconced that a real unity of interest and intercourse might be possible between them and the Africans they seemed so willing to help.

Midday and the heat invaded the shadiest places, so much so that I perspired with the simple effort of wiping away perspiration. In my mind I tried to review the things I had heard in the short time I was in Guinea. Much of it was new to me, some of it very doubtful, probably because I could not help remembering all the things I had previously read and heard about Africa before I set foot in it. Africans had spoken to me about Africa, eagerly insisting on the factuality of their observations; but now, by myself, it seemed to me that they sometimes spoke with no more basis of authority than familiarity with their own village, or perhaps town, or maybe country. Sometimes they spoke of the background to their country's present ambitions, as if no other than indigenous African influences were involved, ignoring the fact of the deep effects of decades of colonization. I had seen here in Guinea people of obviously varied ethnic origin, and mixtures of such origin. I had seen the effect of the spread of the Muslim faith through the country; many of the people favored European dress; many of them spoke French; many governmental techniques new to Africa were being practiced, yet some of my informants spoke as if, before independence, Africa had been a static society. Perhaps the idea was merely to emphasize their advancement. Perhaps.

I thought of what my friend had said about European and American attitudes, especially his reference to what he called evidence of inequality expressed in their disinclination to critical appraisal of African opinion. Perhaps it was too easy for him to say this to me man to man, but I wondered just how willing many Africans, even the intellectuals, would be to receive public criticism. Would it not be viewed as discriminatory? Would even my friend be loath to insist that older-established states be more willing to encourage than hinder? That thing he had about America and Americans? Was it any the less compulsive than what he called American preoccupation with communism? Here I was in Africa, but what was an African? Did the years of slavery and manumission through which my forebears passed completely separate me from these people? Was there any part of me which remained African after all these years? Could I come and live here, among Africans, as an African? If I did, would I too become anti-something or pro-something?

I thought of the young Chinese I had just met, and looked across toward where they had recommenced the game I had interrupted. They were now farther away, and I noticed that their clothing and towels were missing, probably behind a tree nearby where they were playing. How did they really see the Africans and how did the Africans really see them? Did I sound like an American to them also? Was that the reason for their withdrawal from me, or was it a natural shyness, the same sort of thing the British applaud in themselves as their "reserve"? Perhaps these Chinese were Communists. Was that enough to make them acceptable in Guinea? Here I was in a country newly independent and proudly so, yet hampered in its first flights from the crippling security of the colonial nest by these anti-attitudes. If these bitternesses were entertained at high level in Guinea, as my conversations with my friend seemed to indicate, why not find an opportunity for stating the case to the Americans themselves at a similarly high level? If the people of Guinea had the consciousness of their equality, they should be positive in expressing it instead of assuming the negative attitude of defending it.

They needed help, lots of help, and I subscribed to their insistence on keeping that help free of commitments to any political alignment. The Americans and others daily professed their willingness to help the newly independent states; surely there must be some way of bridging these two essentially laudable interests. The Guineans are people. The Americans are people, and they cannot have completely forgotten their own struggles against colonialism, and their own faltering steps toward their present powerful position. America herself was founded on protest; her amazing economic development was based on the essential concept of individual freedom. These things should presuppose a readiness to tolerance and helpful understanding; not only understanding of situations sympathetic to American views, but the deeper, more constructive

39

appraisal of tolerance to differences wherever they appeared. This I believe to be the hallmark of positive leadership. It is very easy to agree with those who share our views, but damned difficult to be patient with those who disagree with us, especially when there is, to us, every indication that those who disagree have little in terms of experience, or carefully directed ambitions to support their attitudes. God, what a whirligig!

I must have dozed off because I sat up to discover that the Chinese had gone and the little beach deserted. I felt a bit groggy from the heat and decided to return to my hotel for a cold shower and a nap. A group of taxis was drawn up near the main entrance of the hotel in the shade of the huge mango trees and the drivers were sitting together chatting and smoking while keeping a watchful eye for possible prospects.

I walked up to them and said, "Bonjour." They replied more or less in chorus, but with a certain deference, probably because they recognized the large towel I was carrying as the property of the Hotel de France (the name was heavily embroidered in blue) and realized I was a guest. I leaned against one of the taxis, took out my cigarettes and offered them around. An old gambit but a good one —the international peace pipe. My French is pretty bad, purely functional; I understand much more than I can speak, but I manage to make myself understood. They were interested to discover that I was not African, and added their welcome on my visit to their country. I explained that I was a writer looking for pieces of information, not people's names, and bit by bit we talked together. Had I been swimming?

"Yes, I was down at the little cove," I said pointing.

"Did you not try the swimming enclosure farther up the beach?"

"No, I did not know there was a swimming enclosure."

One of them stood up to show me a group of tall palm trees just visible over the roofs of some low bungalows. "Over there," he said.

"I was fine where I was," I told them: "water, shade, trees, warm sand. What more could I ask?"

"A cold beer, maybe," someone suggested. "At the other place there's a bar and cubicles for your clothes, and chairs under the trees. Nice."

40

"Only one thing wrong with it," another commented. "It costs money."

"Everything costs money," I said. "Especially this hotel. Millionaire prices without millionaire service."

"Every American is a millionaire."

Laughter. Very funny. I did not bother to explain that I was not an American. Let them have their "tuppence" worth of fun.

"Do you fellows use the swimming enclosure?" I wanted to head them off from the American thing—I was getting bored with it.

They exchanged glances before one replied. "When the French were here we couldn't get in. All this was residential," he said, waving his arm in a vague wide arc. "Now it's open to anyone who can pay, but they wouldn't catch me paying for something I can get free by just taking a little walk."

"Used to be different when the French were here," another added. "More fancy—with things to eat and such, like. Used to pass and watch them, the bastards."

"Ripped the place to shreds before they left," still another said. "You know that jetty place next door, with the winch for hauling up the boats above the watermark? They wrecked it before they left. Lousy bastards, they hated to think we blacks would have the things, so they wrecked them, now all you can see is pieces of rusty iron sticking up all over the place."

All this was said without any sign of anger, in quiet conversational tones; no one passing by would have guessed at the subject of our conversation. I wondered whether they were really dispassionate about it or were controlling themselves just for my benefit.

"How do you feel about the French now?" Probably with a little encouragement they would open up.

"What do you mean, 'feel about them.' They're gone, so to hell with them," from one.

"I don't even think of them," from another, "except when I go to one of the bureaus, like over there"—he pointed to a pleasant bungalow which looked cool and unofficial under its protective canopy of shady trees—"then I see the black faces where I used to see only white ones, and I remembered how it used to be."

"How was it?" I asked.

41

"Well, you know how it is," he hedged. "Not too bad until they had to go. Then they smashed everything."

I had the feeling that remembering required an effort.

"Do you think they hated you because they had to leave after working so hard to make themselves comfortable?" It was my turn to wave toward the bungalows.

"Sure they hated us," one replied. "They didn't say much, but you could see it in their eyes. I used to drive for one of them. He was not bad, but you know what he did? Cut all the lights in the garage, broke everything. Cut up the water hose. His wife stood there looking at him, crying, while he chopped and chopped. Mad. I ran off and left them. He looked as if he would have liked to chop me up, too."

"And you," I asked, "do you still hate them?"

"I don't know," one replied. "If a fare comes along I don't ask him if he's a Frenchman." At this they all roared with laughter.

"It wasn't hating them," someone said. "I don't remember hating them. It was something else. I didn't hate them, but I wanted to see them leave."

"Some Frenchmen are staying in the hotel," one volunteered.

"He'll pay me in Guinea money, so I should care."

The hatred had either died or become forgotten. I suddenly felt foolish pursuing the matter. Perhaps, one day soon, there would be a new *rapprochement* with the French and the willingness and ability to forget would be an important advantage.

"Do you gentlemen own the taxis you drive?" I asked.

First the laughter, then the reply. Maybe the laughter was an ever-ready palliative. Behind it one could say anything, admit anything.

"Do we look as if we could own them?" one asked.

I let it drop. They looked as if they could or could not own taxis. How did a taxidriver look if he owned his taxi? They were all quite young, in the late twenties or early thirties, I supposed; dressed very much alike in linen slacks and gaily patterned sports shirts worn outside the top of the slacks. All wore caps of lightweight cotton material.

"What happens in this town at night?" I asked, purely for the hell of it, to establish something more of a "one-of-the-boys"

42

relationship with them. They again exchanged glances, smiling; and I had the feeling that from here on things would go very much according to plan: they would give me the treatment. I'd play it along for a while to see what I could see.

"Depends on what you want, doesn't it?" one asked.

"Nothing happens and everything happens, if you see what I mean," another said.

"I mean," I persisted, "how do people enjoy themselves here?"

"Well," someone said, "just now it's Ramadan, so there's not much going on, but even so, one can enjoy oneself."

"Or someone else's self," another added, to general laughter.

It was all a kind of game, giving nothing, making no commitment, promising nothing. I thought I'd be a bit bolder, but carefully so.

"Aren't there any dances, girls, things like that, I mean?"

"Sure," one said, "if you know where to look. Girls all over the place, people dancing and singing all the time." He gave his buddies a knowing look, and I knew that I'd get no further with them: this game of question and answers could go on for years.

I stayed with them until the right moment for retreating without indignity, then went into the hotel to shower and take a nap.

After dinner I asked at the reception desk for my account; I wanted to take care of my financial commitments early to avoid rush or delay next morning. A tall, smartly dressed woman was standing at the desk beside me, patiently waiting, as I was, while the clerk performed near-acrobatic feats as he simultaneously operated the telephone switchboard, sold stamps, issued and received keys, answered the queries of guests or junior staff, and attempted to add up our accounts. She was smiling with her eyes, a not very common thing to see these days.

"After another million years or so Man may have to sprout a few more arms in order to adapt himself to the crazy world he has created," she whispered conspiratorially in English. She may have overheard my bad workaday French and correctly divined my native language.

"By then instead of arms we might be sprouting a lot of supersensitive antennae just to show we are ahead of the men from Mars or the moon," I replied, tuning in on her pleasant mood.

43

I was nearly speechless at the total which the clerk presented. Then it dawned on me—the Guinea franc was quoted at near par with the French franc, but everything at the hotel cost in Guinea francs twice as much as the equivalent in French francs. There was nothing to do but pay up. Then came the snag: only Guinea currency was acceptable at the hotel—no personal or travelers checks, no dollars or sterling, and no exchange. I had insufficient Guinea francs and my dollar checks were not acceptable. So the fun began. The clerk argued and I protested and asked for the manager. But he was just as firm. "Nothing personal, Monsieur, but we cannot accept travelers checks; only the banks are allowed to do that." So what's to be done at eight thirty in the evening and all the banks closed, and even the Bureau de Change at the airport closed since six o'clock? The clerk suggested that I hand over the Guinea francs I had and someone from the hotel would accompany me to the airport next morning for the balance.

The lady had less bother. She had kept a careful reckoning of each day's spending and knew within a few francs how much she should pay, and had the amount required. Smart woman. It was with her help and excellent French that I finally reached an agreement with the clerk on the matter. I had a few francs left, enough for some coffee and invited her to join me.

"Thanks for your help," I said when we were seated at a small table in the lounge.

"Oh, it was nothing," she replied. "Which part of Africa are you from?"

"Not from Africa. The West Indies, via the U.S.A., Britain and more recently Paris."

"Oh!" Her face lit up. "And how is Paris? I'm longing to get back. I was born in Paris, you know."

That surprised me. Everything about her said England. The well-polished, sensible, low-heeled brogue shoes, the simply cut two-piece suit of cream Shantung, the neat, sensible coiffure, the round, slightly florid face, unwrinkled except for the nest of laughter lines around the eyes, which were of a clear gray, flecked with gold-brown tints. She wore no jewelry except for a thin wedding ring of whitish metal.

"You sound very English," I remarked.

44

"I've lived for seventeen years in New Zealand with my husband," she replied. "He's a university lecturer, or rather, he was. Now he works for UNESCO as a consultant in education. He's here to take a look at conditions in order to advise his organization on projects they hope to set up."

"Is your husband a New Zealander?"

"No, he's French."

"This your first trip here, to Africa?"

"No." I liked the sound of her voice, so warm and controlled. "We've been in the Sudan, and in the Cameroons, and in the Congo just before the trouble began."

"May I ask what you think of the progress of independence in Africa?" This would be very interesting for me, to hear another point of view.

"Everything depends on how one sees independence, and how one sees the African," she began, her fingers toying with the neat pleats of her skirt in their continuous quest for orderly alignment. "Independence is nothing new or startling. The world has lived with it from time immemorial. History is full of it, but too often we ignore the lessons contained in historical events. From the moment that a country is occupied or controlled by an invading force, or stranger group, peacefully or by might of arms, the process of independence is generated among those so occupied or invaded or annexed, call it what you will. It might take years, even centuries, but always there exists the need to be free of the occupier or invader. This has nothing to do with the type of government imposed or the degree of fraternization or integration between the indigenous and the occupiers, or the extent to which the indigenous ones seem to accept the new standards of education, housing, clothing, etc. It is merely that people, all people, have a natural inclination to freedom and are prone to express this inclination, sometimes in spite of what seems to be in their best interests.

"Every country now called developed has at some time or other experienced this compulsive need for independence, either as occupied or occupier, but we all seem loath to or incapable of appreciating it when we experience it among Africans. We expect that they will follow the pattern we design for 'occupied' people, until we decide to evacuate the territory or relinquish control of it,

45

and we cannot understand or accept that they should be, as we in our turn were, unwilling to wait. Like every fever, independence develops toward a critical point, critical for the occupiers as well as for the occupied. It could end in death, as we saw in the Congo situation, or there might be a reprieve for those who, for one reason or another, were unable to find a cure, a solution, before the point of crisis."

This woman spoke with feeling, as if she had lived very close to people in trouble and sympathized through a deep understanding.

"Strangely enough, as a Frenchwoman I am proud of every act perpetrated by my people in France against the occupying Germans. Had I been there, I too would have sabotaged and killed and done anything else which would have inconvenienced them. Nowadays there are Germans in business in Paris and no one hates or bothers them because the relationship is different. So it is with Africans. They want to be free, but we refuse to see it as springing from the same needs as our own, and we resist it until the point of crisis arrives. Ah! There he is."

Standing near the desk and looking searchingly about him was a short, thick-set man; his square, suntanned face and crew-cut gray hair seemed to belong to the typical athletic coach rather than to the intellectual his wife had mentioned. Catching sight of her he approached in quick, short, bouncy strides. I stood up to meet him. He bent down to kiss his wife, then extended his hand to me.

"I'm Pierre Bissele. I see you've met my wife."

His English had a slight drawl which betrayed his New Zealand association. We shook hands.

"My name is Braithwaite," I replied. "Your wife and I have met, although we had not got around to introducing ourselves. Delighted to meet you, Madame Bissele," I said, bowing to her. She laughed happily at the slightly ridiculous situation.

"We were onto my hobbyhorse," she told him. "African independence."

"Oh, that," he smiled, showing strong, square teeth. "That's become a universal hobbyhorse, because most people don't understand it, including my wife." He spoke soothingly, as one who had heard it all before and was prepared to be indulgent.

46

"This is one of our more familiar points of separate departure," she said to me, her tone easily matching her husband's for sweet patience; "in opposite directions. My husband believes that Africans should be trained, prepared for independence; whereas, I believe they should be helped toward responsible government. The two things are not the same, although they are interdependent. My husband believes that you can teach people to be independent. I disagree, because I believe that people are naturally disposed to independence, although it is true that sometimes it is possible to subject them to conditions which humiliate to the point of demoralizing and killing every last vestige of independence of spirit."

"Don't misquote me, *cherie,*" he interposed. "I admit to part of your observation, but with reservations. The African may wish independence, but he has to be taught how to use it, otherwise the ugly situation in the Congo would reproduce itself all over the place. That is a classic example of people who become independent without any idea of the meaning of it."

"No, darling," she insisted. "All that is classical about the Congo situation is the failure of certain people to appreciate the essential drives and aspirations of others until the point of crisis was reached and passed."

"Mr. Braithwaite," he addressed me, "you as an African might find my remarks difficult to accept, but it would seem that my wife has already been speaking quite frankly to you, so another voice should not be too hard to bear. You and your people have got to realize that established institutions and countries were not created overnight; some of them took centuries to build, yet you seem to think that all you need to do is say 'This land is mine' and you will be able to take effective control where the European with all his advancement to back him up, has not made much headway. You all want to run before you can even crawl. Everything must happen today, or even yesterday. No thought, no planning, because there is no experience to guide you. I see it every day in my particular field, education. Look at these new African States. They all want universities on the one hand and compulsory primary education on the other; but there's nothing in between to keep the balance. And when I tell them that before they can embark on any program of compulsory education they must develop a system of secondary education

47

and give it time to develop, they react as if I'm trying to sabotage their plans. But I know what's behind it; build a university to impress the other African States and introduce compulsory education to impress the voters, and the devil take the hindmost."

He wasn't so cool and detached now; this was his piece of the hobbyhorse and he was bouncing about in the saddle, and, to my mind, not very coherently.

"Your wife made the point earlier," I said, "that the compulsive urge to independence should be recognized and encouraged, and the people helped to understand and cope with the problems of government while there exists a state of harmony which favors such action. I am inclined to agree with her, especially as it is true to say that no new state in Africa became independent without reaching a point in the relationship between the colonial power and the local people when a measure of tension had developed."

"What my wife sometimes fails to consider," he said, "is the near impossibility of understanding the African mind. He does not react to circumstances in the same way as the European, nor does he . . ."

"Oh, what rot, Pierre" she said, with some heat. "What's all this talk about the African mind after all these years of European influence. Do you imagine that Africans are such supermen that they have remained unaffected by close contact with the British and the Germans and Dutch and French and God knows what! Your difficulty is that you see a situation as a Frenchman and you fondly imagine that your view is peculiar and special to you, or maybe only to Frenchmen. When an African speaks French, do you suppose that he is merely a kind of phonograph reproducing words? No, he is also expressing sense, overtones, nuances, all of which is possible only because something inside him has become identified with the words, and forever more that will be a part of himself, and he is therefore never again only African. The same thing is true of English-speaking or Spanish-speaking or any other Africans. And all these indefinable things play their part in this drive toward independence. So when you resist, you are resisting the African plus; and when you cooperate, you are cooperating with something besides the African, something akin to yourself."

As she spoke, she became calmer, assured in the rightness of her thinking, and I felt a deep sympathy with her.

"Do you think any African leader would agree with that?" he asked.

"Why should he, when we find it so hard to believe?" she replied. "Maybe it is because we recognize so much of ourselves in them that we resist so strongly. Maybe we fear ourselves, especially that part of ourselves reflected in them."

"Just for the record," I offered, "I'm not an African. I'm from the West Indies."

"Oh," he said.

"Does that make any difference?" she inquired.

"Not really," I agreed. "No difference at all."

"Of course it doesn't. A black American behaves and thinks as an American, and a black West Indian's behavior is, I am sure, as British as British, no matter what anyone says. The trouble with us white ones is that we cannot forget we once owned or ruled 'blacks,' so we think of the black American as a 'black' rather than as an American, and the African as a 'black' rather than as an African. We see the blackness and our whole attitude to them is colored by that. We have not yet learned that when they look out on the world and at themselves they see people, that's all, and they cannot abide the knowledge that we see them as something less, because, let's be honest about it, if we don't treat them as people, you know, as we see ourselves, then we treat them as something else, something lesser; and what's lesser than people? Animals! That's the crux of it. But I do believe, inside here," she touched her chest, "that the day we see the black people as just people, that day we will discover what respect means, and there will be no need for talk of tolerance and things like that, and it will surely follow that they will know it, and their whole attitude to us will immediately undergo a change—for the better."

She leaned back in her chair, slightly flushed. She had said her piece.

"You returning directly to the West Indies?" he asked. This was safer, easier ground.

"No, I'm visiting a few other African countries before returning to Paris. I live there."

"How do you like it there? How are you treated there? I mean, in day-to-day living?"

49

"I have no complaints. I like it."

"Are you treated decently, tolerantly?" he persisted.

I could see the point he was after.

"What kind of question is that?" his wife intervened. "If he is treated decently in Paris, what does that prove? Must every black man travel to Paris before he can expect decent treatment? And what's so wonderful about it anyway? What's so wonderful about treating a man as a man? Is that any cause for boasting? You see my point now, Pierre? When it is natural to us to see people as people, we will not need to expect any special honors for it." Then, turning to me, she really exploded. Her voice remained low, her hands inert in her lap, but her eyes shone, and her words had the force of hammer blows. "You speak of yourself as West Indian to indicate that you are different, I suppose, from the Africans. Is that it? If you walk down the street, would anyone looking at you recognize anything about you as different? I meet Africans very often who look very much like you, if you'll allow me," she added this with heavy sarcasm. "If wherever you come from," she went on, "you live and work in terms of equality with other people, you should be all the more concerned that everyone else can live and work in the same way. Your responsibility in this matter is as great as mine—not as a black man, but as a person."

I did not reply to her. I did not intend to separate myself from her observations on the universality of human dignity. By my reference to the country of my birth or the country in which I now lived, I was merely trying to avoid being in the false position of having the term "African" attached to me when in spite of my skin I was not an African. In my view this did not conflict with my opinions or sympathies, vis-à-vis human dignity in general and African interests in particular.

"Don't be too hard on our friend here," Pierre said to her, "he might be one of those men who likes to be nice to ladies. My wife," he said to me, "can be pretty tough when she thinks she is right. Have you arranged for transport to the airport?"

I realized that he wanted to be rid of the discussion. "No," I replied.

"Then we can travel together," he said. "I'm still using an official car, so you can ride with us to the airport. I think we'd better turn in, dear. It's up with the birds tomorrow."

We stood and once again there was pleasure in her eyes.

"Good night, my friend," she said. "I do not apologize for speaking frankly to you. The things we have been talking about concern us all very deeply, and we do not seem to realize how terribly important they are. My husband is an educator; I was trained as a nurse. How often do we stop to think of what will happen here in Africa when both education and health are improved to the point when Africans are living longer and healthier lives and are better educated to express themselves and apprehend local, national and international affairs? If things remain as they are now, in terms of poor interracial relationships, we will have to deal with many more Africans who will not only hate us, but be able to express their hatred in the same glib, sugar-coated way in which we often do.

"In short, there will be more of them and they will call the tune. Very soon we might discover that a white skin is a severe disadvantage in many parts of the world unless we work very hard to show that we, all of us, set great store by the man in the skin, not on the skin itself. Good night, and we'll see you tomorrow morning."

They walked away toward the stairs, arm in arm, and I looked on in some wonderment at those two persons who entertained so high a regard for each other that they were not swamped by each other, or afraid to express opinions for fear of being misunderstood. It seemed to me that if the same spirit should operate more widely between people that truth and dignity would not be subject to the dubious advantage of maintaining accord. Being with them had been exciting and stimulating, so much so that I felt no need to retire to bed and went out to walk around for my last look at Conakry. The taxis were gone, the main street deserted except for a lonely-looking dog which dragged itself lethargically along the center of the road.

There was the brightness of starlight, no moon, just a clearness which showed the road a straight, broad cutout between the deep blackness of shadow from the huge trees on both sides. Brighter in the center of town, where the trees gave place to the tall church spire and the ministries. Dark night and stillness, with somewhere near a rustling of living things, trees maybe, or restless birds, or people breathing deep in sleep.

I thought, "So this is Africa, and these trees were here a long, long time. It must take many, many years to make such big trees, and maybe, in the long ago, someone walked here, or slept here and loved here to start or continue the sequence which involved me, produced me. Perhaps. Where are they now, the ones dead and silent so long? If I stand still will I feel anything of them? Where I stand now, did any of my forebears pass here, either freely or bound for the beach and the boats of the traders? All you witch doctors and diviners in which my fathers and their fathers believed, where are you now; can you see that the son who left has returned in the son of his son's son?" I wished that I knew something of my origin to give me the right to say, "In such and such a place my father's people stood and fought. . . ." But perhaps I am lucky in that I have no known point of origin; all Africa is therefore my original home, and I am at liberty to take my choice. Madame Bissele's words came to my mind: "from the moment a country is occupied or controlled by an invader force or stranger group, as from that moment the process of independence is generated." What she probably meant was that the consciousness of independence was generated—that is, if one believed that all men are born with the right to freedom.

For a long time many people are born and live into circumstances of poverty, illiteracy, chronic ill-health and disease, and seem to accept these circumstances until suddenly an awakening and unrest develops and is generally directed against any group of persons or set of circumstances which seem to be, in any way, responsible for their difficulties. How did all this affect me? How did it matter to me? If the things I believed in had any real virtue in them, then I was in fact involved with all mankind, and my involvement in and with Africa and Africans was not because of my black skin, but my kinship with people, any people. All around me was a certain sadness; underlying the warmth and the sunshine and the color and the beauty was the sadness of conflict, the sadness of distrust, of opposed attitudes which seemed to desire to remain opposed and irreconcilable.

All that I had seen so far in Guinea indicated a great and amazing richness of natural resources which still remained untapped. What was the point of boasting of them if none of the people benefited? And where was the value of such amazing potential if they remained unchanneled to serve the urgent needs of the millions of needy, hungry people? A bowl of rice is much more important to a hungry man than an ideology, yet ideological interests seemed to take precedence over the needs of people.

I remembered attending some of the sessions at the United Nations Headquarters in New York last December and listening to important persons talk about the terrible circumstances of people who were living in "low-income countries" at "below-subsistence level." Words, words, words. If some of these important men were forced to live, even for a little while, at below-subsistence level they would more readily apply themselves to examining positive measures to relieve those circumstances. If I must believe the evidence of what I had so far seen and heard in Guinea, then it was clear that efforts made to stimulate national progress were to some extent inhibited by the general preoccupation with distrust of individuals and states believed to be critical of Guinea's political attitudes; but how far was it possible to avoid feelings of hate or distrust when the criticism took the place of sorely needed economic and other assistance? As the man said, a bowl of rice can be a powerful and even final argument.

I wandered toward the beach, where, now at low tide, the sand shelved downward to a black, muddy waterline and seaward to the narrow neck of the inlet, above which perched the lighthouse, which swung a recurrent finger of light at treetop level along the cove. I sat down on the sand trying to convince myself that I should be unhappy to leave this place, but already the excitement of tomorrow had taken hold. Tomorrow I would be in Freetown, Sierra Leone. Tomorrow I would have the wonderful experience of pre-independence fever. Before leaving Paris I had followed closely the gradual build-up of interest in the British and French newspapers, and now I would see and feel it for myself.

Part Two
SIERRA LEONE

The plane maintained a course along the shoreline from Conakry to Freetown, and from twelve thousand feet the main impression was of a succession of swampy river deltas and wide areas of mud; by checking a map I had bought in Paris, I easily located the watershed at the confluence of the Great and Little Scarcies rivers. Everything down there looked desolate, forbidding and savage, with hardly any sign of hutments to indicate human habitation. There seemed to be endless small islands surrounded by expanses of gray mud through which narrow streams snaked their way in a tortuous pattern and reflected the sunlight like the ribbings of some giant green leaf after the ravages of a hungry caterpillar. Farther south beyond this delta along the coastline bordering the Port Loko district, we flew along a wide beach which continued like a golden causeway between the blue-green sea and the deeper green of the inner coastline, to Lungi Airport and beyond.

The plane made a wide circle and I caught a glimpse of the wide, irregular estuary into which the Rokel River, the Port Loko Creek, and a multitude of smaller streams emptied themselves, before we landed at Lungi Airport. My first impression was of quiet order. All the airport requirements, customs declarations, baggage clearance, visas, etc., were conducted with speed and courtesy by a staff that seemed to know exactly what its duties were. I was deeply impressed. These people were evidently all set for the big day, Independence Day, and were ready to assume their responsibilities.

From the airport passengers boarded a bus which would take us a few miles north to Lungi for the crossing by launch to Freetown. During the bus ride I observed the countryside: very much the same as in Guinea, with the huge mango trees in heavy bloom dominating everything; here and there I glimpsed a small hut and the faces of shy children peeping at us from behind tree trunks.

Freetown looked very attractive from across the wide Rokel estuary, its white-painted houses sharply contrasting with the green hillside and the wide Atlantic in the distance. The launch made its way laboriously across the placid mouth of the estuary and tied up at an ancient-looking jetty; disembarking required a few willing hands from the launch's crew. While waiting on the dock for my baggage to be unloaded I overheard a bit of conversation between two youths who were sitting on the edge of the dock watching the passengers disembark, and I felt a thrill as I recognized the 'dialect' they were using: as a boy I had often heard it in British Guiana, especially the market people and fisherfolk, and had even probably spoken it myself. There it was called 'creole,' the pidgin English of onetime slaves. Now I listened as they ran a kind of commentary-dialogue on each passenger: his baggage and possible reason for visiting Sierra Leone—most probably they had already expressed their observations about me. Hearing the dialect pleased me because it represented one contact, at least, with the indigenous people. If it were spoken generally among them I would have very little difficulty in understanding them, and, with some practice, might in time even be able to make myself understood in it.

They must have realized that I was listening to them, understanding them, because they looked questioningly at me, at which I smiled and asked, "What is the name of the dialect you are using?"

"Sir?"

"What kind of language was that?"

"Crio, master."

I looked carefully at the youth, rather surprised and perhaps a bit shocked by the "master"; never before in my life had anyone so addressed me. He was smiling, so perhaps he was just having a lark with me, and the "master" meant nothing at all.

"I understood what you were saying to your friend," I told him. "Where I come from they sometimes speak the same thing."

They exchanged puzzled glances. "You not from Sierra Leone?" asked one.

"No, this is my first visit here. As a matter of fact, I'm on my first visit to Africa."

The smiles broadened and they looked at me with greater interest. Just then the porters from the launch shouted something and the two youths rushed toward the landing steps and grabbed several pieces of luggage, mine among them, and proceeded toward the exit. When my baggage was placed in the boot of a taxi for my

58

short ride to the hotel, I tipped the youth and again heard, "Thank you, master."

The term "master" irritated me. I had never before encountered it in this way, had never in my life used it to anyone, and did not like even the sound of it. Evidently it was common practice here because I heard the term used by other porters. However, I quickly forgot about it in the excitement of being in Sierra Leone. Looking around the dock everything seemed old and somewhat deserted like an English midlands town on Sunday morning. The "harbor" was in fact a series of wooden platforms on piles above high-water mark; against them a few old launches and schooners were moored, and I wondered whether this was a familiar state of affairs or merely one of those days when nothing seemed to be happening. The buildings alongside the dock were, for the most part, old dilapidated structures in sore need of repair and paint. From some distance across the harbor these same buildings had looked clean and attractive in the bright sunlight.

After the taxidriver had stowed away my baggage, we set off for the hotel and, emerging from the fenced-in area of the dockside, I had my first look at Freetown, Sierra Leone. I do not really know what I expected to see; maybe my imagination had been influenced by the lengthy newspaper reports recently appearing in London, and the numerous references to the Sierra Leone's established position as the oldest of the West African colonies, and its supported boast of founding the Institution for Higher Education in the region at Fourah Bay. Now here I was, already damp and uncomfortable from the oppressive heat, which seemed even greater after the cool trip across the Rokel estuary; yet keenly anticipating the reality of closeness to the phenomenon of immediate independence. I had expected to be temporarily a part of something dramatic and exciting, something I would want to remember for a long, long time.

There was not much to be seen from the taxi, which honked its way through groups of people and around lethargic dogs, then uphill where the road followed the curve of a high stone wall beyond which could be glimpsed a white-painted cupola, with a Union Jack hanging limply from a flagpole, past a wide wrought-iron gate at which two soldiers stood stiffly on guard, picturesque in smart khaki uniforms and red fezzes.

"Governor's mansion," the taxidriver volunteered.

About two hundred yards farther on, the taxi swung into a wide driveway and drew up before the covered entrance of a new modernistic building: the Paramount Hotel, Freetown's newest. Several young Africans in khaki uniforms collected my few pieces of baggage, waited until I had registered, then led the way up to my room. I offered each a small tip, which was rather shame-facedly received but speedily pocketed, then each, with palms pressed together in the familiar gesture of prayer, bowed low and said, "Thank you, master." I stood at the door of my room and watched them whispering their way down the corridor, somewhat irritated by their obsequiousness. There had been nothing like it in Guinea, but, more than that, I could not readily adjust to being called "master." Was it the normal thing here in Sierra Leone or was it the required thing at this hotel? But the dock porters had said the same thing, so maybe it was widespread. Perhaps it was even general throughout Africa and only dropped by independent people, as in Guinea. Maybe they will drop it here after April 27, their Independence Day. Christ! These fellows were not behaving as I thought they would with independence so near at hand, but perhaps I was seeing too much in a very simple situation.

My room was very comfortable, well-equipped and air-conditioned, so I took my time with a shave and shower and change of clothing. I thought I might take an easy stroll about the town and try to get in touch with a few persons to whom I had letters of introduction from mutual friends in London. Maybe I could have a meal at a restaurant somewhere in the town.

As I emerged from my room the heat struck me like a blast from a furnace. In the cool comfort of my room I had forgotten all about the heat, and now I could feel the perspiration along my sides under the armpits. I was dressed very lightly in a short-sleeved shirt and lightweight slacks and thought I must look very silly to appear so uncomfortably warm when so much about me suggested familiarity with tropic conditions.

It was now about midday and the sun rode high in a clear sky. I followed the road back to the Governor's mansion and paused by the gate to take a quick peep at that part of the building which I could see, a circular buttress of solid, weathered rock, somewhat

60

like the base of a medieval castle. The guards looked at me somewhat suspiciously, so I moved on. About two hundred yards away from this main entrance to the Governor's mansion I could see a huge tree of the silk-cotton variety; it stood proudly at the junction of several roads, towering upwards of ninety feet and completely dominating its surroundings with wide-branched, leafy majesty. In a direct line from the Governor's gate to this huge tree workmen were busy preparing a piece of wide roadway bisected down the center by a narrow raised concrete trough in which young palm trees and saplings wilted in the heat, not yet adjusted to their transplant. Apart from a small, asthmatic steamroller, all the work on this piece of road was being done by hand.

I walked along the edge of this piece of roadway observing the workmen at their tasks. They were unhurried, joking with each other. I wondered what the significance of this piece of road was, because it ended abruptly at the cotton tree, and there was no sign of other road-making in the vicinity. I guessed that this was in preparation for the Independence Day celebrations, and followed the main road from the cotton tree toward the center of town. Along the way were planted several large flagploes painted alternately red, white, and blue, and I noticed that one or two large official-looking buildings were receiving new coats of paint.

As I walked, I was listening with every part of me for some evidence of that ambience which to my mind was indivisible from so immediate and important an occasion. I listened as I passed individuals or groups; I looked into people's faces in an attempt to locate some sign that they were carrying a wonderful half-secret thing which I wanted to share, and I marveled that I saw nothing, heard nothing. Not yet, I promised myself; not for a while yet, not until I'd learned to read the signs, for signs there must be. These people could not possibly be on the brink of such a wonderful period of their history and remain apathetic. Maybe I was not reading the signs correctly. I needed help, so I set out to find some of those persons to whom I had been given letters of introduction.

It was very warm, and I envied the passersby, black and white, who for the most part seemed quite at ease, probably from birth or long association with conditions. The road led toward the waterfront and the busy shopping center. One large store with the label "Cold Storage" attracted me, probably because of the hint of something cold or cool. Inside it was refreshingly cool, but what was more, there was displayed a wide variety of foodstuffs and cellophane-wrapped packages of fruit. I caught sight of some lovely red apples, and waited at the counter to be served by one of the clerks, of whom there were several, black and white of both sexes. After some minutes one of the clerks, an African, approached, but, to my surprise, addressed himself to someone behind me, an Englishwoman, who without hesitation gave her order from a list she had in her hand. I stood there, surprised and irritated, while he passed her packets to her, and she in turn handed them to an African boy who arranged them carefully in a large basket he carried. I had the impulse to make some protest, but refrained, because I was not sure that she had not preceded me into the store and may have been wandering around while waiting to be served. The clerk's attitude to her was courteous, possibly even deferential, but when her order was completed and she left, he turned to me with a casual, "Yes?"

I asked for a pound of apples, and paid with an English pound note. He deducted the cost of the apples and gave me the change in local currency, which, though similarly in shillings and pence, differed from the English coinage in size, color, and sometimes in shape. I was examining these unfamiliar coins and looked up to observe the clerk, regarding me with evident distaste. He remarked, "Don't worry, it's all there less sixpence exchange charge for the English pound."

Evidently he thought I was being unnecessarily careful with the change because I did not trust him, so I hastened to say, "Sorry, I'm only trying to familiarize myself with your currency. It's a bit strange to me."

"Aren't you a Sierra Leonean?" he asked, surprised.

"No, this is my first visit here," I replied. "My first to Africa, in fact."

His whole attitude changed. He smiled at me and extended his hand over the counter. "Welcome to Sierra Leone," he said.

"Thank you," I replied.

I collected my change and left, wondering about him; he was brusque and offhand for as long as he thought I was a local citizen,

62

but courteous and charming when he realized I was a stranger. Weren't the local black citizens entitled to courteous treatment also? It was comforting to feel that I could so easily fit into the background of black Africa, at least in this piece of it, but it would be even more comforting to see some sign of the dignity and consciousness of equality which should be indivisible from independence.

I now wanted to locate my contact without wandering about too much in the heat and signaled a passing taxi. He promptly swung the car toward me and braked it to a squealing stop. He claimed to know the address and we set off, turning and twisting through innumerable side streets, barely missing chickens, dogs, goats and children at play. Soon I realized that we seemed to be getting exactly nowhere and asked the driver where we were. After some hesitation he admitted that he did not know the street we wanted, so I suggested that we inquire from a policeman we had passed a short while ago. Whenever I've been in doubt about my location I've found policemen very helpful.

We approached this one and I made my request. He stared at me, looking quite bewildered, so I repeated my question, and to help matters, showed him the little address book in which my contact's name and address were written. He made no attempt to take or look at it, merely shook his head and shrugged his shoulders, and it suddenly dawned on me that he was unable to read; furthermore he seemed unable to understand what I was saying to him. I asked the driver to ask the policeman, in creole dialect, to direct us to Kinglsey Street. To this inquiry the policeman shook his head negatively.

"Aborigine," the driver remarked with a chuckle. "He don't know nothing."

Fresh as I was from Europe, and remembering as far back as I could of my early childhood in British Guiana, I could not recall having previously met an illiterate policeman; never, and the experience shocked me. How would he cope with any difficulty which might present itself, especially if it required that he make a written record or report of the event? He was on guard duty, but what exactly did that mean? To what extent could he control or intervene in a situation? Perhaps policemen in Sierra Leone were not

63

expected to be mobile information bureaus, but what would he do if there was an accident, a serious one involving injury or even loss of life?

The driver had the idea that we should inquire about my friend's address from the Department of Public Works, which was quite close to us now. They gave us firsthand information and I was soon able to find the house, a pleasant wooden building in a quiet back street. Then followed a rather heated argument with the taxidriver, who expected to be paid for all the time wasted in locating the place, completely ignoring the fact that he had misled me into believing he knew the address.

Mr. Morris Lindsay was large. No other term would fittingly describe him. Everything about him was large: the protruding eyes, the shiny bald head which fitted snugly into his shoulders without need of a neck, the thick torso from which his large arms seemed to sprout outward, and the thick legs, ending in large sandaled feet.

He had been sitting in a wide rattan chair in the main room of his house when I knocked and entered to his hearty "Come in." With surprising ease for such bulk he stood up and enveloped my hand in a very powerful grip. I introduced myself, while watching him, fascinated by the smooth-skinned immensity of the man, for because of the warmth he wore only a pair of khaki shorts and sandals; and in spite of his size one had an immediate impression of strength rather than obesity.

He read the letter from our mutual friend, then again shook hands with me, bidding me welcome to Sierra Leone.

"So you write," he said.

"A little, bits and pieces."

"And now you want to write about Africa,"

"No."

"No?"

"Not about Africa. About myself in Africa. You see, it would take a long time for me to be able to write about Africa; but I can write about myself in Africa from the moment I landed. You know, impressions—things like that."

"Everybody begins by doing that, but it generally turns out to be what they call a factual report on Africa today."

"Maybe, but I think I'll stick very closely to writing about me."

64

"Good. Our friend has asked me to help you; what would you like me to do?"

"I'm not sure really. Probably talk with me about your country, introduce me to other people if possible, explain things to me, anything you think might help me to understand the things I see and hear."

He smiled, and I suddenly noticed that he seemed to be all of one piece. What I mean is that his face and head were all at one with the rest of him, probably because there was no hair to break the smooth unity of line; when he smiled even the rolypoly creases in the back of his neck seemed involved in the process.

"I'll do what I can," he said, "in so far as my work allows. By the way, I thoroughly enjoyed your book. Is that the only one you've written?"

"So far, but I'm working on two at the moment."

He excused himself, walked to a doorway and shouted something to someone, then returned. "Make yourself comfortable," he said, pointing to a cushioned wooden stool. He settled himself comfortably in his chair, his huge torso settling into sections like a bronze Buddha. A handsome young woman came in with cold beer and glasses on a tray, which she placed on a low table, and, without a word to or from either of us, as silently disappeared. The drink was very refreshing and must have come straight from a refrigerator. Nice living, I thought. He had made no attempt to introduce me to the young woman, though she looked more like a member of the family than a servant.

He asked about my hotel, if I was comfortable, then about Europe, London, where he had studied for a time, and Paris, which he had visited briefly. "You'll find things very different here," he remarked.

I explained that I was primarily interested in Sierra Leone's impending independence and would like to see something of the popular attitude to it.

Suddenly he laughed, a loud, booming sound. "I don't think I can help you much there," he said. "You'll have to look around and make up your own mind. I'll talk to you about anything else you like, but not independence. Let me put it this way, and I'll borrow the words of a certain lady magistrate: 'I am not opposed to independence.' But so far as arranging for you to meet other people and see places of interest, I think I can help. I can run you around in my car if you like, provided you supply the petrol."

I readily agreed, but said, "I hope I shall not make too many demands upon you—interfere with your work."

"Oh, that's no bother," he replied. "My time is my own. I'm an agent, you see, I represent firms in Britain and on the Continent, so I do not have to account to anyone about my time. How long do you plan to stay here?"

"A week or two," I said. "It all depends on what's happening. I could probably stay even longer."

"Good. But let's get one thing understood. No matter what you see and hear, no matter what I say to you, don't quote me. I've got a living to earn, and I'll still have to earn my living long after you're gone. Okay?"

I agreed.

"Are you attending the reception tonight at your hotel?" he asked.

"I didn't know there was a reception there," I answered. "Is it a public thing? Who's giving it?"

"No, it's not public. It's being given by the representative of the United Arab Republic to celebrate something or other—I can't remember. I've an invitation here somewhere. If you'd like to go I guess I can take you in. Everybody likes meeting authors. You'd be sure to meet some of our local bigwigs there." He laughed. "Maybe they will tell you about independence."

"I'd like that very much" I told him.

We agreed to meet in the lobby of the Paramount Hotel at 6 P.M., and after some further conversation I left him.

The sun had swung away from overhead, and the shadows under the trees and along the sides of buildings were areas of comparative comfort, although every movement along this side street struck up clouds of thick reddish dust which clung as a discoloring film on all the bushes and low-hanging branches nearby. Most of the houses were set some little distance away from the street, surrounded by trees, mainly orange and mango trees. The houses were all of wooden construction, most of them shabby-looking either from an urgent need of paint or even more urgent need of structural repairs.

The yards around these houses were generally very untidy, littered with rusty scraps of old cars or bicycles and the discards of tinned foods, with here and there ugly little pools of greasy water which had collected from frequent washing up. In one yard a few women were busy around two large cooking pots on an open fireplace which was a simple structure of several large stones set closely together, allowing room between them for sticks of firewood. There were small children everywhere, the youngest naked, the others in thin shorts or dresses of lengths of printed cloth secured waist high and flowing about their feet. Some of these young children were girls in their early teens and quite unself-conscious of their delicate young breasts. All these children looked smooth-skinned and healthy in spite of the swarms of flies and mangy dogs everywhere.

Where the side street joined the main macadam road, which I had taken on the way in, I was still some distance from the center of town and could see no sign of a taxi, so I set out to walk it. The road was barely wide enough to permit two cars to pass each other in safety, and was edged on both sides by deep, narrow, concrete gullies for drainage. These gullies looked very dangerous and I wondered what happened at night to the unwary motorist who might swerve too close to the roadside. There was no pavement along the road, nothing more than a narrow lip of ground between the gully and the entrance to the shops and dwelling houses which lined the roadway in an unbroken, untidy line.

The general impression was of untidiness, with litter everywhere. The buildings were a hodgepodge of wooden latticework and convoluted sheets of galvanized iron, and I felt that each one was overpopulated. Men and women everywhere, hanging out of windows, sitting in doorways, standing in small groups wherever there was some shade, as if everybody had lots of time to spare; lots and lots of time.

The nearer I came to the center of town, the more crowded it seemed, not of people, but of these ugly, untidy dwellings. Nobody seemed to be houseproud here; there was no sign of flowers being tended, even in window boxes. At some of the doorways women sat with large trays of peeled oranges for sale; I was amused by the small collections of pulpy discard near to each of them, for it seemed that they themselves ate as much as they hoped to sell, and would probably eat all of it if there were no buyers. I did not think I would want to buy fruit presented in that way—years of exposure to certain standards of hygiene cannot easily be ignored.

All the time I was looking for some means of making contact with some of the people at this level, but didn't quite know where to begin. One shop carried the sign "Ritz Bar" and advertised beer "ice cold." I went in. A dingy room with a counter and two or three wooden chairs; probably the patrons had their drinks standing up or the place did not cater to more than three patrons. Behind the counter was a curtained doorway. No one was in sight so I knocked on the counter. Presently a man appeared from behind the curtain, red-eyed with sleep and asked, "Yes?"

This seemed to be the current form of address in these parts. I asked for a cold beer and he disappeared behind the curtains; perhaps that doorway led to his living quarters. I noticed that there were no shelves of bottled liquor anywhere in the room, nor cases of beer or even mineral water. Some bar! He reappeared with a bottle of beer and a glass, one in each hand. The beer looked frosty-cold and I waived the glass, deciding to drink straight from the bottle. I had the feeling that the glass might not be well washed, that this sleepy fellow might not be too careful about such things. I tilted up the bottle and took a long swig.

"That's good," I said.

"Mmmm," he grunted.

"Terribly hot outside," I said.

"Ummm," he grunted. Not much of a conversationalist, it seemed. Try again.

"My first visit to your country," I said. "I've been walking around having a look. Very interesting."

"Ummm," he grunted, this time passing a large hand across his face as if to wipe away whatever was befogging his mind.

"With independence so near this must be a very exciting time for you," I said, teasing him into some sort of comment.

"What?" At least this was better: one word, but better than a grunt.

"Independence," I repeated. "How do you feel about it?"

"Where are you from?" he asked. "Nigeria?"

So many words all at once, it sounded like a speech. "No," I said. "British Guiana."

"What?" His wide face wrinkled in puzzlement. "You mean Guinea?"

"No, it's in South America." He peered closely at me, examining me.

"You look like you're from Nigeria," he said.

"About independence," I prompted. "How do you feel?"

"To hell with independence!" he exclaimed. "What the hell good is it to me? That's for the politicians up there." He pointed through the main doorway, toward the center of town.

"Doesn't the thought of independence excite you?" I asked.

"Why the hell should it excite me?" he countered. "I'll be no better off. Do you think I care? To hell with them."

Evidently a man of few words, few and pointed words. I decided to play it along some more in the hope of learning something more about his feeling and the reasons behind them.

"But soon you'll have your own government and the experience of being free people."

His laugh was short and bitter, like spitting without mucus.

"Free for what? Who's been telling that? Free? Why the hell do you think they won't have elections before Independence Day?" He spoke as if I understood about the local situation; I didn't know anything about an election proposal or the Government's refusal to consider it.

"What freedom are you talking about?" he went on. "We might get rid of the whites, but the black bastards who take over will be lots worse, take it from me. If you even open your mouth they'll get you, take it from me. Shaka Stevens will find that out soon enough."

He was progressing from strength to strength, but I still did not understand much of it. Who or what was Shaka Stevens, and what was he likely to find out? Anyway, easy does it. Maybe a cold beer might encourage him to say more and I would try to unravel it later. His speech was heavily inflected and broad, but easily understandable.

"Who is Shaka Stevens?" I asked.

"Where did you say you were from?" he countered.

69

"British Guiana."

"Oh yes," he said, probably not knowing or understanding, but satisfied. "Shaka Stevens used to be in the Government. Now he wants them to have elections before independence, but they'll throw him in jail, I'm sure."

None of this made sense to me because I had no background in it. I'd try another gambit. "I've not heard anybody talking about independence although it's so near at hand."

"Who the hell cares?" he said.

He was losing interest. "Have a beer with me," I invited.

"Sorry," he replied. Then "Ramadan" in explanation.

This rather surprised me. I had not been surprised to find Mohammedanism in such a force in a onetime French colony, but somehow it seemed out of place in a British colony; perhaps I was thinking of Africa in the same terms as I remembered British Guiana, with Christianity generally predominant though sectionalized. I bade him goodbye and walked out once more into the warm afternoon. The road continued on toward the town center and I saw the cotton tree towering up ahead; now I knew my way and was soon back at the hotel.

*

Just before six o'clock I was in the hotel lounge, freshly shaved and changed into a lightweight suit of dark blue material, black shoes, white shirt and dark blue tie. This, I expected, was just right for the occasion. I sat in the lounge, ordered a drink, and watched the people come in: Europeans and Africans, some of the latter in national dress, bright-hued affairs of flowing robes which looked at once comfortable, cool and pleasantly decorative.

Mr. Lindsay appeared soon after six-thirty, wearing a kind of loose garment of native cloth, alternately striped blue and white, and shaped rather like a Spanish poncho; it was worn over European slacks and shiny black shoes. His round, strong face smiled beneath a fez handsomely decorated with an intricate pattern of silver and scarlet threads.

70

"Sorry to keep you waiting," he greeted me, "but this is Africa; you'll soon get accustomed to our time."

"Like hell," I thought. It always irritates me to wait on tardy people, and I could not see that being in Africa should make any difference.

"Let's go." I followed close behind him, marveling at the ease with which he carried his great bulk, like a dancer or prizefighter.

The reception was held in a lovely, ground-level, open patio which opened off the main dining room of the hotel and was surrounded by a high wall and rows of trees and low bushes trimmed to form a hedge. The central floor of polished stone was surrounded by a lawn of coarse grass; running through the surrounding trees were strings of colored lights. I was introduced to two or three Arab dignitaries, who received us most graciously at the entrance to the patio. Inside there were many men and women, black and white, standing about in small groups, chatting and sipping drinks which were served by busy waiters with laden trays.

"Ah, the Old Man's here," my friend whispered, nodding in the direction of a small group which included a thin, gray, elderly man who seemed to me rather ill and pale beneath his dark skin in spite of his decorative national dress and the slim fez erect on his narrow head.

"Is that the Prime Minister?" I whispered.

"Yes, that's the Old Man," he replied.

I had read of Sir Milton Margai and seen photographs of him in English newspapers, but had somehow got the impression of a vigorous, aggressive person, totally unlike the man standing a few feet away.

"Come, I'll introduce you," my friend said, and steered me to the group. He waited until there was a short break in their conversation, then presented me. The Prime Minister held out a limp, bony hand and made pleasant sounds without seeming to pay much attention to me. He seemed to be preoccupied, but mostly he seemed to be ill. "God," I thought, "how can this feeble old man undertake the task of leading his country through the initial phase of its independence?" A new independent State needed vigor and health—yes, health, and probably youth—but this man looked old, even feeble. But perhaps I was missing something here. "Remember

71

Churchill," I reminded myself. "Think of de Gaulle, and Adenauer. Old men in years, but forceful, dominant, vigorous. Maybe this man is the same. Maybe right now he is ill, but that might be a very temporary state of things."

We left the group and my friend said, "What did you think of him?"

"A bit old, isn't he."

"So?"

"He looked rather feeble, or ill."

"Take your pick."

God, this one was such a matter-of-fact fellow, admitting nothing, committing himself in no way.

"How did he make it?" I asked. "I mean, aren't there younger men to challenge him for leadership? Seems to me this independence thing calls for youth, as in the other African States."

"Oh, some tried," he smiled. "That's all you can say for them— they tried. Don't be deceived by his frail looks; he's as tough as rope and he's forgotten more political tricks than most of these younger ones will ever learn. Looks near to death, doesn't he? Some have been fooled by it before now. One bright young fellow, who shall be nameless because he also is in the Government, once gave the Old Man one week to live. Lousy guesser."

"Oh, why did he do that?"

"Medical opinion. He's a doctor. But the Old Man fooled him. You see, he too is a doctor." He grinned mischievously. "In this game you've got to do more than wish."

We circulated and he introduced me to several government officials and their wives, among them two ministers, one of whom was a slim young man who wore a filmy silk poncho over his European clothes and a fez. We chatted with him and his wife for a minute or so, when he looked at his wristwatch, murmured something about being late for something or other and led his wife away.

My friend laughed, "You're very fortunate," he said. "He allowed you all of a minute of his precious time. Usually you can figure on him checking his watch after standing still for a few seconds. Always on the run, that one, mostly from himself, because nobody's chasing that I can see. But he's smart enough to run in the right direction, so far."

72

"Don't you like him?"

"Who me? Friend, I like everybody." His voice was sweet as honey.

I met the State representatives of Liberia and Nigeria, and their wives, and representatives of the International Cooperation Administration, together with local personalities. One young newspaperman asked if I was the author of *To Sir, With Love*, and on my admitting it, said he would like to interview me for his newspaper. I agreed and we arranged to lunch together the following day. There were several Britons present, officials of one sort or another who seemed to be on terms of easy relaxed *camaraderie* with the Africans. "This bodes well for post-independence relationships," I thought.

It was altogether a very pleasant affair, but it required a real effort of will to remember that I was in Africa and not at some cocktail party in Europe. Only very few of the Africans wore national dress; most of them favored English worsteds and tweeds and succeeded in looking even more formal than the British. Around seven-thirty people began to drift away and I invited my friend to dine with me at the hotel.

"Sorry," he said, "I must break my fast with the family. Some other time." I then realized that I had not seen him take a drink during the evening. We agreed to meet late the following afternoon, and he left me.

Dinner was very much in the British tradition: whispered conversation, subdued laughter and servants hurrying on near-silent feet. The servants in the dining room seemed to be of two categories, i.e., those who waited at tables and were obviously illiterate, having much difficulty in either understanding what was said to them or in making themselves understood, and those who supervised them. These latter were literate and wore red cummerbunds to distinguish them from their lowlier brethren; over both these groups was a major domo, a courteous, intelligent young man far removed from the sickening obsequiousness in which the others indulged. Perhaps I am not as liberal and objective as I would like to be, but I must confess to feeling an acute irritation every time I saw one of these young men bowing so servilely to the guests, halfway to touching the ground. What the hell kind of preparation was this for independence, or hadn't these young men heard about it? Would they continue to do this after April 27, or would they suddenly stop, in mid-obeisance, so to speak, when the guns roared and the bells pealed the good news? Would it be good news to them? Did they know anything about it?

After dinner I took a short walk around the environs of the hotel. It was cool now and people were sitting in doorways, chatting and laughing together, while small children played noisy games in the dusty street when, in my opinion, they should long ago have been abed. Try as I might, I just could not get the feeling that something important loomed ahead for this country, for these people. I was very surprised and somewhat disappointed.

*

The newspaper reporter arrived on time next day and I suggested lunch.

"Fine," he said, "but not here. I can't stand this place, with its stiff atmosphere and bowing flunkeys and sky-high prices. I'd rather eat somewhere else."

"Is there somewhere else?"

"We could try the City Hotel, a short walk down the road, or we could drive out to the Government rest house on the edge of town, but I'd recommend the City Hotel. Lots of atmosphere; everybody goes there sooner or later. It used to be *the* hotel before this one was built. Part of its fame derives from the fact that Graham Greene lived there while writing *The Heart of the Matter*.

"Sold," I said. "Let's go."

He was right about the "short walk"—but I couldn't be sure about the atmosphere. I saw a large wooden three-storied building very much in colonial-American style, with double-entrance stairways and railed portico. It had once been painted white, a long time ago, but had finally given up the unequal struggle against daily layers of red dust. In one corner of the portico an African peddler had spread his wide collection of curios: tanned snake skins, handmade sandals, beads, carved heads in gleaming ivory or ebony, crudely made handbags of crocodile or alligator hide; a

74

miscellany slightly different from that for which his ancestors had sold their land or their brethren into slavery. The wheel had certainly turned around.

The lounge of the hotel was cool, unpretentious and comfortable. Yes, comfortable, not in its furnishings, for these were simple, contrived wooden arrangements; but in the immediate welcome which the room itself seemed to extend, as well as the hearty, heavily inflected "Hi, fellers" which the owner shouted from his perch behind the bar. And here, for the first time I saw black and white men and women sitting, drinking and chatting in the friendliest and most relaxed terms. I guessed that this was what my companion meant by "atmosphere."

A waiter *waddled* over to take our order. No other term could effectively describe his odd, splay-footed gait and the way he swung his arms, as if to help propel himself forward. A loose-limbed, ugly fellow with the cheeriest of smiles, he seemed to know and be on very personal terms with everyone, and either greeted them by name or with the word "boss," which he used indiscriminately to man and woman alike. We ordered ham sandwiches and beer.

"Well, Mr. Braithwaite," my companion began, "what do you think of Freetown?"

"Is this the interview?" I asked.

"Yes, part of it."

"I don't know what to think of Freetown yet," I replied. "I've seen very little of it in physical terms, but the thing I want most to to see is either very elusive or nonexistent."

"What's that?"

"Attitude, feeling, atmosphere, call it what you like, a sort of general air of anticipation of independence. I expected it to be the chief talking point on everyone's lips, the major topic of news, but so far I've been unable to hear anything, feel anything."

"Things are happening, though," he said.

"I'm sure they are. I've seen a nice piece of road being built from the Governor's house to the cotton tree, all of a hundred yards or so, and I've seen some bright-painted flagpoles, and some fairy lights in trees, so I'm sure things are happening. But what about the people, what's happening with them?"

"You mean you expect to see us excited?"

"Frankly, yes. I'd be very excited if British Guiana were to become independent in a few days, I can assure you."

"You must understand, we in Sierra Leone are a very reserved people; we take things very calmly, no matter what it is. It would take a lot more than independence to make us fly off the handle."

He was serious about it, too. Young, relaxed and neatly turned out, his young face sporting the newest of beards, he was probably stating what he believed. Good God! This African was telling about being reserved about something which was a battle-cry throughout the world, and has always been the *prod excelsior* wherever man has struggled against indignity and enslavement. He said it with the same casual pride with which Britishers often defend their insularity: they too claim to be reserved. Reserved for what? What was this fellow talking about?

"Extraordinary." I could think of nothing else to say to him.

"Not really. We can jump around and dance and wave our arms as energetically as anyone else, but what's to be gained by it? If you're here on Independence Day you will no doubt see that we can enjoy ourselves very enthusiastically. Then you'll see all the fever and spirit and atmosphere you want."

We were not on the same wave length. Or perhaps he was deliberately evading the issue. Damn it, one would expect the people to sing and dance on The Day, as they would at Christmas or Easter or any major local feast day. I was talking about a consciousness of arrival, of achievement, of national and political stature, of meaningful identity in which there was popular involvement. I was talking about a death and a birth: death of colonial control and everything the term indicated; and the birth of a new entity, a new State. I thought that these things should be more than enough to generate excitement and fever among these people, as they have generated excitement and fever among people throughout history. What was so special about Sierra Leoneans that they were immune to this fever? Had they become so deeply colonized as to be completely emasculated politically?

"Here in Sierra Leone we have established a tradition," he was saying, "of restraint in all things, and that tradition will be fully vindicated in the next few weeks and afterwards. There is no

76

possibility of the sort of breakdown which happened in the Congo when they got their independence."

"My friend, I'm not even thinking of that kind of thing," I told him. "Aren't you personally excited at the thought that your country's independence is imminent? I'm not hoping for or expecting any unpleasant occurrences; I'm merely surprised at the almost complete absence of interest in what should now be a popular preoccupation." I wondered who was interviewing whom.

"What did you think of the P. M. last night?" he asked. A neat change of subject.

"He seems rather old," I said. "Rather surprising. What sort of government does he head?"

"Our Government is based very much on the British parliamentary system," he replied.

"Who leads the opposition?"

That seemed to stop him in his tracks.

"Well, at the moment there is no real opposition," he replied, "because we need unified effort to see us through the first stages of independence. Later, perhaps."

Where had I heard this sort of thing before? Oh, yes! My friend in Guinea had hinted that the opposition in Sierra Leone had been somehow invalidated.

"Are there enough trained Sierra Leoneans to run the country efficiently after independence?" I asked.

"Not enough, but for some years now we have been gradually replacing overseas personnel with local people, and I expect that this process will continue for some time yet."

This was a lousy interview, or whatever it was. He was not asking me any questions of interest to me, and I could get nothing more than very general and vague comments out of him, so gradually the conversation drifted around to more earthy things. He pointed out some of the clientele sitting around like ourselves over beer and sandwiches: the consuls general of the United States and Liberia, a diplomat from Yugoslavia, the French consul general, a magistrate, a few good-looking girls, whom he referred to as "good company."

"They prefer to eat sandwiches here than dine at the Paramount," he said. "Here everybody is friends with everybody. Drop

77

in any Saturday afternoon around four and you will see about everybody who is anybody. They all come in here for a while."

We parted shortly after two o'clock and I returned to my hotel for a nap.

Mr. Lindsay called for me soon after five. We sat in my room in air-conditioned comfort.

"How did it go, your chat with our newspaper friend?"

"It didn't, except for one thing: I discovered that you are a reserved people."

"How's that?"

"You are immune to the excitements of independence fever."

"That what he said?"

"Yes."

"That's creole talk."

"Is he a creole?"

"Sure."

"And you?"

"I come from the hinterland, or protectorate. The creoles refer to us as aborigines."

"What's the difference?"

"These creoles are the descendants of the emancipated slaves who first settled the coastal strip, which later became the colony of Sierra Leone; it extends inland a little way beyond Freetown. The rest of the country is protectorate, peopled and owned by indigenous tribes. From the beginning the settlers looked down their noses at us, and considered us uncultured savages. With their advantages of education and other evidences of contact with Europeans, they isolated themselves from us and only within very recent times have we been able to have any voice in the country's affairs. But things are changing. Since the last elections we are in the majority in the House of Representatives." His voice was low and earnest. "The Old Man is an aborigine. He was educated at Bo then went to study medicine in Britain. Do you know that when he returned to Sierra Leone, a qualified practitioner, he could not practice in Freetown? The creoles would have nothing to do with him, considered him an aborigine and socially inferior to them. So he returned to the hinterland and worked among his people, then later turned to politics. Now that the tide of affairs has turned, he

78

has the support of all the Paramount chiefs, and none of the creoles are big enough to unseat him."

"But I can see no difference, physically, between you and the newspaperman. How would I know who is or is not a creole?"

"It's not important that you know," he replied, "but it is easy for us to distinguish them."

"What's your feeling about this 'reserve' he spoke about? Are the aborigines equally reserved about independence?"

"Speaking for myself, I would like to say that it's a lot of crap." He spat out the word with nose-wrinkling distaste. "It's merely an excuse for lack of popular interest in the whole thing. Let's put it this way—an outsider might form the view that the whole independence idea has been a sort of political arrangement between Britain and the Government of Sierra Leone, and that at no point have the people been consulted or taken into our leaders' confidence, and he might assume that independence has not come to us as a result of popular pressure or agitation, and therefore there is no real popular involvement. Furthermore he might form the view that the Government has so effectively silenced any opposing voice, that no one can express criticism of its actions."

"And would such an observer be accurate in his deductions?" Two of us could play at this game.

"Im in no position to say," he replied, "but as you move around you'll have a chance to see things for yourself."

"Good, when do we start?"

"How about tomorrow, Saturday? There's to be a function upcountry at a place called Moyamba, about ninety miles or so from Freetown. Crowning of the local beauty queen, should be interesting for you to see how we indigenes live. In any case you'll see something of the country.

"Okay. It's a date."

*

On Saturday we set out soon after midday, driving through the depressing ugliness of Freetown along the narrow macadam road, through attractive but impoverished-looking villages which bore

79

the startling names of Waterloo, Wellington, Allentown and Newton, into the wide-open cool countryside, green and soothing with acres and acres of rolling ground devoted to the cultivation of Sierra Leone's chief crop, palm oil. The road wound its way under the overhang of huge trees, hugged the shoulders of low hills and crossed innumerable gullies, deep or shallow, each spanned by a narrow bridge, wide enough for only a single vehicle.

"Considering that this is your main arterial road, these bridges are frightfully narrow, aren't they?" I asked him.

"Not surprisingly so," he replied, laughing. "When the British built this road they did not conceive of the possibility of development beyond horse and buggy traffic."

Songo marked the border between colony and protectorate and also the end of the surfaced highway. From then on we traveled in a swirl of dust which increased to a blinding, choking cloud whenever anything passed us in either direction. The countryside now became wilder with no sign of planned cultivation. Here and there we passed a tract of scorched earth, which my friend assured me was deliberate: the first step in seasonal cultivation. First burn the ground to get rid of as much as possible of creepers, grass and saplings, then clear away everything except tree stumps, then plant your crop in the hope that it will outgrow the new weeds and bush. Soon after harvest the same patch of ground will look as virgin as before, and remain so until next year or later.

Sometimes the road cut through thickly wooded areas, the bushes alongside the road thickly grimed with layers of red-gray dust, then broke out into open country, wild-looking enough that elephants were conspicuously absent. About twenty miles beyond Songo the road ended at the bank of the Ribi River, wide, deep and blackly opaque, and we cooled our heels while waiting for the hand-operated ferry to take us across.

"Part of the legacy we'll inherit with independence," my friend remarked. "This country is really a nest of rivers joined together by land, and there are more bridges per mile of roadway than in any other country on God's earth. Ergo, we'll have to build new bridges, if this country is to be economically developed. That means we'll have to start learning how to win friends and influence people internationally. The British taught us a hell of a lot about government, now we'll have to find somebody to help us with development."

"Like who, for instance?"

"Like anybody. The United States, perhaps. Nobody can doubt that we are Western-orientated, I think that's the term." His easy laughter followed, and I wondered how to heed him; how much was mockery and how much was meant seriously.

"Maybe when we are officially proclaimed free and sovereign we can begin to cash in on the 'Peace on Earth, Good Will Towards Africa' campaign."

He continued, "The Americans are with us already, wanting to help to educate us, you know, technical schools, libraries, things like that. There were one or two of them at the reception the other night. You know, if I were a black American I would move heaven and earth to land a job like that, something which kept me outside the United States. Marvelous. I could then be a black American and a human being at the same time, without any sacrifice of dignity."

I let it ride; if I tried to tease any comment out of him he promptly reminded me that he was speaking off the record, or else he evaded answering. This way he said his piece, somewhat obliquely, but he said it.

"Are the Americans the only foreigners actively wanting to help here?"

"Oh, no, we have all kinds. You name them and we have them. Germans, Israelis, Yugoslavs, and others. Much of the new building in Freetown is being done by Israelis. Low tenders but good workmanship, I hear. Then there's our own special minority group, the Lebanese. You name it and they own it. Everything except the land itself and the owners of the land are usually heavily in their debt. You know, an uninformed outsider could jump to the conclusion that independence is merely a word in these parts."

"And what would an informed insider like yourself say about it?" I asked.

"I'd say that it must be damned hard work winding that ferry," he replied, pointing to the huge metal float which was being inched

81

slowly across the river by two men using notched sticks to pull on a steel cable stretched waist-high across the river. Crude but effective, yet hardly indicative of progress.

As soon as it grounded on the sandy bank, we rolled aboard and began the leisurely trip across. Looking up or downriver from midstream, one could see huge boulders jutting upward and creating innumerable eddies and rapids which flashed and twinkled in the sunlight, presenting a picture of rare, wild beauty. Some fishing enthusiasts in Europe would rave about a place like this.

On the other side of the river, near the little landing stage, a group of young women were washing clothes, standing waist-deep in the dark water, bare backs and breasts gleaming wet, their faces clean, wholesome, untroubled. All this natural loveliness was new to me and I must have stared, fascinated, because he nudged me in the ribs and said, "Take it easy, boy, there's lots more where those come from."

Now we drove through flat, sparsely wooded country, and always the road bisected the villages through which we passed, these were mostly thatched huts except for the residence of the headman, or chief, which might be a sprawling, roomy structure of wood, thatch or stone. We drove carefully through these villages to avoid harm to the children, dogs or goats which abounded. We often passed women on the road, trudging through the dust under terribly heavy loads, closely followed by their menfolk, burdened with nothing more than a long staff. I noticed that these women were generally unlike the women of Guinea. Their bodies were permanently distorted by the heavy loads they carried on their heads: their spines curved inward so that their stomachs protruded forward and their rumps extended grotesquely backward. Years ago I had read that African women derived graceful deportment from carrying things on their head. Agreed, provided the "things" were not heavy enough to distort them so dreadfully. Often, in addition to the load on the head, the woman would have a small child strapped to her back; many of them had ugly, pendulous breasts which swung abnormally low and seemed to indicate that the babies, strapped securely as they were, pulled the breasts backward to feed and produced the fearful disfigurement in quite young women. Occasionally I saw a woman with one rounded breast while the other,

82

usually the right breast, was unnaturally elongated, as if the small child favored it and fed from it exclusively.

"Life seems to be rather awful for women around here," I said.

"Life is awful for everyone around here," he replied. "It merely happens that women are built in a way which shows it up more easily. Life has changed very little for them, in fact, in spite of all our talk of progress, I'd venture to say that all the women we pass on the road are illiterate, belong to polygamous households, and can hope for little change in their circumstances. They might not be happy, as we think of happiness, but they might not be discontented either, having been taught from early childhood that their role is to serve their men in every way."

Evidently the mere male taught that, too.

Mabang, Masanki, Rotifunk, Banya, Voygema, names fitted to the land. But this was like parkland gone wild, nothing really savage about it, nothing of the "bush" I had read about. Then suddenly the road widened and there were houses—not huts—houses, pleasant bungalows on cleared plots of ground.

"We're entering Moyamba," my friend said.

I saw large buildings, shops, and a powerhouse, a hospital gleaming white in the gathering dusk, a thriving town along a narrow dirt road.

"Rather poor communication with Freetown, don't you think?" I asked.

"I suppose so. There is a better alternate road north of this one, but it's about forty miles longer. Let's pay a call on the Paramount chief."

"Wouldn't he mind our just dropping in on him without warning?"

"Not 'him,' *her*."

"A woman?"

"Why not? We're a democratic people," he replied, grinning. "We've several lady Paramount chiefs, but this one is perhaps the best known; she's also a member of the House of Representatives."

We swung off the main road and followed a narrow lane into a high-walled courtyard in which were several low, white-painted buildings; the central one was brightly lit within and I could hear the sound of Spanish-type music coming through the wide doorway and windows. We approached this building and leaving the car outside, we entered a large, cool room, well-lighted from pendant electric fittings and furnished with several comfortable-looking armchairs and cushioned stools. Several people were standing about chatting and laughing, and a group of young women was gathered about a large phonograph.

"Well, look who's here," my friend whispered. "Gathering of the clan."

He led me to a small group and introduced me to a thick-set, robust man whose thick, brawny arms protruded from a short native poncho; there was much more than mere physical strength in his square face, and when we shook hands, his clamped on mine like a vise.

"Mr. Albert Margai, I'd like to introduce a friend of mine, a visitor from Europe, Mr. Braithwaite."

The man's deep, rumbling voice welcomed me. "From Europe?" he asked.

"Recently from Paris," I replied. "Originally from British Guiana."

"Welcome to Sierra Leone," he repeated, renewing the pressure on my imprisoned hand.

"Mr. Margai is the Prime Minister's brother," my friend explained, "and is minister for natural resources."

We chatted together and I had a chance to observe the man, the apparently youthful power and drive, the toughness of him. He seemed good-humored, his laughter coming easily from behind strong white teeth set in a square bulldog jaw. He was on very friendly terms with everyone and joked with the young women, who giggled shyly. He told us that the Paramount chief, Madame, was dining with the Governor and his family, who were visiting Moyamba, but we would have an opportunity of meeting her later that evening at the dance arranged in conjunction with the beauty contest.

My friend took me on a short tour of the town, an interesting example of the juxtaposition of tribal life and modern technical progress. Not far from the chief's compound was the barrier, or local court, a large-roofed concrete platform with a low concrete railing on three sides and furnished with heavy wooden chairs for

84

the officials, and rows of wooden benches for the public. Set in a piece of open ground, it presented a clear view to anyone interested. I thought it was ideally arranged that "justice might be seen to be done." We passed the mosque, outside of which the overflow of worshippers knelt in prayer, and the Catholic mission, a group of school buildings, church and residents' accommodation; the residence of the district commissioner, elegantly remote in its neat grounds, rest houses. Everything indicated that this was a thriving, lively community.

"He looks tough," I said.

"Who?"

"The Prime Minister's brother. One might think that he rather looks the part of leader of a new independent state."

I was falling into the same third-party kind of talk in which my friend was so skilled.

"First of all one would need to understand a few local moves," my friend said. "Things like personal and tribal loyalties and pressures. One would need to appreciate that it is not very easy to achieve political ambitions at the expense of other members of one's immediate family, no matter how good one's chances for success might seem. It would also be unwise for one to underestimate the Old Man's personal influence with the Paramount chiefs or his own wily ways. Yes, my friend, one could lose when everything indicates that one would win."

"Did he have a shot at the premiership, then?"

"He did, and suddenly, when success seemed assured, he stepped down. Now he is minister of natural resources. However, don't weep for him; he's quite young and anything can happen."

"Yesterday the newspaperman told me there was no opposition group in the Government." I thought this as good an occasion as any to get some answers out of him.

"Your trouble, my friend," he replied, "is that, like too many others, you see democracy only in British parliamentary terms; anything else is suspect. Why should there be an opposition as such, when every important matter is fully thrashed out in the House of Representatives anyway before action is taken? What good could be served by merely aping what is done in London's Whitehall? Maybe what you mean is whether any voice is ever raised in criticism of any Government measure or policy. My answer would be no, because I take very little cognizance of the rabble-rousers who quibble merely to attract popular attention without any knowledge or examination of the circumstances. I hold no special brief for the conduct of this Government; I would be the first to admit that it would be the easiest thing to discover evidence of corruption involving many of its highest officials. But an effective opposition would presuppose personal qualities and group loyalties which too many of our politicians either do not possess or cannot afford. Perhaps, in time, things will change. After all, our people have learned new lessons about service and responsibility."

A heck of a long speech for him. I wondered where he fitted in all this.

Twilight had given way to starry night, and there was now plenty of activity: people had completed their period of worship, youngsters were shouting to each other, promising to meet at the dance, cars were flitting to and fro, their horns sharply impatient of the leisurely pedestrians.

"Why did the younger Margai step down from the premiership?" By swinging away from a subject and then back to it I might catch him off balance.

"Pressure from the Paramount chiefs," he replied. "They've seen what happened in Ghana and Guinea and they are not the least bit anxious for any reforms to disturb their position or lessen their power. Perhaps someone whispered in their collective ear that young Albert planned to do exactly that. Who knows? ... You seem to be in luck; if H.E. is here you might be able to meet him."

"H.E.?"

"His Excellency, Sir Maurice Dorman. H.E."

"Does he become ex-H.E. after April 27?"

"Oh, no. He becomes governor general."

"What difference does that make?"

"Constitutionally, a great deal. But in terms of his relationship with the people—none. You'll understand if you meet him."

We noticed that the honking motorcars and laughing people were all headed in a certain direction and followed them till we came to the site of festivities: a piece of ground surrounded by an impromptu fence of interwoven palm fronds and illuminated by

86

strings of multicolored electric bulbs; an aperture served as a doorway, and here was placed a small table, behind which three or four persons did a brisk trade in entrance tickets and rosettes. The color of the rosette determined whether one sat among the high or the low.

We bought tickets and inside I noticed that the enclosure contained a flat, grassy knoll in front of the local police court, a low building open on three sides and adjoining the police station. This building, of painted concrete, was now clear of all furniture, and polished smooth for dancing. On a raised platform in one corner were musical instruments, ready and waiting for the musicians.

Already many people were assembled in the enclosure, chatting over drinks, laughing and jollying each other, but I was surprised to see that the majority of the men were wearing formal European dress—dark suits, white shirts, black bow ties, black shoes—and I felt somewhat out of place in a linen shirt and slacks, but hoped I would be recognized as a stranger, unfamiliar with local custom. The women, however, were wearing very colorful costumes: short, flared jackets and ankle-length skirts which looked becomingly lovely and "belonging."

My friend introduced me to several persons of his acquaintance: nurses, schoolteachers and local dignitaries of one office or another.

I met a very charming young man, the director of Sierra Leone broadcasting services, who was there to report on the festivities. It transpired that he knew of me and had presented several recorded programs I had made in London, so we were soon chatting away very cozily. Gradually I swung the conversation around to independence, but from his guarded answers it was clear that he did not wish to commit himself to any observations. I did not press the matter, appreciating that he was, after all, a civil servant, and must keep his personal views very much to himself. I discovered that he was very well informed, interested in the arts, and was himself a writer and musician of some repute. He was of mixed Lebanese and African ancestry.

"Does that make you a creole?" I asked.

"I'm not sure," he replied. "By association I suppose I would be called a creole, because I live in Freetown and practically all my friends are creoles; but I was born in this district, at Rotifunk, and am at liberty to assume my mother's heritage and call myself an aborigine."

He in turn introduced me to several persons, among them his father and mother. There was now a general air of expectancy, a kind of buzzing anticipation, and presently the murmur went around the place: "H. E.'s arrived. His Excellency's arrived."

Into the enclosure came, first of all, an African woman, followed by an English couple and a young girl of perhaps sixteen or seventeen years. The African woman was of medium height, small-boned and probably around forty years or so; very difficult to assess the age of these smooth-skinned, attractive women, but the striking thing about her was her dress. I suppose it was the national costume, but it was worn with all the grace and chic of a Balenciaga original. Her skirt and flared jacket were of a colorful silky material which did all kinds of wonderful things to her slim, compact figure; from beneath the skirt occasionally peeped high-heeled golden sandals, while on her head was an intricately folded winged headkerchief of pinkish gauze with a predominant gold thread.

"The Paramount chief," my friend whispered.

The Englishwoman was tall and casually elegant. Some women do not need to be beautiful, what with their abundance of grace and charm; this one seemed to be as completely at ease here in a small African township as she would be at the Queen's garden party. The man with her was a few inches taller than six feet, ruddy-complexioned, with the physique of an ex-rugby player, dressed in dark trousers, white linen jacket and black tie. I had the impression that clothes, as such were not very important to him. The daughter bore a very striking resemblance to her mother.

The musicians must have collected before the group appeared, for now with a roll of drums they played the familiar "God Save the Queen," at which everyone stood up. This ended, everyone else remained standing until the Governor's party and the Paramount chief had seated themselves. Soon afterward the dancing began and the night was filled with the insinuating sounds of African dance music, more especially the now popular "high life," an import from Ghana. In this dance there was the very minimum of contact between couples, each partner seemed primarily concerned with his or her own freewheeling interpretation of the music and occa-

88

sionally opposed each other in a kind of impromptu competition. I noticed that the Governor's daughter, partnered by a young African, was in the thick of things. Her movements were as graceful and natural as those of any other person present, and it was clear that this kind of familiarity with such a dance was not obtained by mechanical tutoring. Teased, urged and completely seduced by the music, I found a partner and was soon completely victimized by the wonderful atmosphere.

Afterward I circulated among the people, hoping to get nearer to the Paramount chief, but she was closely involved in the preparations for the beauty contest. Then someone, who introduced himself as the district commissioner, told me he was "required" to take me to the Governor.

"Your presence has been commanded," he joked.

He took me where the Governor and Lady Dorman sat; she was slightly flushed from her recent turn on the dance floor. It transpired that both of them had read my first book, *To Sir, with Love,* and, hearing that I was present, wanted to meet me.

"Our careers have much in common, Mr. Braithwaite," Sir Maurice said. "I too was a schoolmaster, and later was engaged in welfare work."

"Yes, sir," I replied, "but not by the remotest possibility could I become Governor of anywhere." He laughed at this, an easy, deep-throated, amused sound.

"And for that mercy you ought to offer much thanks," he quipped.

His wife was as charming and gracious as my first sight of her had suggested, and very soon we were chatting away quite easily.

"You're visiting Sierra Leone at a very interesting time in the country's history," Sir Maurice said. "In a few weeks the country will have its independence. I am now on trek, traveling throughout the hinterland, telling the people about independence, and in some cases, selling the idea to them."

It was some little while before the import of his words sunk into me.

"Extraordinary!" I exclaimed.

"You find it so?" Lady Dorman asked.

"Yes, ma'am. Never before have I heard or read of a people

89

having to be talked into becoming independent; in the history of colonial peoples the opposite is true. With every respect to both yourselves, I would have thought that you would be representative of whatever resistance there was to the idea. I find all this very confusing. In the short time I have been here you are the only persons who have willingly and readily discussed the matter; everywhere else I meet a wall of silence or indifference where I must confess I had hoped to find nothing but energetic enthusiasm." I had spoken bluntly because I felt that I could say my piece to them.

He hesitated before replying, fixing me with his clear gray eyes. "There is some danger in jumping to conclusions about what you see here," he replied. "You should not read too much in what seems to be the absence of energetic interest or militant enthusiasms. For many years the colonial administration has been working toward the day when Africans could take over the reins of government, and we are not displeased that it is about to occur in an atmosphere of calm and orderliness."

"You may be right, sir, but I am naturally bearing British Guiana very much in mind, and Ghana and Nigeria and Guinea and others. In each case there has been popular agitation for self-determination. Here I can see no evidence that the people, the common people, are in any way involved. How is it that you find it necessary to 'sell' them the idea? One would expect that the selling would long ago have been done by the indigenous leadership, that is, what little 'selling' would be necessary for a package which should be already 'sold' long before it is offered. Would you say that the people of Sierra Leone are in any way different from other Africans?"

"Tell me," he countered, "what have you observed since you have been here?"

I confessed that I had not been able to see much or speak much with anyone in the little time I had spent in the country.

"Then take your time," he advised. "Talk with the people whenever you can, but try to avoid comparisons with what you know or have heard about other places. Sierra Leoneans are not special Africans in any way, but many of the conditions you will find here are peculiar to this colony. I would very much like to meet with you

90

again after you have spent some time 'round and about, and then we can perhaps more fully discuss the matter."

"Tell you what we'll do, Mr. Braithwaite," Lady Dorman said. "We'll have an open date for dinner. When you have about completed your visit, give us a ring in Freetown and we'll have dinner and a chat."

I readily agreed and thanked them, more than ever determined to go whenever possible and follow up on our discussion. If there was something special about the country or the people which would explain the prevailing apathy, I would try to discover it.

The dancing continued until just before midnight, when the beauty contest got underway. There were only four contestants, and my friend explained that the idea of presenting themselves publicly for examination was sufficiently new and frightening to discourage all but a very few of the local girls. Even those four went through the sequence of changes from national dress and the briefest of bathing costumes to European-style cocktail dresses with an air of hesitant shyness. As one might say: "Neither willing nor reluctant." One of these, however, bolder than the rest, introduced, whenever possible, a few hip-swinging movements which set the crowd off in peals of laughter and hand-clapping, although it was obviously superfluous to her slight but fulsome body, which seemed to become interestingly agitated with every least movement.

"She's French, from Guinea," my friend whispered, as if in explanation of her more relaxed performance. "She knows how to put it over."

The judges must have been in full agreement with him, because the little lady was unanimously chosen the winner and presented with a gilt crown and loving cup by the Paramount chief.

After this ceremony the dancing resumed. My friend suddenly grabbed my arm and hurried me to where the Paramount chief was standing alone, surveying the dancers.

"Madame Gularma," he said, stopping in front of her, "I'd like to present a friend of mine who is on his first visit to Africa."

Close up like this I noticed other things in her face: strength, gentleness, and when she spoke in reply, I heard the modulated tones of good breeding. We danced together, at least I tried to match her easy improvisation, the swaying movement which flowed

91

downward from the waist yet was in pliant harmony with arms and neck. Tonight was the very first time in more than twenty years that I had danced with a Negro woman and the experience was inexplicably heady. I had seen newsreels of dancing Africans, but always the dances were thrilling set pieces, with drums providing a throbbing, dictating counterpoint. This was so very different, so essentially African, yet easily international.

My friend and I said our goodbyes at two o'clock in the morning, although the dancing was in full swing, and took the road north out of town, the long road back to Freetown which would completely bypass the ferry.

"Did you enjoy it?" he inquired.

"Oh, yes. Thoroughly. That Madame Gularma is simply fabulous."

"You were having quite a chat with H.E."

"I found him very interesting, you know, direct. I'm hoping to see him again before I leave Sierra Leone."

"He'll be with us a long time, I predict," he said. "I have an idea that he enjoys more of the trust and confidence of the people, both in the colony and the protectorate, than does anyone of our national leaders."

"I suppose after Independence Day there will be no more talk of colony and protectorate?"

"You suppose correctly, and thereby hangs the beginnings of what might become a very real and lively problem. At the moment the difference between colony and protectorate means more than the separateness of creole from aborigine; it also involves a serious question of land tenure. Anyone, as long as he is a Sierra Leone national, can own land in the colony. All protectorate land is held in trust by the Paramount chiefs and cannot be disposed of by sale. In short, no creole can own land in the protectorate. In an independent Sierra Leone, there can be no distinction between nationals, and, if development is to be achieved, it must move inward from the coast to affect the protectorate areas. How far the Paramount chiefs will be prepared to accept land reforms is anybody's guess, and once the movement inward begins, it also marks the beginning of the end of Paramount chiefs as such.

"Part of the reason for the apathy you have noticed may be due

92

to some fears within the protectorate about possible land reforms, on the one hand, and, on the other hand, in the colony about possible engulfment by the aborigines, who already account for the large majority of seats in the Government and in the House of Representatives. One might suppose that, in such a situation, nobody wants to sound off too loudly about independence, because it does not mean the same thing to all parties concerned."

"That sounds reasonable enough," I agreed, "but I had always thought that the need to rid themselves of the colonial yoke was so primary and immediate to all these people, that any other issue was secondary, no matter what it involved."

"That's where you are in error, my friend. You must consider also the background to the present situation. Most of the people in the colony are the descendants of freed slaves, who, with British help and guidance, arrived here from England in 1787—think of it, as far back as that. These people were allowed to form a fully autonomous kind of Government, with their own laws administered by elected officials, but the results were calamitous, and their first taste of independence a terribly bitter draught."

Hurtling along the dark road as if dragged behind the powerful double beams of headlights, his voice had a strange compelling quality. For a little while he was not slipping away puckishly behind half-assertions and innuendo, as if somehow I had touched something close to his pride in his country and his concern for its future.

"From that point the British took over, in the form of the Sierra Leone Company of London, administered locally by a council of eight Britons, mainly traders. Later this was changed to a Governor and two other elected officials, and finally in 1808, when Freetown became a Crown colony, the Constitution was changed so that the Governor was appointed by the King and the laws were approved by the British parliament.

"Since that time the pattern of affairs has not altered very considerably if one accepts the fact of general progress. The Europeans have set the pace in practically every aspect of daily life and the African has merely followed, not learning from the European in order to extend and develop his own potential, but aping him, concerned more with conforming to his mores and cultural behavior than with the extension of educational and other facilities to their less fortunate brethren. Even today there is nothing which might be called African leadership in that it represents a movement of Africans toward economic and cultural development. Sure, we are soon to become independent, but our lack of excitement is dictated by caution; we have so long been dependent in every way that we fear to trust ourselves to the first unaided step, and are still looking over our shoulder for reassurance of the presence of the Great White Parent."

There was no mistaking the bitterness and hopelessness which may have been long housed within him, thinly guised with an easy affability, an ever-ready badinage.

"You came here expecting to find us all practically standing on our heads in an ecstacy of freedom gained. Freedom! You heard or perhaps read of others fighting and dying for freedom and you thought that if other parts of Africa are like that, Sierra Leone cannot be different. You couldn't be more wrong. We're different because we never fought for anything. I'm talking about the Sierra Leone the world knows, that little piece of it which is called the colony, because the protectorate is still mostly unknown territory. The freed slaves who settled here never really got over being slaves; they persisted in their slavish habits and treated the indigenous Africans as badly, if not worse, than they had once been treated. To them the British settlers and traders were not oppressors or exploiters, but examples which they assiduously copied in dress, speech, religion and attitudes. There is no genuine background of mistrust and antagonism here between the black settlers and the white, and not very much between the black indigenes and the white administrators either. But the indigenes had had very little reason to love the creoles, who were for the most part Western educated and maintained a kind of black elite group in the colony.

"From about 1924, when Africans were first elected to the legislative council, until after World War II, these creole elite were the real power, but since then, especially since the revision of the Constitution in 1956, things have changed drastically for them, and now they see the last vestiges of their power rapidly disappearing. Can you wonder that they are not enthusiastic? Did you realize that, if it were possible, many of them would sabotage independence even now?

94

"So you see, my friend, there is no anti-colonial feeling, as such, to be found here, and the virus of African nationalism has not yet reached us. It may be that it will come to us, but perhaps differently from others. We may suddenly awaken one day to the responsibilities of self-determination, and decide to step away from the Queen's skirts to prove ourselves. Perhaps. We have the human potential, what we need is the consciousness of it, and the dignity of responsibility. Other African States with much less than we have are standing tall, free and uncommitted, while we still echo the opinions of others."

Without noticing it, we had slowed down. Now he stopped talking and the car jumped ahead, the speeding tires throwing innumerable bits of gravel against the bumpers in a continuous metallic tattoo. Some time after five o'clock we approached Freetown, cool at this early-morning hour, but haphazard and untidy after the pleasing irregularity of the interior. Outside my hotel he stopped for me to alight.

"How would you like to spend a few days upcountry?" He asked. "I could borrow a land-rover from a friend and we could follow the roads as far north and west as the borders of Guinea and Liberia. It would give you an opportunity of seeing the real people of the country, those who have always been here, and from whom must eventually come the leadership that will truly matter."

"I'd love it," I replied.

"Good. You pay for the petrol, okay?"

"Okay."

"Fine, we'll get some sleep and I'll meet you at the City Hotel around one o'clock for a beer and sandwich. I'll probably fix it to have the land-rover in a day or two."

Soon after entering the wonderfully cool room I was fast asleep.

*

We lunched at the City Hotel on bottled beer and sandwiches. We sat in a group including an Indonesian and the Liberian consul, who inquired about my trip and my observations so far. I told him that I had visited Guinea, where I noticed that the French influence

95

was very marked on nearly every aspect of life, as much as I had already noticed the clear imprint of Britain on life in Sierra Leone; I had read of Liberia's very close relationship with the United States of America and wondered whether, when I visited that country, I would see similar evidence of close, lengthy association. He expressed grave doubts that I would see any such evidence, adding, "In Liberia you will discover that we have a culture of our own, unique and quite independent of any other."

I told him I was very pleased to hear that, and would make a point of checking while I was there.

Later on some of the town's "bright young men" drifted in, among them, Bankole Timothy, author of a very fine biography of President Nkrumah, who in turn introduced me to some of his friends, who were similarly interested in literature.

There was some excitement about the possible outcome of a competition in which some of them were involved; soon it would be announced whose play had been selected for presentation as one of the special features of the independence celebrations, and some very lively discussion on literature and the contributions made by local writers. I received invitations to visit Fourah Bay College and address the education students and to participate in a radio forum of Negro writers. I enjoyed being with these lively intelligent young men, sharing in their interests, responding to their immediate acceptance of myself. But I could not forget the words of my friend during our drive through the early morning.

These young men behaved and sounded like Europeans; everything about them reflected their English training, education and thought, and significantly, but for the relationship between the winning play and independence celebrations, there was no comment or discussion about independence. Once or twice I tried to bring it in, because I felt that these bright young men would be able to supply some answers; there was no doubt of their intelligence and ability, so surely, such an important event could not overtake them without their awareness and comment. But, skillfully and adroitly, they swung away each time, without any embarrassment to myself, but leaving no doubt that there was no wish or intention to discuss it.

When the group broke up my friend told me that he'd secured

the land-rover but it was undergoing some repairs in a garage; a thorough overhaul was necessary before starting out, because for most of the trip we would encounter rather poor roads and we could not expect to find any dependable servicing en route. He expected that it would be three or four days before the vehicle was ready, and meanwhile I could take a further wander around town and do some swimming at the beach. We walked about into the hot afternoon sunshine, headed toward the cotton tree—all roads seemed to lead to the cotton tree. Opposite the cotton tree, in front of a row of shabby buildings, numbers of young men were standing about in groups or sitting on the dusty sidewalk: some were fast asleep, crouched against the railings in the shadow of an overhanging tree. Looking up I noticed the sign "Labour Bureau" on one of the buildings. This was the labor exchange, but at three o'clock in the afternoon it was very unlikely any hiring would be done. The young men all seemed relaxed and unconcerned, but what surprised me was the fact that there were so many of them.

"Is it always like this?" I asked my friend.

"Yes. The unemployment situation here is chronic. By this time many have gone home or are strolling around down by the water-side or around the market. If you come here early in the morning you'll see three or four times this number. At the same time you can find hundreds of them sitting around the markets or just wandering about. An observer might get the impression that the situation is chronic."

"How long has it been like this?"

"Since the war, mainly. During the war Freetown was quite an important stopover and watering place for convoys; the harbor was always full of ships and there was plenty of work of one sort or another and many people came in from the protectorate and settled here. Those days have long gone, and no other avenues of employment have opened up for the people. The numbers of these unemployed increase every month, from the protectorate migrants and from young school-leavers. There are simply no outlets. At the moment a few men are employed here and there on small projects for the Celebrations, but after April 27 most of them will be out of work and back here again."

"Just how extensive is this unemployment situation?"

"Purely by accident I overheard someone say that not less than ninety per cent of our potential wage earners are unemployed." He had fallen back into his third-person role.

"And do you accept it as a reasonable estimate?"

"That does not come within my sphere of activities, but an outsider looking around for himself might eventually arrive at a similar conclusion."

"Are there, then, no foreseeable prospects for these chaps and those boys and girls who are soon to leave school?"

"I couldn't answer that, but you could look around for yourself. I often get the impression that every section of the civil service has reached the saturation point, maybe beyond it. You might think that what is urgently needed here is not only money but ideas: ways and means of providing outlets for the youth of the country before they become frustrated and demoralized. I hear tell that in Ghana they have a scheme called the 'Builders' Brigade,' where youths of both sexes are trained to meet the needs of new industrial development. Whether that would work here or not is not for me to say, but an outsider might conclude that something is urgently needed, if not long overdue."

"Is there no uneasiness among these people about their plight? Don't they ever demonstrate or agitate for some change in their circumstances?"

"Friend, you are in Sierra Leone, remember? Demonstrate? Agitate? What are you talking about? That sounds like Communist talk, and we do not tolerate anything here which sounds like Communist talk. When you have been here awhile you might think that there is a certain deep-seated lethargy which permeates all of us, at all levels. You might imagine that we are the victims of an unusual type of colonialism, the type which conditions the mind to complete acceptance. Struggle of any sort seems foreign to our nature, and we can as easily accommodate ourselves in the dust and filth as on the silken cushion among the scornful. We adjust to things. These out-of-work chaps adjust themselves to their chronic unemployment and would continue so for years, especially if some known relative is employed, then they batten on him and consider it their prerogative to do so. We call that maintaining our tribal ties. Friend, I have an idea you came to Sierra Leone to see

98

a birth. Some might think you are witnessing a kind of death."

"But I can't understand you!" I exclaimed. "You speak as if this country were completely cut off from the rest of Africa. Surely the people must be aware of what is going on all around them. Don't they read about Guinea and Ghana and Nigeria and the Congo and all those other places? Don't they know that Africans everywhere are awakening to a new and vigorous sense of destiny and responsibility? And why do you speak as if you are in a special little capsule, separate from the rest? Have you no share in the responsibilities, too?"

"Take it easy, friend," he said, calmly. "Don't forget, everyone will tell you that we are a reserved people, so let's not get all worked up and bloodthirsty. What do we know of what's going on around us? Who tells us? The newspapers? Read the local ones any day of the week; nothing of consequence ever appears until it is old, stale news. I hear that they deliver them free in your hotel. Do you ever read anything in them that's important and current? Do you ever read current stuff about the Congo, or any of the hundred and one earthshaking things which are happening each day all over the world? But that's not all. One can buy overseas newspapers and journals, but these are always at least one week old when they arrive here. I'm not saying that it's deliberate; I'm just telling you that this situation exists.

"So much for newspapers as a medium of current information. Now radio, that wonderful miracle of this scientific age. From it you get nothing more of news value than you get from the daily papers, except for news bulletins from the B.B.C. relayed through the local system, and none of that is likely to excite or incite. Don't preach to me about responsibility, my friend, until you have lived a little longer among us and can see for yourself that we are, in fact, separate and cut off in this neck of the woods."

He turned to point a dramatic finger at the towering cotton tree. "That tree is supposed to be the symbol of a free people. It appears on our postage stamp and we are forever talking about it—it may be significant, however, that it also spreads its branches daily over these poor wretches, who are as tightly enslaved by chronic poverty as if bound by the shackles which their forefathers buried among those eternal roots. But their enslavement is even worse—look at

99

them! Don't they seem relaxed, even content? Remember, my friend, we are a reserved people, so damned reserved that we have lost the will to struggle against any kind of adversity, or perhaps we have even lost the personal dignity which stimulates the need to struggle."

Just like that, sudden as the puffs of wind which blew the dust into tiny, whirling funnels, my friend would quickly flog himself into passionate exhortation, temporarily forgetting his proclaimed middle-of-the-roadness.

"Mr. Lindsay, if you feel so deeply about things, why don't you do something about it?"

"Don't jump to conclusions, my friend," he replied. "I was not speaking for myself. Even so, what is there to be done? Any voice raised in protest would be quickly and completely hushed. First of all the protesting person would be labeled a Communist, in the pay of subversive foreign elements, then he would be hauled into court on some trumped-up charge and after due process of law, probably jailed. No one backs the Government, no one opposes the Government."

"But you have an official opposition and a leader of the opposition."

"My friend, I am not concerned with the theory but with the practice of government, and I think it is fair to say that there is no real opposition. There is only one political party, the S.L.P.P., or Sierra Leone Progressive Party, headed by the Prime Minister. Any other so-called party is merely a name, meaningless and ineffectual. They do not count, no matter who heads them. Do I sound despondent and bitter? I'm not really. Think of the things I've said and take another good look at these carefree, indifferent, jobless fellows. The time will come, the time may soon be here, when they will suddenly wake up and begin to ask questions and the fat will really be in the fire."

"I'd like to talk with them, you know, find out if they do have any interest in approaching independence."

"Go ahead, but I don't think you'll get anything."

I walked over to a group and said hello in greeting. My friend spoke to them in creole, explaining that I was a visitor from Europe and wanted to chat with them. They looked at the camera I had

100

slung over my shoulder and asked whether I wanted to take their picture. Thinking that this would be a good opening I said yes.

"How about some gash?" one asked, rubbing the fingers of his right hand together in a sign unmistakable the world over. "Gash" meant money.

"Give them a few shillings," my friend advised, "they need it. And taking their picture provides them with an excuse for asking."

I snapped a few shots of them, handed over a few shillings, and leaned against the fence, very much as some of them were doing.

"How long have you been out of work?" I asked.

"Long, long time, maybe six months," said one.

"Long time, a year maybe," answered another.

Some of them merely spread their hands, fingers outpointed, as if to encompass as much time as possible by the gesture.

"Do you come here every day?" I asked.

"Yes, except when it rains."

"Why not, nothing else to do?"

"We all come here, every day."

They laughed nervously together. I thought I'd try another line. "I've come to your country to find out how you feel about independence. In a few weeks this will be an independent country."

They looked at each other as if unsure about how to answer that one.

"Yes, independence is next month," one said.

"Then the Old Man will go live up there," said another, pointing up toward the barely visible cupola of Government House, from which the Union Jack gaily fluttered in the breeze.

"Yes, the Old Man will turn Governor," another agreed.

"Then the white men will go back to England."

"Maybe then we find work."

"Them Lebanese will go back where they came from, and we take over them Lebanese shops."

"Them Lebanese own all the shops around waterside. When independence comes only black people own the shops."

"All the big shops, like Kingsway and Cold Storage, all them big shops."

"And the banks. Lots of money in those banks. Just walk into a bank and say, 'Gimme that money there.' "

101

As he divulged himself of this piece of fantasy and the mental picture it conjured up, the speaker rolled on the ground in glee, kicking his heels high in the air, while his friends laughed heartily in sympathy, slapping their thighs loudly in accompaniment. I laughed too at the ridiculousness of it all.

These young men were a long, long way from responsible conduct. My friend had not overpainted the picture. I remembered conversations I had had in Guinea with young men like these, probably from the same kind of background, but with vastly greater social consciousness. Was it because of Guinea's recent turbulent experiences? Was the same kind of turbulence necessary here as a stimulus to effort and responsibility? A few more years of this inactivity and these young men would be permanently useless to themselves or their community. Idleness is a serious social disease. My friend looked at me with raised eyebrows, as if to say, "Well, what did you expect!" So, with a word or two more, I left them, diverting themselves with magic dreams of ease and plenty after independence.

"Let's forget about social injustices for a while," my friend said. "We'll follow the road around the colony and out along the coast and perhaps have a swim out at Lumley Beach."

We found the car, stopped at his house and my hotel for our bathing trunks and set out from Freetown, through villages which were all very much the same, rather shabby, and built on both sides of the narrow ribbon of the macadam road. Leicester, Regent, Charlotte, Hastings, Waterloo, Campbell Town, Russel, York, Sussex, Hamilton, Godrich, the British imprint was deep, probably permanent. In the warm afternoon sunshine everything looked peaceful and quaintly picturesque, the houses sheltering in the cool shadows of cocoanut palms and huge mango trees, people sitting in the shade chatting together or dozing, dogs half-heartedly giving chase to the car or lying carelessly in the roadway as if accustomed to being bypassed.

At the approach to Lumley Beach, on the right-hand side of the road, I saw the smooth, carefully laid-out greens of a golf course, now somewhat brown for lack of rain; a large notice board announced that the golf club was for private members only, and not open to residents of Freetown.

102

"Don't you think that that notice board is in rather poor taste, especially at this time?" I asked.

"No, my friend," he replied, "for as long as our people are not offended by it I think it should stay there."

It sounded rather cryptic and I did not pursue the matter. Further along I saw the clubhouse, a low, rambling building which sat primly on the edge of the course; several European couples were sipping drinks in the forecourt, which offered a splendid view of the broad reach of the Atlantic.

"Is this notice in any way indicative of the social relationship between black and white?"

"Some people will tell you that, in this country, Europeans and Africans meet and mix socially. Others might affirm, that though they work together there is very little social intercourse. Here and there you see a mixed couple, but this has no bearing on the matter. Very rarely are Africans invited into European homes, and I think it would be true to state the little mixing which does occur dates very largely from about the end of the second World War; in fact, anything which might reasonably be called social or economic progress here, dates from not much more than ten years ago."

The beach at Lumley was a beautiful and impressive sight: the soft white sand fell away from the rutted macadam roadway in a gentle slope until it flattened out in a short plateau before dipping sharply to the sea. At the moment huge rollers were rushing inward to hurl themselves against the lower lip of the beach and expend their whistling froth in a fruitless struggle up the plateau.

"Rather dangerous here for bathing. Let's try further along," he said.

About a mile beyond the golf course the beach curved gently in a shallow crescent; several long boats manned by briskly paddling Africans were darting to and fro in among the gentler waves, while on shore scores of African men and women were gathered in long lines, holding ropes which led to the edge of the water and out to sea.

"This is really something you should not miss," he said. "Let's get down there and watch the fun."

At close hand those on the beach were lined up, each like a tug-of-war team ready and waiting for its opponent; each of these teams consisted of twenty or more men, women and children most of them wet to the skin from contact with the waves; the younger ones, boys and girls, were clad only in a kind of flowing loincloth. Some of these laughing children were truly beautiful, their smooth skins generously pearled by water droplets, eyes and teeth flashing in enjoyment; the young girls, some of them in their early or late teens, full-breasted and completely unshy. Running up and down some short distance from the teams, shouting and waving his arms seaward, was a large African clad only in a pair of discolored shorts and a grotesque wide-brimmed straw hat; his stentorian voice yelled instructions to the boat crews, who paddled furiously or paused at his signals, while those on shore, at a word from him, hauled so vigorously on the lines that often several members of each team would tumble over in the sand to the delight of the others. Suddenly the conductor, for such he seemed to be, signaled rapidly seaward and all the boats immediately swung 'round to point inland, the paddlers working furiously as they raced simultaneously toward the beach. Meanwhile the lines of the pullers on the beach raced up the easy slope and soon the first ends of the nets appeared. Now ensued a frantic pulling on the ropes, hand-over-fist, as they hurried to land the twisting, heaving, silvery catch, their voices raised in excited yells, laughter and exaltation. The boatmen raced their craft until they grounded, then leaped out to draw them up above the waterline before turning to lend a hand with the catch. And what a catch it was! Fish varying in length from two to three feet or more; fat, succulent things which flopped and slithered as they were hauled to form a huge silvery pile which glittered in the rays of the slanting sun.

As if informed by some kind of bush telegraph, several lorries and cars appeared along the road, honking their contribution to the din, and disgorging groups of fish vendors and middlemen.

"I did not know about this bit of local activity," I said to my friend, who seemed as excited and entranced as I was by the skill and harmony of the whole cooperative procedure.

"It isn't local," he said, "except for those who've just arrived, all the people here are Ghanaians; they are the only ones who fish along the coasts; they're tough and capable and wonderful fisher-

104

men. Let's go closer and watch the sales and you'll notice something."

The selling was a rather complicated affair of bid and counterbid, with bundles of pound notes changing hands. In most cases the Ghanaian women seemed to take charge of the money, stuffing the bills into bulging leather pouches attached to their waists.

"You mean about the women hanging on to the cash?"

"Yes. These Ghanaians are quite well-off. They don't squander their money or raise hell in town as soon as they have a pound or two. They live over there," he pointed to a low valley some distance inland, "in their own little communities, and keep very much to themselves."

"Will they sell all this fish?" The pile somehow seemed tremendous.

"Most of it. Of what remains they will reserve some for their own use, then bury the rest deep in the sand."

"So quite a bit of each catch is wasted."

"Yes, but such is life, no way of avoiding that."

We walked some little distance down the beach away from the sound and smell of the impromptu fish market and swam awhile in the warm, refreshing water.

In the days following I familiarized myself with the town and made many friends, among them the families of Dr. Jean Neale and Dr. Max Bond, both of them I.C.A. field operatives working in Sierra Leone on technical-aid programs. For a time Dr. Bond and I lived in the same hotel and I was able to benefit greatly from his very wide experience in planned educational projects, gained from field work in several countries. The man's humility was astonishing, and even now, when I hear or read of some instance of bigotry associated with American conduct, I think of Dr. Bond and his colleagues, who are quietly but effectively forging links of international understanding.

*

He and I were involved in a rather odd incident one morning. He had moved from the Paramount Hotel to the Government Rest

105

House some distance out of town and I had run over there to see him. We were chatting over beer when a smartly dressed gentleman approached and sat next to us. As was usual with Dr. Bond, he soon said something to the newcomer which drew him into the conversation with us, and before long we were chatting away together in the friendliest fashion. Our new friend introduced himself as a visiting official from one of the Arab States, he too was residing at the Rest House. Our conversation was occasionally interrupted by the noise of power drills, hammers and workmen's shouts which flowed around us from the building operations nearby (Rest House accommodations were in process of extension by a firm of Israeli engineers and everywhere one could see well-muscled, bronzed, energetic young Israelis, not only supervising the construction, but working shoulder-to-shoulder with the African craftsmen and laborers).

"Don't you think this is a rather dangerous thing for Sierra Leone, to have all these Jews flocking into the country?" our Arab friend asked. "These people have a way of digging themselves in that could prove very dangerous if it were not recognized and curbed."

He knew that neither of us was a native of Sierra Leone, but may have supposed that our dark skins was sufficient guarantee of immediate sympathy with everything African.

"Let's look at it this way, friend," Dr. Bond replied. "I'm an American Negro, which makes me part of a minority group wherever I am. Even here in Africa, although I'm black, I am American, so I am again in the minority. It would hardly become me to speak, act or even think adversely about any other minority group. I would presume that these engineers are here because they are needed, at least they seem to be getting on with something very needful. If I started thinking badly about them merely because they are Jews, how do you know I would not soon think as badly of you merely because you are an Arab? By the way, I'd like to visit your country one day to learn something about your educational system." And thus, without causing any hurt or embarrassment, he steered the conversation into more general waters.

One evening I dined with an Englishman, his wife and a group of his friends; he was a staff member of Fourah Bay College, in the English department, and asked me to address a group of education students at the college. A few days later I addressed the group of young Africans in one of the lecture rooms; they were mostly Sierra Leoneans, and a few from Nigeria and Ghana. I spoke about my own experiences as a teacher, and of the urgent need for teachers to develop a broad outlook which acknowledged and examined all the educational processes to which children are consciously or otherwise exposed, including radio, newspapers, conversation with adults, or their own ilk, books, cinema, church. I expressed the view that the classroom was most effective when everyone, teachers and pupils alike, was involved in conscious interchange of ideas and experiences.

I told them the following story from my own teaching days: One of my students, a mischievous boy named Tich Jackson, one day interrupted a lesson in geography by waving aloft a magazine folded to show a cartoon of a group of savages sitting around a large cooking pot, licking their lips in anticipation. Never one to miss any opportunity for having fun at my expense, he asked loudly, "Is this how it is where you come from, sir?"

Many of those sitting in his immediate vicinity saw the cartoon and laughed, as he had hoped. Watchful from numerous previous occasions of the same kind, I took the magazine from him and held it open so that everyone could see the drawing. I said, "I'll answer Tich after everyone has seen the cartoon and had his laugh."

Naturally there were merely a few giggles. I was quickly trying to think of some way of taking the play from him without embarrassing either him or myself. Then something occurred to me. "No, Tich, that's not how it is where I come from, but that's very much how it is here."

There were snorts and murmurs of disapproval at that, but I continued. "Let's try to examine what I mean. That cooking pot is very much like this classroom, in which something or other is cooking all the time; we are like the men around the pot, for each of us is hoping to pull something out which will satisfy us and strengthen us for whatever tasks await us. Some of those men might like fat, some lean, some might like the sparerib, some the heart or liver, or what-have-you. Each man to his taste or needs.

"So it is with us. Each of us has a special need, and here we hope

107

that day by day our abilities are developed, our needs met, our interests directed; but let's take another look at this drawing. What do you think is cooking in the pot, Tich?"

"Dunno," he replied. "Stew perhaps."

"Could be," I agreed, "And for a stew we need more than the meat. These fellows are licking their lips, which suggests that whatever is in the pot smells good. Somebody must have popped in some salt, another some herbs, just as is done in your own home. Similarly with us. Each day, we come here, forty-seven of us, each bringing something of himself or herself, some idea, or bit of experience or information or knowledge which sweetens the pot, perhaps just the tidbit someone else needed to enrich his own experience or elucidate some little problem. In short, each of us provides something to making the stew, and all of us take what we need from the pot."

From this little story I hoped to show them that the teacher should be willing to create circumstances within his classroom favorable to the student, giving something as well as receiving something. At the end of my talk I invited comment or questions. Several students were opposed to the idea that the teacher could learn anything from his pupils.

"Perhaps that is possible in Europe," one said, "but not in Africa. Whatever teaching is done must come from the teacher."

"I expect to teach in the protectorate," another said, "where the people are very primitive and the children believe in witchcraft and all kinds of similar things. It would be impossible for any of them to make any contribution to the teaching process. What would you do if you had to teach children like those?" he said in a clear voice which betrayed his pride in the distance between himself and the "primitives" to whom he referred.

I thought over his question very carefully before replying. "If we accept that my training would have been oriented to the situation I would find there, then, immediately upon contact with them, I would try to learn all I could about their beliefs, practices, environment, etc., in order to find ways of making the things I wanted to teach meaningful to them; and the persons best qualified to inform me on those practices would be the pupils themselves, because, given the opportunity and favorable circumstances, they would

108

teach me gradually while learning from me. For an African teacher who expects to work in the circumstances you describe, I think it would be imperative that he learned all he could about the prevailing conditions."

They were very skeptical about my ideas; evidently they considered themselves somewhat superior types, probably by virtue of their studentship at such a renowned institution as Fourah Bay College. After all, they would be working in places where education was still a very important symbol, and teachers would be expected to conduct themselves as the "fountainhead of knowledge." I could only say my piece and leave it at that.

*

The day before I started out on trek with my friend I had a rather unhappy experience. Early that morning I received a notice from the post office that a parcel addressed to me awaited collection at their parcels depot. I judged it would be a parcel of books my London publisher had sent out to me.

After some difficulty I located the parcels office. Behind the public counter one young clerk was reading a paperback novel, and some distance away several other clerks stood together in quiet discourse. I approached the nearer clerk with the green notice in my hand.

"Excuse me, please, but I'd like to collect this parcel, if I may." I placed the green slip before him.

He must have seen it, but without lifting his head from his book he rapped on the counter and a khaki-clad messenger appeared, took the green slip and disappeared, to return quickly with a small string-bound package, which he placed on the counter beside the clerk, who, without interrupting his reading even to glance at me, said, "Open it."

At first I thought he was addressing the messenger, but that young man had departed immediately after placing the parcel on the counter.

"Open it," the clerk repeated, this time favoring me with an annoyed glance.

I was both surprised and irritated by his manner and could only stare at him.

"Open it, I said," he repeated irritably.

Suddenly I lost my temper at this public servant, this paid servant who so brazenly occupied himself with a novel and treated me so casually because I had interrupted his reading.

"Look here, mister," I told him, barely able to control my anger. "I already know what is in that parcel. If you want to know what is in it, then you open it."

It may have been the tone of my voice, of the fact of my anger, but his whole manner changed, yet he insisted but in a somewhat conciliatory tone.

"The customer is supposed to open his own parcel."

By now I was having none of it and retorted heatedly.

"I'd like to believe that you are paid to render a public service and not to sit on your backside reading and ordering customers about. If you want that parcel opened, then you'll damned well do it yourself."

He looked about him in some confusion. Someone detached himself from the group further along and approached us, asking, "Is something the matter?"

"This gentleman refuses to open his parcel," the clerk said.

"I rather resent the attitude of this young man," I said. "He could not be bothered to even look up from his book but merely ordered me to open my parcel and I refused."

He quickly took in the situation—novel, parcel, clerk and myself —then said to the clerk in mild reproof, "You should have explained to the gentleman that the regulations require the customer to open his own parcel." Then to me, "I am the chief clerk here, and I'm sorry about the misunderstanding, but if you'll open the parcel with this," he produced a razor blade, "we'll soon have it cleared. It is a kind of safeguard to ensure that your parcel was intact when you received it, and to allow us to check the contents at the same time."

His manner was polite, dignified, gracious. I slit the package and exposed the contents: six copies of my first book, *To Sir, with Love*.

The chief clerk examined a copy; they were evidently both

110

impressed by the fact I was E. R. Braithwaite, the author, and the young clerk apologized for his behavior. I thanked them, tied the package together and left. Later I mentioned the incident to Mr. Lindsay.

"I'm not surprised," he said. "We Africans do not respect each other. The clear intention was to impress you by being as casually disrespectful as possible, only he does not see it as disrespect. He is an example of the kind of disease which is prevalent throughout our civil service and can be found wherever a black man holds office, no matter how lowly or badly paid that office might be. He would either have seen you enter, or he saw your hands as you extended the green notice to him; that was enough. You are black and he felt under no obligation to be courteous to you. If a European had entered that office, the novel would have disappeared like lightning and the clerk would have been on his feet. The only black exceptions are the more familiar local dignitaries. We simply do not respect each other. Simple. The European does not respect the African, and the African, in emulating European conduct, exhibits very little selectivity, and merely follows suit. Furthermore, that clerk is a civil servant even though he might be at the lowest rung of the ladder, and he is merely doing what he has seen done by his seniors, black and white."

"But if Africans do not respect Africans, how will independence ever become a reality?"

"Perhaps when we finally develop the spirit of independence. As I said before, our colonialization has gone deeper than most; so deep that we willingly and readily disrespect ourselves. That postal clerk is only a short distance removed from the houseboys at your hotel in his attitude to Europeans. Even I, and this is somewhat of a confession, am never quite at ease with Europeans, because I have never had much opportunity for meeting and dealing with them as equals. You know, you shouldn't stay in this country too long or you'll soon become as bitter and frustrated as I am."

Later that evening I had occasion to remember what he said. I had persuaded him to dine with me at my hotel and was waiting for him in the lounge. Two young Englishmen and an African girl entered, sat nearby and ordered drinks. The girl, a well-rounded, fulsome creature, wore, in my opinion, too much makeup; she was evidently very ill at ease and nervously giggled at every remark made by either of her companions, both of whom were young and obviously making the most of being a long way away from home and inhibiting influences. Soon the trio was joined by another Englishman, slightly older-looking, and now the three men entered into conversation which completely excluded the girl; she sat there, taking occasional sips from her drink and looking around the room, bored and unhappy. When my friend joined me the three men were still talking over her head, as if quite unconcerned about her.

My friend noticed and said, "That is about as far as most black-white associations go: lonely men, ambitious women. When I say 'ambitious' I limit the term to the material advantages as might result from such an association, for let's face it, the black boys have no money. Now and then there is a marriage, but, for the most part, this is about the limit of black-white social relationships."

Later we went down to dinner in the open-air patio. It was like being part of a scene dreamed up for a film romance—the over-hanging trees dappled with light from the colored electric bulbs hidden in the foliage; the star-filled sky, which seemed near enough to touch; the gleaming napery and silverware; the waiters in white tunics, black trousers and flamboyant red sashes; and the four-piece band, weaving a sweet pattern of soft sound, unobstrusive yet recognizable over the murmur of whispered conversations. Everyone "dressed for dinner" at this hotel: the filmy, bright dresses of the women in pleasant contrast to the men's dark lightweight suits. The tables were scattered around the patio, clear of the central dance area; on each flickered a candle, which added its seductive contribution to the night and the music.

After dinner the guests remained to sip drinks or dance; the band now came into its own, filling the African night with foxtrots, quicksteps, waltzes, all very correct and pleasing, yet somehow controlled, ordered, like listening to Victor Sylvestor. There was a small party of two African couples who had dined together and were now watching the European couples on the dance floor. One of them signaled a waiter and whispered to him, and at the end of that dance, the waiter as unobtrusively as possible, went over and whispered to a member of the band, who smiled and nodded in the direction of the African couples. I might have guessed! The next

112

number began with a series of bass chords from the piano, not loud, but deep and suggestive, like an impatient lover calling in the darkness, over and over, but yet unhurried, until it meant something pleasing, enticing. And now the other instruments slipped into the strain. The strong compulsive notes prevailed, but over, around and through them the trumpet, saxophone and clarinet, wove an intricate, exciting lacework of sound. Following the first opening bars, the African couples took the floor, fitting themselves easily and naturally into the music. It was delightful to watch them, their faces aglow, their bodies slightly arched forward to better accommodate the hip-swaying, graceful movements as they circled each other in free individual interpretation. Fluid, exciting and completely African, immediately in harmony with the night and the stars themselves; seductively challenging to the earlier ordered sounds, interjecting a new spirit, a promise of things to come, things yet a long way off. I listened and watched, entranced. An English couple sat at the table nearest me. The husband was keen to "have a go" at the dance. It seemed so easy, so natural, he wanted to join in; but his wife resisted, whispering that she did not "know" the steps. No other couple ventured on the floor, and the Africans, dancers and musicians continued for a while in their wonderful conspiracy of sound and movement. When the dance ended, the African guests gathered up their belongings and left.

"Great," I said.

"Sure," my friend agreed. "Pity it's an import. But in time we'll have our own."

Later that evening, using a small survey map of Sierra Leone, we made plans for our hinterland trip, laying out a route which would take us over most of the country in the shortest possible time. We'd follow the road southeast through Bo to Limi, northeast to Karlatun, then north to Kabala and back to Freetown through the Bombali and Port Loko districts. For provisions we took some bottled beer, tinned biscuits and fruit. These were mainly for my use and my friend assured me that he would find plenty of local fare, made available by numerous relatives and friends. It was inadvisable that I eat the local "chop," as the sudden change of diet might prove disastrous, at least until I stayed long enough to develop certain immunities. The trip was expected to take two or three

113

days. We would travel very light, taking one change of khaki shirts and shorts, towels and shaving kit, all stuffed into dustproof plastic bags. My friend told me that while on trek he would be exempt from fasting. We would be traveling day and night, taking turns at driving.

*

We started out at 4:30 A.M. on Monday to take full advantage of the cool morning air and the traffic-free roads. A heavy mist hung low over Freetown, and as we climbed the slopes toward Waterloo, I glanced back at the saucerlike depression in which the capital slept under its blanket of mist.

The land-rover fled along the macadam road as if as anxious as we to make plenty of headway before the sun came up. Now I was better able to observe the country through which we had passed a few nights before on the way back from Moyamba—green country, rich with its abundance of shrubs and trees out of which the oil palms raised proud, leafy heads. The road was a thin black ribbon slipping and winding a way through the trees, frequently interrupted by small wooden bridges over dry, shallow gullies. We slipped past village after village, the huts still closed like defensive armadillos, with dogs and goats sleeping on the dusty forecourts, hardly stirring as we flashed by, a packaged blast of noise which quickly passed before it had really disturbed them. Near Jonibana, the macadam road suddenly ended and we became the spearhead of a whirling column of thick dust which completely obscured the road behind us and followed us like a revengeful genie uphill and down short slopes, adding to the thick discoloring layers which coated the trees and shrubs on the sides. Before long I noticed that my friend's hair was powdered red as if made up for some festive masquerade— head, eyelashes and eyebrows were red-touched, giving him a grotesquely comical appearance, like Falstaff gone mechanically mad. I laughed, so absurd he looked: his fat, large hands loosely on the wheel, the khaki shirt stretched taut and damp across his thick chest.

"What's so funny," he asked.

114

"You. You're all made up for the 'Darktown Strutters' Ball.' Red wig and eyelashes are being worn these days."

Instead of replying he glanced up at the driving mirror, then twisted it toward me; I looked aghast at the red-wigged fellow who looked aghast at me.

"That old thing about stones and glass houses," my friend laughed.

By this time the sun was slanting over the trees, an indefinite area of gold-white against a background of pale grayish-blue cloudless sky in which buzzards hung unmoving, black, spread-winged shapes. At Taiama, we crossed the Jong River by a long steel bridge, excellent in construction, but as narrow as any of the flimsy wooden structures we had crossed.

As if sharing my thoughts, my friend said, "As you can see, we were not planning for development."

We paused halfway across the bridge to watch the wide, swift river, starved by the long dry season until, here and there, the boulders scattered about along the bed formed innumerable small rapids which converged and split again into racing, gurgling hazards. It looked very dangerous and forbidding.

"During the rainy season this river becomes navigable for small craft for nearly its entire length," my friend said.

Mano, Bumpe, Tikonko, and on to Bo, the main township of the southwestern province. It was surprising to find this bustling town deep in what I had hitherto thought of as bush. The road leading into it was a dusty, rutted dirt track, but in the town itself was a neat network of macadam streets between neat government buildings, schools, churches and administration compounds. The center of the town was crowded with overstocked Lebanese shops, warehouses, filling stations and dwelling houses, deteriorating on one side into tin-roof shanty huts and cutting itself off sharply on the other to accommodate the clanking, rolling stock of the tiny railway. My friend told me something of Bo's history and of the Bo Boys' secondary school, which had originally been established as a boarding school for the sons of Paramount chiefs and now was regarded as one of the foremost secondary schools in the country.

"Nearly all our outstanding men were, at one time or another, trained here at Bo school—people like Dr. Nicol, principal of

Fourah Bay College, our internationally renowned scientist and most of our government ministers."

He spoke with a certain air, as if he wished he too had enjoyed such a privilege.

We stopped at a filling station to have refills of petrol, water and air. While the land-rover was being attended to, we strolled around the town, chatting briefly with persons of his acquaintance. Now and then I attempted to introduce a question about independence or education, but there was very little response, somewhat to my friend's ill-concealed amusement.

"You can't believe that they're not interested, can you?" he asked. "Most of them either don't know or don't understand. The others may know enough to suspect that it might mean relinquishing something personal—you know, like power or influence, perhaps. Not only is it true that most of them don't know, but it is also true that nobody is making much of an effort to explain it to them. The Governor does what he can, but he is limited by having to keep his remarks as objective as possible; he cannot afford to become too enthusiastic, because, apart from displeasing the politicians, on whose future platforms he might be encroaching, he would earn the suspicion and distrust of the rank-and-file, who would immediately assume that if the white man was so keen on it, he, not they, had the most to gain."

"You make it all sound so hopeless," I remarked.

"No, not hopeless. I merely want you to see behind their indifference. They don't know what's going on now, but one day the fact of independence is going to hit them, then there will be changes."

On our way again, through country now flat with few and stunted trees among low shrubs and tough-looking grass. The ground on both sides of the road was chewed up into an ugly proliferation of shallow excavations, as if someone had made several halfhearted attempts at ploughing the ground and had, on each occasion, given up in disgust after doing little more than disturb the ground to a few inches in depth.

"Diggings," my friend explained. "Diamonds."

"What do you mean diggings?" I asked. "Do you mean to say that diamonds are found lying there on the surface? The ground has been scratched no deeper than to plant rice."

116

"Well, they find the stuff there, that's all I know," he replied. "All this area through which we are now passing is part of the Sewa River basin—we'll cross the river in a short while—and the people have been finding diamonds literally on the surface of the ground. As you can see, they never dig deep, perhaps because they have neither the patience nor skill. They scratch around in the same inefficient and wasteful way as they do their farming."

"Are they wealthy, these local people with diamonds in their backyards?"

"No, not wealthy; few are even reasonably well-off, because there is little sense of application. Everyone wants to strike it big and become rich overnight. The people who do best out of it all are the Lebanese. They trade in diamonds and they trade in everything the diamond-diggers need, so they can't go wrong. Very often they put up the money for a mining venture, including licenses, and then receive a tribute or percentage of everything found. As you can expect, a hell of a lot of thieving and smuggling goes on, but the Lebanese are familiar with all the tricks and know how to protect their interests."

"Do the Lebanese themselves mine the diamonds?"

"Rarely. It's not easy for a foreigner to get a license; so the next best thing is to put up the money for someone else to get it. In some places, you'll find that the children of Lebanese-African marriages or associations become licensees and provide the necessary openings for their fathers' financial ventures, because any child of African extraction is considered African. Sometimes some Africans form a company, but usually they either scratch around independently or work for the Lebanese. They will do better and more consistent work when they're employed than they would ever do for themselves."

The scarred country looked tragically ugly; it seemed an awful shame that the ground was thus relieved of its riches and left naked and abused. As we approached the Sewa Bridge, I saw the miners working upstream, and we parked to take a closer look. It was not as I had expected; these men were literally diving for diamonds, scooping up the fine silt from underwater in shallow buckets, then washing it on improvised rockers. There were several groups, or gangs, of Africans working at different points in the river. On

117

the bank, opposite the divers, a Lebanese sprawled in a kind of deck chair, beside which were a large hamper and thermos jug.

"He's keeping an eye on his interests," my friend remarked.

Traveling through Bendu to Keribondu, then north toward Blama, with everywhere the scarred earth. Sometimes we crossed streams which had been dammed, the water diverted through a shallow channel, the section pumped dry, and the diggers hard at work on the exposed sand and gravel of the riverbed. Here and there we passed a single digger and sometimes two of them, knee-deep in a water gully, backs curved as they peered into the shallow cone-shaped pans.

"Is everybody doing this kind of thing?" I asked.

"It's a kind of vicious circle," he replied. "They've deserted the farms to seek diamonds, so now they often have to buy the food they eat and pay heavily for it, and very often they run into debt when digging is not profitable and have to return to farming until they can either start digging again for themselves or dig for someone else."

We stopped at Blama to pay a courtesy call on the Paramount chief, then went on north to Boajibu, a village which diamond-mining had turned into a sort of boom town with German, American and British cars being driven furiously through the narrow, dusty streets by excitable young men with heavy pocketbooks and the urge to raise some hell.

"What do you think independence could mean to these fellows?" my friend asked. "All they ever ask of life is that they occasionally strike it rich and that nothing interferes with their licenses. Look at the cars they're driving on these roads—Mercedes-Benzes, Buicks, Peugeots, luxury cars intended for smooth roads and graceful living; then look at the miserable huts in which some of them live! None of them would be interested in taking any responsibility for improving their own living conditions. Sometimes, one of them will get the idea of building a house, so he decides on an elaborate affair and sets out to build it without much thought for over-all costs. The result is that, scattered over the Protectorate are partly finished houses of all kinds, abandoned because the money ran out too quickly, or the labor force soon deserted, or something else."

118

*

Soon after leaving Boajibu, on the way east to the Kenewa and Kailatun districts, we encountered a group of about a dozen girls, whose ages ranged from about seven to fifteen or sixteen years. They were standing beside the narrow roadway with their backs to the oncoming car, as if to protect their eyes from the clouds of dust which the car stirred up in its progress.

"Those are girls from the Bundu Bush," my friend said. "Let's stop a little way ahead and come back to chat with them."

We drew up a few yards farther along and walked back to where they stood closely together, regarding our approach with large dark eyes, their faces unsmiling but unafraid and composed, as if aware of their ability to deal with whatever situation might arise. They were dressed very simply in a kind of wrap-around garment which covered them loosely from waist to ankle; around their long slender necks were necklaces of colored beads, sometimes interspersed with the teeth of animals or shaped pieces of ivory; some wore armbands of twisted hair or colored string. They were beautiful in a pleasing, natural way, their skin silky, smooth over rounded muscles, their breasts firm and shapely. Each one carried something on her head, casually balanced, and as they stood there, arms limply by their sides, heads and necks swaying slightly in automatic adjustment to balance the objects on their heads, I realized that at last I was seeing something of Africa that had hardly changed after centuries. My friend spoke something to the girls in greeting. Immediately their heads moved close together, like the points of a jellyfish retracting. They whispered briefly, then replied to him in a chorus, a startling, pleasant sound there on an otherwise deserted dirt road in the African hinterland, ranging from the slight thrilling treble of the youngest to the harsher but still-pleasant voices of the older ones.

"Good Lord!" I exclaimed, wondering where they could have learned to do this.

He spoke to them again in a dialect of sounds which seemed to explode from his throat without much control or modification by

119

his lips, and once again their heads flowed gently together before they replied in the same chorus of easily blended sounds. Now they removed the parcels from their heads and placed them carefully by the roadside, then they knelt on the ground in a circle and began a strange chanting, weaving their hands in graceful movements as they sang, always in chorus.

Suddenly, as if by a prearranged sig ial, they sprang up and following one behind the other in the same tight circle, presented a series of dances, some of them strange, stiff-jointed movements, accompanied by rhythmic stamping which kept the thick red dust in an eddying cloud about their feet; others were to me intensely beautiful, each body flowing, sinuous and separate, yet somehow a part of the others, dependent, necessary to the gently rotating circle. Throughout the dances, their faces remained calm, controlled and gentle, as if they were doing what they had always accepted as necessary to be done, like obedient, unquestioning children. But if their faces showed no sign of emotion, their bodies betrayed a deep and perhaps compulsive enthusiasm, for together with the precision of cooperative movement was a certain grace and charm which suggested surrender. The dance completed, they collected their parcels and replaced them on their heads, then stood together again, silent, shy and innocent—yes that was the word which best described them: innocent. It was the first time in my life that I had seen a group of young people of such varying ages who so conspicuously wore the mark of innocence. We said goodbye to them and they were soon lost behind the thick red screen we stirred up.

"You're a lucky man," my friend said, "to meet them like that; they're just out of the Bundu Bush and on their way back to their village."

He explained that the girls were all in various stages of training and preparation to assume the responsbilities and burdens of womanhood. From the age of six to seven, the girls become novitiates in the Saude Society, the women's secret organization, where they are taught the herbal secrets and folklore, together with household crafts and skills. At the age of thirteen or fourteen, the girls are initiated into the society and circumcised (the clitoris is removed). They are now ready for marriage. In explanation of their choral singing, he said that during their training all their duties and chores are performed to the accompaniment of songs, so the girls who train together soon develop the facility for singing or speaking together. Among the things taught to them are weaving of indigenous cloths, ceremonial dances, respect for their elders and obedience.

"What's the purpose of the circumcision?" I asked, my limited knowledge of physiology made such an operation seem to defeat the basic purpose behind all the careful training and preparation of the girls, because it was supposed to reduce or severely inhibit sexual desire.

"What's the use of teaching the woman how to be a useful woman and then, at one fell swoop, reduce her to little more than an obedient drudge?"

I suppose the very idea horrified me and I must have spoken somewhat excitedly, for my friend said, "What you read in your scientific books is one thing; I can tell you from firsthand knowledge that in my, shall we say, limited experience, there is nothing inhibited about our women in their sexual behavior. But, anyhow, there is no reason why you should take my word for it, you can have plenty of opportunity to find out the truth for yourself." He roared with laughter, his head tilted back as far as his thick neck would allow.

The countryside had changed and now our road wound its way through thick growths of trees. Here and there my friend pointed to what he called cocoa or coffee farms, but though I occasionally caught sight of some yellow cocoa pods on low trees, these were so thickly involved with the other forest growths that I could see nothing which deserved the name "farm." Then I realized that I was expecting to see a certain order, with a clear demarcation between the cultivated areas and the rest of the forest, whereas methods of cultivation here allowed the crop to grow in close relationship with the forest.

"I think we'll stop at Kenewa," he said. "I've some friends there and we can be sure of a bed and some chop."

In Kenewa, we drove to his friend's home, a large comfortable wooden bungalow set well back from the road in spacious grounds; inside, it was well equipped for convenience and adequately furnished. After a leisurely bath and shave, I sat down to a meal with

121

my friend and our hosts, Mr. and Mrs. Anibojin. They were a charming African couple and the meal was most welcome and enjoyable. Later we sat out on the veranda in the cool African night sipping drinks. Mr. Anibojin was a senior Government official who had recently arrived in the district to take up a new appointment. I made some flattering comment about the house and he replied, "This is my second visit to these parts. I well remember the first occasion because I was then a very junior officer sent here as temporary extra help to the district commissioner. I was never then allowed to use those front steps."

He pointed to where the white-painted steps were now half-hidden in gloom and the thick leaves of bougainvillea.

"Why?" I asked. "Who lived here then?"

"The district commissioner, an Englishman. Things have changed somewhat since then. While he lived here, those lawns and flowering bushes were all well-watered and trimmed and everything kept spick and span by a lot of cheaply available labor. Nowadays the D.C., an African, gets nothing like the salary or other emoluments once paid to Europeans, so this place is as it is and gradually becoming worse. As Africans we are not expected to want the same treatment and advantages which Europeans enjoyed and we ourselves cannot afford to keep the place up."

Here was someone who seemed willing to talk, so I pressed the opportunity. "I take it that the policy now is to replace all European personnel by Africans?"

"Yes, that is the general policy," he replied, "but that's as far as it goes. The African official exercises less power and influence because everyone looks upon him as one of themselves: someone who either grew up among them or who was related to someone who did."

"But," I argued, "it seems to be part of the larger picture of independence."

"I wouldn't say that," he replied. "The changeover had to come because there had to be an outlet in the civil service for the large numbers of Africans who are becoming more and more able and qualified to hold commissions. Independence is another matter. Personally, I cannot see that it matters much at the present time, because there are no known practical schemes planned to make it

122

a reality to the villager, if I might take such an example. We'll become independent on April 27, and I am wondering where, when all the shouting has died down, we can find the money to provide good all-weather roads to link up our main towns and even to join up with roadways of Guinea and Liberia. We need good wide roads as much as we need schools, hospitals, electricity—things like that.

"Independence will mean very little to us unless we are prepared to tackle certain unpopular but important problems, including land reforms and a new appraisal of our natural resources. As a civil servant, I cannot say more, but in our present state, independence might well seem to be a kind of luxury we cannot really afford. It does not come to us as the result of any popular uprising, so some other kind of stimulus is necessary to jolt us into the kind of effort necessary to justify us in our new role. But there is no sign of any beginnings in that direction. The Old Man would deal very summarily with anyone or anything which in his view was calculated to disturb the present rather questionable calm, and they'd be labeled Communists, or something like that."

"Has there been any Communist activity in Sierra Leone?" I asked.

"There he goes again," Mr. Lindsay observed. "How could we know the answer to that one? How would we recognize a Communist? By the color of his skin, or is he supposed to be a wild-eyed, ranting fellow who goes about advocating the overthrow of the Government? In this country one worries because there is no voice just now which is heard and understood by the people. Perhaps when it comes it might be the kind of voice we least expect—you know: quiet, reasoning, understanding; the kind of voice which will claim no one. Personally, I should welcome any movement, be it Communist or anything else, which gave my people a sense of faith and responsibility, an awakening to the need to live like free men rather than as has been the pattern all these years; like freed men, congenially grateful to their liberators and incapable of the luxury of anger against the deep sloth which enslaves them."

I suddenly had the urge to needle them a little. Here they were comfortably expressing opinions on what ought to be done, so . . . "Very often, it is more important to decide the measure of one's personal involvement in a situation than to suggest how someone

123

else should deal with it. It should be more a matter of 'What can I do?' or 'What will I do?' than 'What they ought to do.'"

Neither of them replied to that and shortly afterward we retired for the night.

Next morning we left Kenewa at six-thirty after breakfasting with our host and followed the road through the heavily wooded Pola Forest toward Pendumbu and Kailatun. Overhead, troops of monkeys gibbered noisily in the branches as they swung from tree to tree with fantastic agility. Some of them were brown, skinny creatures, all spidery arms and legs; others were white-faced, with long white tails.

"Every once in a while we organize a monkey shoot," my friend said, "because these animals are a menace to the crops; thousands are killed each year, and the Government pays a bounty on each tail."

*

At Kailatun we refueled and retraced our steps, passing again through Kenewa, then Grema, Gegbwema and down to Zimi, a few miles from the Liberian border. Beyond Zimi, we crossed the wide Moa River at Baudajuwa by hand-operated ferry and headed west for Papetun. I could not help thinking that so much seemed to depend on the roads, yet so little seemed to have been done about them. This was the dry season—during the rains, life must be really grim for all concerned. From Papetun, we headed north for Magburaka, where we hoped to spend the night. My friend wanted to visit one of his wives, who lived there, and remarked, "I think I'll take the opportunity of getting some medical advice while I'm there."

"Does your doctor live there?" I asked. It seemed an awfully long way to travel for medical attention.

"Oh, I've got a doctor in Freetown," he replied, "but this is different. This is what you might call a native doctor—he can deal with things which are not found in medical textbooks."

"Is he a witch doctor?" I asked.

He looked at me, then roared with laughter. Whenever he did that, I had the feeling that he saw me from a long way off; thought

124

of me then with something like pity, as if he considered me naive and uninformed beyond belief.

"Wherever do you get such terms?" he asked. "You say 'witch doctor' in a way that clearly expresses your unbelief and European disdain for something about which you know nothing."

It had truly shocked me to hear this cultivated, intelligent man speak with such casual acceptance and faith about something which had always seemed to me to be mumbo-jumbo. I had heard of witches and witchcraft and read of the part such beliefs and practices had played in the historical development of many countries. I had read many reports of such practices and beliefs as related to Africa and Africans, but I suppose I had stupidly assumed that they belonged to the primitive element, which still remained comparatively unchanged by contact with Europeans. In my mind, I somehow expected that education presupposed a rejection of such beliefs and I found it difficult to associate this charming, educated man with charms and fetishes.

"Sorry," I said, in puerile excuse.

"You know," he continued, "you've been away from Africa too long, too many generations, so you talk and think like a foreigner, like a white man. You'd be surprised to know what really goes on in this bush we're passing through. You call him a witch doctor, but he can do a hell of a lot more for us than all the patent medicines you can name. Besides, some things cannot be cured by medicines."

He then recounted instance after instance of strange illnesses which had suddenly overtaken friends or acquaintances, so that they sickened and would very probably have died but for the intervention of the native doctor. In each case, the illness defeated analysis by the European-trained doctors in Freetown, but promptly responded to what one would call the "witchery" of the native doctor. Evidently he believed and, for me, it was another lesson I needed to learn. Although I could not understand much of what he said, I felt a deep respect for the things which, in spite of his travel and education, bound him so securely within the very spirit of Africa.

We reached Magburaka after dark and found our way to the house of one of my friend's relatives, a solid-looking concrete

125

building, single-storied, with a corrugated iron roof, and already shuttered tight although it was barely eight o'clock. My friend knocked loudly on the door, which was soon opened to release the bright light from indoors. After much exclamation of delight we were drawn into a large, comfortable room where six men sat in cushioned wooden armchairs and were introduced around. Our host was a slim thin-faced person whose thick-rimmed spectacles gave him a serious, scholarly air. He introduced the others: two young men from Kenya paying their first visit to Sierra Leone, short, thick-set fellows, one with a thick, scraggy beard; a local civil service official; a schoolteacher, and a young man from Freetown on his way by car to Liberia. My friend and I were shown where we could wash ourselves, and although there had been no advance warning of our arrival, our host assured me that a bed would be made ready for me.

"What about you?" I whispered to my friend.

"I'll be fine," he said. "I'll send word to my wife and she'll see to it that everything is laid on for me." He grinned broadly.

We were fed then returned to the room to join the group of men. The conversation must have been about Kenya, because the bearded young Kenyan was explaining something about Kenya's political struggles, and though he did not openly defend the Mau Mau uprising, he expressed the view that it was the result of unacceptable colonial policy.

"It is not always possible to anticipate the nature of degree of violence which might arise from any given situation," he said. "We who are concerned with the liberation of our country from colonial rule would wish to achieve this without violence, but if forced to employ violent measures, we cannot then concern ourselves with the niceties of killing. I can see no difference to a dead man if he is shot or has been hacked to pieces with a panga.

"I cannot understand some of you," he continued. "You talk about Mau Mau just as the British do, as if you too are not Africans and do not understand what it is we in Kenya are fighting for. I am against killing, but we were left no choice. The British press referred to us as primitive, bloodthirsty savages. That's not surprising because the British are concerned with methods rather than with principles. They are more interested in the method by which they

126

think independence should be achieved by people than in the principle of independence and freedom as human prerogatives."

"Our independence has been negotiated and will be achieved without any need for such extreme measures," the schoolteacher intervened. "Everything depends on the way in which we set about these things. We have been able to do it without rabble-rousing the rank and file. The British Government will hand over to us and we can proceed to build our country without bitterness on either side."

"Rubbish!" exploded the young man from Freetown. "That's what makes all the talk of our independence stink to high heaven. We don't need extreme measures because we have nothing to fight for. We are content to receive whatever the British give us—including this independence—and the most noticeable thing about us is our gratitude. And we'll continue to be grateful while our people have no work to do nor food to eat; we'll continue to be grateful while the elected representatives fatten themselves with producing nothing. We're the world's most grateful people—and soon we'll be independently grateful."

"The trouble with you hotheads," the civil servant said, "is that you are always in too much of a hurry."

" 'Too much of a hurry,' he says," boomed the young man from Freetown. "What do you care and others like you? You're safe in your jobs and your pension and as long as nothing interferes with that you don't care. We can't be too much in a hurry for change in this country, because change is too-long overdue, and everytime anybody says so he's called a hothead. Sure the British Government will hand you independence, because they know damned well that you'll do nothing and they can withdraw themselves from any responsibility for it."

"What would you like to see here?" the teacher asked. "The kind of blood bath they had in Kenya? What would that prove? And, in spite of it, they're not yet independent."

"But they're fighting," the bearded Kenyan said, "and everyone in Kenya is involved, so that the day we finally achieve independence, it will be something valuable to us—having been bought and paid for with our blood."

"We're winning it without blood," the teacher persisted.

"Not winning it," the young man from Freetown retorted,

127

"merely getting it. That's why hardly anyone knows anything about it and very few care. It's nothing personal to them, they have no stake in it; and the only thing they have to do about it is to be grateful."

"Our young friend here cannot understand how it is we are approaching independence without excitement," Mr. Lindsay interposed.

They all looked at me as if expecting some comment.

"Where are you from?" someone asked.

"British Guiana."

"Where's that?"

"South America."

"Is it a colony or are you independent?" This from the teacher.

"We're not yet independent, but we're struggling for it," I replied.

"I know," the smooth-faced Kenyan said. "The British have to send gunboats and troops to keep you quiet down there. I met one of your countrymen in the U.S.A. at Harvard and he told me that soon after the troops arrived, your womenfolk rendered them harmless—an interesting way of dealing with an invasion."

"What were you doing at Harvard?" I asked.

"Reading political science and learning about Americans. The one was complementary to the other because the more I saw and experienced of discrimination and indignity, the harder I worked at my studies, because I knew that, for all their fancy talk, the Americans will never respect us black people until we are independent of them. To the mass of Americans every black man is a 'nigger,' whether he be a black laborer from the Southern cotton fields or the highest-ranking diplomat from an independent African State. All they see is the color of his skin—and I found this to be generally true in the North as well as in the South. They view our struggles for independence and our exhortations for equality as the antics of rather clever monkeys and firmly believe that we are congenitally incapable of directing our own destinies, so the time may come soon when we'll have to show them and others like them that the things which we now fight and die for, we will also live and work for."

"Good for you," said the young man from Freetown. "We in

128

Sierra Leone do not fight because nothing is important enough here for us to die for."

"Were you both at Harvard?" I asked the Kenyans.

"I am attending the African Institute at Hamburg in Germany," the bearded one replied. "I was in the U.S. for seventeen days last year, but I was happy to leave it. If I had stayed, I would have got into serious trouble. I believe that some of those people in America are inhuman. They behave in a way that makes you want to kill them. But they don't give a damn. I couldn't for my own sake be exposed to that sort of thing much longer. It's far better in Germany. I wouldn't go again to the U.S. for anything.

"But at any rate you know who your enemy is," said his companion.

"That doesn't make it any easier to bear. I can't imagine any African student leaving America with anything but hate for the country and the people. If you hate, it doesn't help to know whom you hate, it only strengthens the hatred by directing it." He banged his fist on his knees. "How the hell do the Americans hope ever to convince Africans that they are kindly disposed to us? Take the Guinean students, for example. In order to protect them as much as possible from humiliation and indignity, their government never allows them to mix with Americans during vacation time; they all go to their embassy in Washington, where they can be together and are protected under their diplomatic umbrella. With what kind of opinion, will they return to Guinea? What would they really know about the American people? But, at the same time, why should they be exposed to the risk of physical harm and spiritual bruising in order to have some closer contact with the American people? Is the U.S. a jungle? Why should any man not feel safe among other men merely because his skin is darker than theirs?"

He spoke softly, but with deep emotion, as if these things had long lain close to his heart and were at last being given an airing.

"After all is said and done," he continued, "all the fighting and killing and speeches and arguments are not because we want work, or food or better clothing; there is something which is much more fundamental to us and to all other men, something which drives us on to further fighting and dying, something which makes us wield the spear or panga or even a club in defiance of guns and bullets.

129

You know what it is—it's human dignity. Without it man is less than the basest animal, but the moment he feels its fire he is like a god, and nevermore will he be willing to be subject to anything which offends it or attempts to inhibit it."

His calm, somewhat pedagogic manner held everyone's attention. He went on, "Dignity cannot be conferred like a charter of independence. It is a human prerogative, but it is necessary that human beings appreciate it. I've been in this country for nearly three weeks, and you'll excuse me if I say that I have seen little evidence of an appreciation of dignity. The dignified man is also a responsible man, who knows that though dignity cannot be earned, it can be projected by positive endeavor; therefore he works increasingly toward progress and improvement. He fights, not necessarily with guns and pangas; perhaps he fights only by improving the immediate conditions in which he and his family live, but he cannot feel the fire of dignity and remain inactive and uninvolved. He cannot be content with his own acquired advantages while others are being repressed and ill-treated.

"You are asleep in this country, and the few gestures you make here are the unconscious movements of the sleepwalker. In Kenya we have a saying that things must get worse in order to get better, so that is perhaps what will happen here. Dignity will one day catch up with you and you will then learn some of the hard realities of living as free men."

"That's just a lot of talk," the teacher said, a rasp of anger in his voice. "We know as much about dignity as any of you. Take a look at any of our ministers or our Paramount chiefs and you'll see men of dignity. I've heard that kind of Communist propaganda before. Some of you are jealous of the fact that we in Sierra Leone are becoming independent without terror and bloodshed. In spite of all your Mau Mau and murders you're still no better off."

"My friend, we don't seem to be talking about the same thing," the Kenyan replied in his quiet, measured tones. "The dignity I'm talking about is not something a tribal chief or government minister acquires with his office. It is something to which every peasant is heir on equal terms with kings. You talk about Communist propaganda. I'm not a Communist, but I have visited East Germany and Yugoslavia and Poland. I have also visited the United States

130

and Britain. In the Communist countries I was treated with courtesy and consideration. Perhaps you will argue that black faces are still a rarity and where there are only few of us there is no problem, but what matters is that, for whatever the prevailing reason, a man is treated as a man. No more and certainly no less.

"On the other hand, in Britain and in the United States I was under pressure twenty-four hours a day to prove that I was a human being. I could not eat here, I could not sleep there; no blacks allowed in schools, in churches, or even in graveyards. Perhaps such things mean nothing to you, but they assault my spirit.

"You say that for all the fighting we are still no better off. Perhaps. But we are doing the only thing which men of dignity can do. We are fighting for our right to freedom. And just in case you imagine that we in Kenya are in a unique position, look around you at the rest of Africa—Algeria, the Rhodesias, Tanganyika, Angola, the Congo and South Africa."

"You are not unique, friend," the young man from Freetown intervened. "We are the unique ones, because through all these generations we in the colony have not outlived our slavish ways, while here in the protectorate every little chief and every big chief is concerned only with hanging onto whatever power and influence he has. To them that is much more important than the dignity and freedom you talk about."

So it went on, each one adding his views, objections or arguments, sometimes heatedly and emotionally, yet never offensively. At one point the bearded Kenyan suddenly laughed out loud and remarked, "In my country these things are a matter of life and death; here they serve as an intellectual exercise, and you fellows take yourselves so damn seriously."

It was well after midnight when we dispersed, but it had been an informative and stimulating experience for me.

*

Next day we headed north for Kabala. We soon left the forest lands far behind and passed through mile after mile of scrub land with hardly a tree to offer the least shade from the dazzling sun.

131

The road was now little better than a track, which sometimes wound its way through flat, swampy ground; paddy fields, my friend assured me, and he explained about the size and importance of the rice crop. This was very different from the geometrically arranged and weed-free paddy fields I had known as a youngster in British Guiana, but I was gradually learning the unwisdom of comparisons with other things and places, because, for the most part, the agricultural methods employed in this country were still rather primitive, and the yields were the result of much backbreaking toil. We skirted the Gbenge hills and once more the countryside was thickly wooded, the road a narrow, rutted pathway which wound its way up and down as it skirted hill after hill.

Driving became a tiring business as we carefully negotiated the narrow bridges, steep inclines and frequent blind turns. Scattered at irregular intervals along the road were the rusty skeletons of cars which had either been involved in accidents or developed major engine trouble far away from skilled assistance.

"If your car fails far away from help, and you leave it unattended," my friend said, "chances are that you would return to find it completely stripped of its wheels, and everything else which can be removed. That is why it's always safest to travel with a companion. The people are not thieves, as you might think, but they annex anything which seems to be abandoned, even for a little while."

"You speak as if it's generally assumed that people will steal." Even as I said this I remembered something which had puzzled me but suddenly seemed clear. "Tell me. Come evening, nearly every house in Freetown carries one or more outside lights. Is that an attempt to combat burglars?"

"Yes, I'm afraid so," he replied. "Sometimes, in addition, those who can afford it employ a watchman whose duty it is to keep a sharp eye on private property. With the present state of unemployment and no sign of an early improvement in the situation, it is not surprising that thieving has become so widespread. The need to survive can be a very compelling type of pressure, you know."

We reached Kabala in the early afternoon. A dusty, dirty little town which sweltered drowsily in the afternoon heat—young men and old men half-asleep on the street-level verandas of the

Lebanese shops which lined both sides of the dusty road in the town center; women moving about slowly with large bundles or water-buckets on their heads and sleeping infants strapped to their backs; dogs and goats dozing in the middle of the road as if there to escape the myriad flies which swarmed over the garbage scattered near the roadside.

My friend drove some distance from the center of town to the home of a friend of his who he hoped would accommodate us for the night, but was told that the gentleman was away on a trip to Ghana.

"Miracles will never cease!" he exclaimed.

"What's so strange about his visiting Ghana?" I asked.

"It's not just Ghana, it's anywhere," he replied. "It requires such a great effort to get someone even to visit the next town that it always comes as a bit of a shock to me to hear of one of them visiting any of the neighboring countries. You would be very surprised at how little communication there is between us here in West Africa, and how little we know about each other as a result."

"What would you say is the reason?"

"Lack of money and poor communications. The few interconnecting roads are very poor at the best of times; there are no railways; air and sea travel costs more than most of our people can afford. Don't forget that in spite of an abundance of natural resources we are mainly very poor folk and will remain so while the country's wealth remains where it is—underground."

We drove back along the main street to the center of town and parked before one of the Lebanese shops. I followed my friend in. Apparently he knew the proprietor well, for they shook hands and pummelled each other in a way which denoted comradeship of long standing. I was introduced and my friend mentioned that we had hoped to spend the night in Kabala but because of his other friend's absence he was in some difficulty about accommodations for me. Without hesitation the proprietor suggested that I stay with him; he explained that there was plenty of room in the living quarters behind the shop and forthwith called out instructions to two African houseboys to prepare a room for me. He invited us to have a drink with him, introduced us to his charmingly youthful wife, and left us to fetch the drinks.

"Good friend of yours?" I asked.

"Well, yes, but that's not the reason. If you had come up here by yourself and were stranded for accommodations, he would have put you up just the same," he told me.

"What about you? Where will you stay?"

"Don't worry about me, there are lots of places I can stay. Besides, there's a special little call I want to make later on," he said, winking at me.

We had some cold beer with the proprietor and were invited to wash ourselves free of the thick dust which covered us. After a short rest my friend took me on a tour around the town and its immediate environs. The town was situated in a shallow basin surrounded by a series of low hills. Most of the buildings were low wooden or concrete cottages roofed with corrugated galvanized iron which shone silvery bright in the sunshine. Here and there along a narrow side street was the tree-shaded modern bungalow of a shopowner. Cars and heavy lorries rushed up and down keeping the thick red dust in continual motion, forcing the pedestrians to step off the roadway and cover their faces with handkerchief or shirttail.

Now and then we saw Lebanese women chatting together in the forecourt of a bungalow or playing with their children under the mango trees. They seemed completely at home. We visited the administration buildings. Here again the wide, landscaped lawns were gradually becoming overgrown, the paths rutted, the paint or thick whitewash peeling from the scattered buildings. By now I was recognizing the signs and asked, "Has an African District Commissioner taken over here?"

My friend smiled in acknowledgment of my meaning. "Not exactly. There is an African D.C. here at the moment, but he's only acting—he may be approved later."

He took me to see the local hospital, which he claimed was one of the best in the protectorate, and I was introduced to some of the medical personnel and shown through some of the departments. Once again I had to remind myself about comparisons, as I was sickened by some of the things I saw there: the sight and smell of human excreta, the filthy sheets on which patients lay, the swarms of flies, and the all-pervading odor of sickness in poverty. I could

134

not stand much of it. One of our guides showed us the midwifery section, speaking with pride of achievement. I could only stare in horror while desperately telling myself that all this was better than nothing: a sick person here was undoubtedly better off than lying unattended, or poorly attended, in some hut; a child born here had a greater chance of survival than one born in a hut with no one but an unskilled native midwife in attendance. Yet none of these silent arguments helped me to better stand the sights and smells, and to realize that these were human beings served by other human beings doing their best with terribly limited resources.

I visited the medical officer in charge of the hospital and district. A young African doctor who had been trained in Britain, he was at home in a pleasant bungalow among shady trees and flowering shrubs inherited from his English predecessor, and nursing a rather bad cold.

"Had to stay at home today," he explained. "With this cold I would be more of a danger than a help."

We talked about his hospital and the health of the people of his district.

"Each person you see walking around in this village is a miracle of survival," he said. "The same is true of any other village and town in the protectorate and colony—the same is even true for Freetown. Given a combination of polluted water, poor diet and inadequate housing, it is a miracle that so many of our people survive. You might even say that only the fittest survive. I would not ask your opinion of our hospital; it is the only one we have here and we make the most of its limited facilities, but I entertain no illusions about its standards. We need new buildings, trained personnel, and a whole range of equipment and medicines. But all that costs money, which we have not got."

He walked up and down as he spoke, a tall, broad-shouldered, handsome young man, on his face that mixture of resolution and concern which is the hallmark of the dedicated. I remembered that on the way to see him we had looked across the valley at the new powerhouse which was being put up, and I said, "I see that a powerhouse is being built in the valley below. If money can be found to provide electric lighting for this town, cannot some money be found also to improve your hospital facilities? I took a look at

135

your midwifery section. Aren't the lives of newborn babies a matter of high priority here?"

"Unfortunately, I have no say in the matter of priorities," he replied, "and nowadays electricity in a town or village seems to be a more attractive proposition than the health of the inhabitants. Electricity is visible, a kind of community status symbol, whereas a dead child is soon disposed of and nobody bothers. Our water system is a continuous threat to the lives of all our people, but I suppose no one will take our complaints seriously until there is some tragic epidemic. Anyhow, we'll probably have plenty of light by which to count our dead.

"We're not the only sufferers," he went on. "Throughout the country the same problem exists, yet somehow people survive. Perhaps things will change one day."

"After independence, perhaps?" I quipped.

"Whatever happens now must happen after independence," he replied soberly.

*

We drove around and in the main street I saw the secondary school for boys, a single-room affair in which the schoolmaster taught all subjects to about twenty youths, aged about fourteen to sixteen. I went in and spoke briefly to him. Afterward we visited a school for infants, a tiny, unpainted, single-room hut set in a disused field. The little tots sat in rows on low benches, their bare feet on the rough floor, eyes large in their inquisitive faces. The teacher was himself tiny, small-boned and frail-looking, but tight-lipped and brightly aggressive, as if aware that these children were a special responsibility. He told me of his struggle to get the children into school and maintain attendance in spite of indifferent, apathetic and even hostile parents. He was a teacher and he was determined to have a real school and sow the seeds of learning. He was impatient with my questions about independence; what mattered more to him was finding ways and means of attracting children to school. Their parents were not interested in learning for its own sake, or learning as the open sesame to better employment and progress. For the most part they did not care. But if, perchance, a

136

way could be found of providing a meal for the children while they were at school, then more would come to avail themselves of such a great benefit and stay to learn.

Listening to him, I remembered the early travail of my own career as a schoolmaster and breathed a silent prayer that his physical and spiritual fortitude would prove equal to the enormous task ahead of him.

"Let's go look at another school," said my friend. "This one I'm sure will cheer you up."

We followed a narrow, winding track which led away from the town and up the brush-covered slopes of a hill, circling it in wide, easy spirals until we reached the top and parked on a flat, grassy plateau on which several neat, modern buildings sat snug and comfortable among the long shadows cast by some tough, low-branched trees. Several children, sombreroed and two-gunned, were shooting it out to the death among the branches or from behind imaginary boulders, and the air rang with the sound of hissing bullets, wild whoops and the death cries of the fatally wounded. The hilltop had been leveled flat and carefully planted with grass which was now trimmed to a neat lawn, though slightly the worse for lack of rain and the wear and tear of tireless juvenile feet. The buildings were arranged on the periphery to allow for as much playing space as possible.

Our presence caused a temporary lull in hostilities, and one fair, crew-cut cowboy approached us rather shyly.

"We'd like to see the superintendent," my friend said.

"Aw right, I'll show you where he is," the boy said, leading the way to one of the buildings.

Before we reached it a young man emerged, fair-haired and crew-cut as was the tiny cowboy, and dressed in crumpled khaki shorts and shirt. My friend introduced himself and me, and then I learned that this was a boarding school for the children of American missionaries working in Sierra Leone.

The superintendent expressed his pleasure at our visit and showed us around. First the classrooms—neat, airy and well-stocked with books. I met some of the teachers and they told me of the curriculum which was planned to keep the children abreast of others of the same age in the United States.

The whole layout was marvelous—individual desks and about three teachers for the twelve or sixteen children. We saw the small power plant which supplied electricity to the schoolrooms; the central building, in which were combined children's dormitories, dining room, lounge, sick bay, etc., and some comfortable bungalows which housed the staff. Everything had been carefully planned and designed. The hilltop offered an impressive view of the countryside for miles around, and there was a continuous cooling breeze.

"What about water?" I asked.

A well had been sunk some distance away and water was pumped up and sterilized before using; there was an adequate supply for all their needs.

"Are American children the only ones accommodated here?"

He said that so far only the children of American missionaries were catered to, but there would be no objection to accommodating local children, provided they had the necessary initial qualifications and there were vacancies. Furthermore, he told me, it should be borne in mind that the syllabus they followed was fully American, and should any parent other than an American one wish to have a child taught there, he must be prepared to accept the fact of an American syllabus.

"But surely what special features there are in your syllabus can only relate to the orientation of history," I said, "anything else at this stage comes under general knowledge."

He did not agree and insisted that American methods might be found to be somewhat in conflict with British methods, and that such conflict could lead to confusion in the mind of a child.

I looked at my friend and observed the quizzical expression on his face. He had deliberately brought me here to see and hear this with something ulterior in mind. This was without doubt a fragment of America persisting in the American way of life. It seemed strange to me that missionaries would deliberately deprive themselves of the very positive contribution these children could render to their ministry by giving living evidence of the equality of humankind which is basic to any teaching of brotherhood. By isolating them from contact with Africans while in Africa they were ignoring a wonderful opportunity to live religion instead of preaching it. Probably at this very moment some of these children's parents were

138

laboring in a remote place, teaching African children to read and write, to pray and believe in a God who was supposed to be completely impartial to considerations of race, color, sex or creed. Perhaps, after all, any parent should have the right to decide what was best for his children, in education as in other things, and there was no reason why missionaries should be exempt.

The superintendent told of the work involved to choose the site, clean it, then carefully level the top before constructing the buildings. There were plans for further development still.

On the way down the hillside my friend asked, "Well?"

I thought I'd play him out. "Nice," I replied. "Nice people, nice layout and wonderful view."

"Quite a school, eh?"

"Yes, nice school,"

"A bit different from those in the valley."

I got his drift, but I wanted him to say his piece, not hedge with me. "From here I can see many other hills," I said. "Nothing to stop anyone from doing the same thing. No point in being jealous or envious of what he has done up there when you can do the same thing anytime you like."

"Easy to say. Where would we get the bulldozers to cut down the top, or the money to erect buildings?"

"So you'll just have to get along as best you can without them. I'm sure, however, that you don't need bulldozers. There are enough idle hands down there in the town which, together, could clear and level a hilltop if they were put to work."

"That's all very well," he retorted, "but it's a lot easier for the local people to dislike the Americans through sheer envy than to emulate their efforts. Some of them have been whispering about that school up there—for white Americans, they say."

"I cannot see what could be achieved by allowing one or two black children to attend. Far better to agitate for better schools for your own children than create ill feeling by forcing the issue like that."

"You're missing the point," he said. "The very principle is bad. These people are in Africa because they say they want to help us. Can't they understand that things like that school only serve to separate us from them—no matter how hard they toil and preach?"

139

We were still discussing the school in particular and education in general when we returned to the Lebanese shop where I was to spend the night. The proprietor invited us to dine with him, and while we waited for the meal to be served we chatted together. We told him of our visits around the town and he said to my friend, "Nobody wants to work at making improvements around here, but they're all talking about what they will do after independence."

"Talking about independence?" I asked, and explained that I had hitherto encountered no one who willingly spoke about that dreaded subject.

"Oh, they talk about it all right, but only when they're mad at somebody. Some fellows came into the shop today and wanted me to give them credit. They already owe me money, so I said no. You know what one of them said? He said, 'After independence you Lebanese won't be so high and mighty. We will not ask you any favors, but just come and take what we want.' "

"Oh, don't worry about fellows like him," my friend suggested, "you're sure to run into a few loudmouthed crackers now and then. They're quite harmless, only full of hot air."

"That's fine for you, my friend," the Lebanese replied, "but I take everything that I hear seriously. If these fellows say something like that it means that they've been talking about it. They sleep about the place all day long and don't care about working, but they think that after April 27 all they have to do is take whatever they like—and it would not take much to start them going. I know."

"Has there been any serious discussion about independence here?" I asked.

"It depends on what you mean by 'serious discussion,' " he replied. "Governor Dorman was up here the other day and every-one turned up to listen to him talk about independence, but I'm sure that much of the time they neither heard nor understood what he was saying. As soon as some of these people sit still they fall asleep, or else they merely nod their heads wisely without paying much attention. . . . Since he left, nobody talks about it. Look at those fellows out there." He pointed to a group of young men sitting on the grass verge on the other side of the road, talking, laughing and frequently spitting. "As long as they have enough for cigarettes and a drink now and then, they don't worry. I've lived among these people for over twenty-five years, and I like them, but I don't think that independence will mean anything to them, yet. Not unless something or somebody stirs them up. Then anything could happen."

This man was really concerned. He lived each day among Africans whose lives were a constant struggle for survival, and he appreciated that they must often look with envy on the comparative comfort in which he and his family lived. He seemed to be a well-balanced kind of person, so his fears may have been justified.

When my friend was ready to leave, he took me outside and broadly hinted that if I were interested he could "get me fixed up for the night." I guessed he meant that he could arrange female companionship. Since we had been on the road I had encountered very few women whom I considered attractive. Here and there the shy young wives of a chieftain were the exceptions, but most of the women were work-twisted drudges, just not my cup of tea. I said that I was fine, but what with the heat and the bumpy roads I was not in the mood.

"You ought to sample what Africa has to offer," he advised, but I said that I was more interested in putting in some sleeping hours.

"Perhaps you're thinking this is like Europe," he said. "I'm not taking you to a whorehouse or to prostitutes. In Africa we have our own way of making our guests comfortable, and there is nothing for you to worry about."

I decided to try another line. "But suppose I came along and afterward the woman became pregnant? What then?"

"What then?" he repeated. "Women become pregnant every day. The child would be just another child in the woman's household. That's all."

Into my mind came the picture of the maternity room at the hospital. To my friend and to other Africans, women were there to serve their pleasure, expendable. Perhaps, as he had said earlier, I was too far away from Africa and African ways, but the thought of spending the night with one of the women I had seen about the town held no appeal for me. He gave up, considering me a rather hopeless case.

141

After he left, my host and I sat on the veranda in the cool night talking about things like his business, a trip he hoped to make to his homeland, the growth of the town during the time he lived in it. I found him a delightful interesting man, as the French would say, *"tres sympathique."*

*

A car drew up in front of the shop and a young African approached us, crisply neat in short-sleeved sports shirt and light-weight slacks. He had heard that I was in town and, having read my first book, decided to take the opportunity of meeting me. He was the veterinary surgeon to the district, recently appointed, and lived with his wife in a new bungalow on the slope of one of the near hills. I was delighted to meet him. I am always delighted and very flattered to meet people who have read and liked my book. He was well known to my host, so was invited to join us in a drink.

Soon we were talking about conditions in the town and its environs, and naturally talk of independence was introduced at some point. He was not hopeful of any observable results or reactions in the district, because the local people did not know or understand what it meant. They were not aware of any involvement in any of the processes.

I asked about the young men, like himself and the medical officer, and probably others who were educated and trained and able to understand and appreciate the circumstances. Probably they could help to translate it to the rank-and-file in terms they could understand.

"You must not make too much of the fact that some of us have been trained overseas," he replied. "That can be a mixed blessing. First of all we have a job of work to do taking care of the health of the people and their livestock, and hampered every step of the way by bureaucratic obstacles and the age-old prejudices and beliefs of the local people. Then, there is the matter of communication. The African who spends three or five years away in Europe returns to discover that he is much more than three or five years away from the people and environment he once knew and understood.

142

"All kinds of changes have taken place in his absence, some so subtle that they pass unnoticed. New or different forces might have been at work to change the old leadership; people have died and have been born, and all these things have been happening in his absence. Also, he has been associated with different and probably higher standards of food, clothing, housing, hygiene; different mores relating to association with groups or individuals, and sexual matters. Sometimes, without his being aware of it, his exposure to these things, quite apart from the new techniques he has acquired, have produced some irrevocable changes in him. He is no longer an African African, if you see what I mean, although this is what he might most urgently want to be.

"You know, I have a theory. I think that some of the African leaders who seem to be the most reactionary, deliberately assume that role in order to quickly bridge the gap between them and the stay-at-homes. It is a dramatic way of selling themselves and their ideas to the rank-and-file, who, though fully involved in the struggle for freedom and independence, can easily find time to dislike or mistrust their leadership on the flimsiest of pretexts, and the pro-European label is very easily stuck on."

"But how do you yourself view your country's approaching independence? What do you as an educated African expect to see in Sierra Leone as a result of independence?" I asked.

"I cannot answer your questions because I must confess I have not seriously and sufficiently taken myself to task about them. To be frank with you, I feel no burning enthusiasm about independence, nor any resistance to it. I may be considered apathetic, although I do not think that that word would adequately describe my position. I was in Europe at the time another African State became independent, and I, like most other Africans in Europe, felt a close identity with that State and its achievement. I felt an immediate identity with those who had struggled to be free and were finally reaping the reward of their struggles.

"Somehow, here at home, there is no struggle, no cause, no stimulus. I feel no excitement and no commitment, and I cannot work up an enthusiasm for something I can't feel. Way up here in Kabala I feel remote from whatever is going on in Freetown, probably because I feel no urgent involvement. Perhaps that will come later. Perhaps some form of struggle will present itself into which I, and others like me, will be drawn or deliberately engage ourselves, but, as things are, I must address myself to the job I am paid to do, which has become much more than a job to me. The health of livestock in these remote districts is very important to all of us, and my job is to keep every animal hereabouts in the best possible condition, and to help the local people to appreciate the need and economic advantages of healthy livestock."

"Are you making any progress?"

"Perhaps. More than half my efforts are directed to breaking down barriers of legend and myth, besides being forced to accept certain realities in spite of one's scientific training. For instance, it is very difficult trying to persuade someone that any infected animal should be destroyed in order to safeguard the rest of the stock, especially if he can see little evidence of illness. Then, there is the matter of feeding. It will be a long time before Africans accept that animals cannot survive healthily by merely foraging off the land. Why should they buy special feed for cows or chickens? But gradually we are gaining ground."

So the evening passed in pleasant conversation with two men of different background, both loving the country and each in his own way concerned about its future and willing to make his contribution. To see their reaction, I mentioned my visit to the school for the children of missionaries up on the hill.

The African said, "I've been up there. It's wonderful to see what those people have done in so short a time with land nobody else wanted. Personally I think it is a good thing for everybody that the school is there, and if we are worth anything, we Africans can learn an important lesson from it. They didn't use magic to do what they've done, but knowledge and hard sweat. We've got to learn to work in order to enjoy better standards in every aspect of our daily life. The time may come when somebody, some strong leader, will put the chronically idle hand to work, and then it will be discovered that what the Americans can do is not beyond the scope or imagination of Africans."

"That's fine," the Lebanese said, "but it might be a good thing if one or two African children attended the school and

144

learned something at firsthand about Americans instead of only seeing them from a distance and thinking of them now with a kind of awe but probably later with distrust. At the same time the American children could do a lot worse than find out who an African is besides someone whose black soul their parents are striving to save."

He spoke with a quiet fervor which I found surprising. I had probably imagined that men like him were occupied only with thoughts of adding to their business, and this deep interest in sociological things was very revealing. Perhaps amid the clutter and squeeze of business in Freetown and the protectorate, others like him entertained the same deep concern, because for them Africa was now home.

Maybe in time they would cease to be Lebanese living in Africa and become truly Africans.

"They are not the only ones carelessly making a big mistake," he went on. His choice of words was refreshingly direct and expressive.

"We Lebanese are just as bad. All business, nothing but business. It would be good to see Lebanese teachers in the schools, Lebanese farmers, nurses, carpenters and," he hunted around in his mind for the word, "even laborers. You know, being just like the local people. At the present time we're set apart, a recognizable minority group, and no matter how earnest we might be in our wish to fully identify with Africa, there is a distance between us and the local people, and we are mainly responsible for maintaining that distance. If we are truly concerned to make our home here we must take some responsibility for the country's development, not only economically but socially.

"As I see it, my son will go to school with the African boys and will learn with them. What is important is that he'll learn about them and to respect them. Perhaps," and here he grinned, "as part of his education he will fight with some of them. Some African boy might knock the stuffing out of him, but he will learn to see them as people. As a matter of fact, such a beating might save him from further beatings, and even worse later on. My responsibility and my problem is to teach my son to live in Africa, and not to be merely another Lebanese in Africa.

145

"It's not going to be easy," he went on, "because we have a lot to live down. My skin is white and that identifies me with everything which, historically, is associated with the white man's presence in Africa, especially those things for which he is despised and feared by Africans. I have to face facts, my friend. So far the Africans have had no reason to love us, and nowadays they believe they have every reason to hate us. Look at this shop. An African comes in and sees the shelves packed with tinned food-stuff and clothing and other things he needs but cannot afford. He knows that these things belong to me. That places me in the position of having what he has not. Then he asks for credit because he and his family are in want, and I refuse. What happens next? This is not like Europe or America, or even the West Indies, where people understand that business has nothing to do with personal feelings. I know that if I give him credit he might never be able to pay me. Can I run my business like that? So he hates me because he can see the stuff he wants lying there on the shelf. I can see the hate in his eyes, but if I give it to him I might as well pack up and leave because I would have to do the same for everyone else. And my refusal is another link in the chain of ill-feeling and hate which is forged down there among the huts where they do not have enough to eat or wear, but plenty of time to long for the day when they can walk in here and take it all. How the hell can I tell them I care about them when I don't give them credit for the asking? And it's the same with all the Lebanese. We're known as traders, and that means exploiters, because we must make profit to survive. So we daily contribute to the backlog of hate with the best will in the world, but also with that peculiar blindness which would not let us see the writing on the wall."

"You're overstating the case," the vet said. "I can't believe that in this town the Lebanese are hated. All around me I see them mixing easily with the local people on the friendliest of terms."

"Perhaps I am," our host agreed, "but I have lived here long enough to learn something about the people. Perhaps they don't even think they hate me, but I would like to see some changes here before they get around to thinking about it. I would like to

146

see some schemes for giving the people work, so they can come in proudly and buy from me, or if they don't like my prices, tell me 'To hell with you' and go somewhere else. When that happens I will feel better and very much safer."

As we chatted I was half-hearing a persistent sound of intermittent drumming and singing. Now from a narrow side street some distance away there came into view a long, twisting line of torch-bearing dancers escorted by drummers, and a noisy crowd of small children and adults bearing homemade Chinese lanterns, all shouting and singing without much concern for tonal nicety or the drummers' valiant efforts to maintain some rhythmic order. Nearer, I could see that some of the dancers wore masks, grotesque white-streaked affairs which seemed strangely lively in the flickering light of the torches; these, held aloft by nearly invisible black arms, seemed to be floating against the tide of an unstable black stream, as their flames pointed backward from the revelers' advance.

What rather jolted me was the fact that, at this very late hour, there were so many small children in the procession, prancing about in the dust when they ought to have been soundly asleep. Perhaps it did not matter whether or not they attended school the next day.

As the procession slowly passed by, several voices called out to my host, and he replied in the same dialect, evidently encouraging their efforts. Laughing, shouting, singing, completely blocking the roadway, they continued on their way, and long after their voices were but a faint buzz in the distance, the dust remained a thick, uneasy cloud hovering over the ground.

"What was that in aid of?" I asked.

"It's the Procession of Lanterns," the vet said, "observed by the Muslims a few days before the end of Ramadan. If you're up here on Saturday night you'll really see them in action, the real stuff, dancing and feasting and everything. After all the months of fasting they really make up for it on one big glorious night. Then on Sunday they gather together from all the neighboring villages for a big open-air ceremony. It's very impressive."

"Are you a Muslim?" I asked.

"No."

147

We talked awhile longer, about the social and cultural limitations of the town, among other things.

"Life is not all beer and skittles for us," the vet said. "Up here I often feel desperate for stimulating conversation. One reads books and occasionally meets with the boys for an evening's chat, but when it's always the same people, after a while conversation tends to become ingrown and we are soon able to anticipate each other's thoughts and reactions."

So it went on, and when I finally went to bed I lay awake for some time, my mind buzzing with the things I had seen and heard.

*

Next day we left on the long haul back to Freetown. My friend seemed rested, refreshed, in excellent form; he must have had a good night.

"We'll change our route at Makeni," he said, "to bring us through the iron mining region at Marampa, then on to Freetown."

Now we were driving more slowly and I could take better note of the countryside and the villages through which we passed. Although I was constantly reminded by the heat that this was the dry season, all around, as far as I could see, was predominantly green; a deep, lush, strong green which somehow softened the sun's glare. What I saw while riding down the gentle slopes of the hillsides, looking down on the mist-shrouded valleys, was so unlike the picture of Africa I had hitherto entertained. At any time we were within at least a mile of some habitation; we saw men and women along the road, or disappearing into the bush where, my friend assured me, their farms were located. At no time did I feel out of touch with people.

"You don't know what you missed, last night," my friend broke in upon my reverie.

"I'm sure you dealt adequately with the situation," I replied.

"What are the girls like in your country?" he asked. "I mean, are they different from the girls over here?"

148

"Women are women wherever they are." I wanted to know exactly what he was after before committing myself.

"Oh, come on," he chided. "I could see you were not interested last night, so it must be you don't find the women attractive. What's the difference between them and the women of your country—you know, British Guinea?"

"Guiana," I corrected.

"Okay—Guiana. Well, what's the difference?"

"Well, let's put it this way," I was borrowing his gimmick for the occasion. "If I had some money to invest in this country, I would set up a corset and brassiere factory. Strictly utilitarian, nonluxury products."

He looked at me a moment, then roared with laughter till the trees threw the echoes back at us.

"Ah, so that's it," he said between guffaws. "Sort of shift the center of interest, eh?" The idea tickled him as it played about in his mind.

"More than that. It seems to me that with a little artifice here and there your women could present themselves much more attractively. To be frank, some of them allow their bodies to become terribly distorted, especially after motherhood."

"They seem okay to us," he said. "Perhaps you see them that way because you're new to them, while we are accustomed to them and they don't seem odd to us."

"And perhaps you don't see them at all." His line of argument emboldened me to make a direct point. "I get the impression since I have been in your country that after her early youth, when a woman can naturally present her physical charms, she is expected to be functional rather than decorative, and even when dressed up the emphasis is on parading her clothing and jewelry rather than her face and figure. Perhaps you men require no more of her than that. In British Guiana the women are as sensitive about their bodies as they are about their clothing, and when one has become accustomed to a certain physical presentation it is rather difficult to easily accept something else."

He thought of that for a while, then said irrelevantly, "We Africans like our women solid, you know." He grinned. "None of your skinny, bony, fancy stuff for us."

149

"That's fine," I replied, "but it would do no harm to have the solid stuff attractively disposed, don't you think? Everything in its place and a place for everything."

Again his strong laughter rang out. It was fun chatting away like this with him. His conservation was easy, without the watchful reserve and "don't-quote-me" condition.

Once again we descended into the swamplands, through the wide, flat, rice-growing areas. He told me that rice was the country's main food crop, and that the Government had instituted a program for reclaiming more sections of mangrove swamps to provide more land for its cultivation. "Excellent," I thought, but could not help the fleeting mental picture of the neat, weed-free paddy fields in British Guiana; perhaps it would be like that here some day. "There's such a hell of a lot to be done," I said, more to myself than to him.

He suddenly swung the land-rover as far off the crown of the road as possible and braked to a halt; then he leaned back in his corner of the cab and looked at me, his face grave. I thought that he might have felt ill or tired, but he spoke in a strong, somewhat angry voice.

"Sure, there's a hell of a lot to be done, but who knows what should be done first or when or how? Look, my friend, I made this trip with you because I wanted you to learn something for yourself, but it seems that you are likely to leave this country, perhaps even Africa, as uninformed about the realities as when you first arrived. Perhaps you have misunderstood my answers to your questions—you may have thought them evasions for my own safety. You were wrong, damned wrong. I was trying to let you make up your own mind without too much bias because of my thoughts or attitudes.

"The thing which seems to concern you most is independence, and the way in which we react to its approach. You are clearly disappointed by what you have seen and equally by what you have not seen here. I think I ought to explain something about independence to you. Every African State wants to be independent of or from some colonial power or other. That is not too difficult in the present state of affairs; the difficulties involved vary only in degree. But there is another kind of independence,

150

which, so far, only very few African States seem to be able to appreciate—that is, independence to grow, to build, to work, to achieve. Do you get my point? The first type is a kind of political charter. After receiving it and waving it around awhile in the first flush of glory and excitement, many states discover that, in fact, their position has not really changed. Not only is the economic life of the country still fully controlled from outside, but that control penetrates in devious forms to the political and cultural life as well. The reason is simple. Some states immediately upon becoming, as is claimed, independent from a colonial power expect to blossom forth in all the splendor of advanced economic and social development—you know, universities, hospitals, blocks of flats, fancy government buildings, educational and social reforms, the lot. Those things cost money, so where is the money to come from? Well, back they go to the former controlling power and the money is forthcoming as long as there is the right kind of collateral—either concessions in the development of the country's natural resources, if any, or concessions in terms of that country's strategic position in the event of the threat of war."

He shifted his bulk to a more comfortable position, then said, "Independence, like any other luxury, has to be paid for, and the sooner we learn that the better for us. We cannot pay for it with our natural resources, which lie buried in the ground, until those have been fully developed; but we can begin to pay for it by putting ourselves to work. Look at Israel, my friend. Do you know what is the secret of Israel's development? Work, and more work, for every man, woman and child. Have you ever seen a group of Israelis? Well, I have, and they are fine, strong, resolute and intelligent people, all proof of the fact that hard work is good for body, mind and spirit.

"Independence will not mean a damned thing here or elsewhere until the children suck the fire of it from their mothers' breast and learn their responsibility for it with each school lesson. The people of Africa have more reason to make themselves into free, independent entities than even the Israelis have, but they are too blind to the importance of first principles. We talk of Africans, but we don't know each other, we don't understand each other, we don't talk with each other. It is easier for you to

151

fly from Dakar to Paris, than from Dakar to Freetown. Our border is contiguous for three-quarters of its length with Guinea, the rest with Liberia, yet we have little contact with Guinea because they speak French and we speak English. Liberia is in an even worse position, literally surrounded by French-speaking Africans, yet having very little contact with them.

"This is the situation, my friend. Before you write about us, think over these things. Don't be too harsh on our seeming apathy. As you say, there's a hell of a lot to be done, but we still don't know who will do it, or lead us to the doing. Some of our leaders spend so much time living up to the titles and honors conferred on them from outside that they are now only African in color. I love my country but can see no virtue in talking about independence unless the responsibilities are considered, as well as the benefits. Sierra Leone is only a piece of Africa, a small piece. Try to understand us, and for the time being, expect no more from us than we are able to give."

Saying this, he started the motor and we resumed our journey.

On reaching Freetown we found that our way to the Paramount Hotel was blocked by a military procession of some kind. Up ahead I could occasionally glimpse the flash of color, glint of polished button, and now and then the upflung shining white staff of the bandleader as the music came floating toward us behind the advance body of small boys and unemployed men who seized on any occasion which offered a moment's diversion. Following the crowd of men and boys came the band marching crisply in neat khaki uniforms, their eyes glued to the musical score clamped on their instruments. Each drummer wore a red-trimmed leopard skin, which added a bizarre touch of color. As they passed by I felt like cheering, stimulated by the music, which ricocheted in late echoes from the buildings and trees along the street.

"Pretty good, that band," I said.

"Not too bad," he agreed, "considering that hardly one of them knows how to read or write."

"But if they can be taught music they can be taught to read and write," I said. "After all, music is merely another kind of language."

152

"Sure, oh sure, but nobody seems to have realized that, so our soldiers and policemen remain illiterate. When we read of illiterate soldiers and police in the Congo and think of the same situation here, the possibilities are a bit frightening."

At the Paramount Hotel there were two notes for me; the first, an invitation to an investiture at the Governor's mansion that very evening, and the other, an invitation to dine with the Governor and his wife on Sunday evening.

*

I dressed carefully and took it very easy walking the short distance between the Paramount Hotel and the Governor's mansion, to be as perspiration-free as I could possibly manage, yet though I was some minutes earlier than the time stated on the invitation, I found myself part of a long queue which snaked outward from the main gateway to some distance along the dusty, tree-shaded road. Black and white minor dignitaries and their wives were dressed up for the occasion, uncomfortably elegant but gallantly patient in their determination to give a memorable send-off to the final appearance of an old and familiar institution. There was an interesting reversal of role—the African men, with rare exception, favored European tweed and serges, while the European men made every concession to the heat that lightweight clothing and the formality of the occasion allowed.

Observing the dress of the women, it seemed to me that in Freetown, at least, there had occurred a kind of synthesis between what had been the national costume and near-current European styles, and if the results were not exactly *haute couture,* at least they were colorful and interestingly varied. I thought of my earlier remark to my friend about artificial aids to the arrangement or rearrangement of the female form, and believe that, had he been present at this gathering, he would have been persuaded to agree with me.

When we finally reached the reception hall we were received by the Governor and his wife, then ushered out through a wide veranda overlooking spacious, shady lawns to a smaller enclosure, where chairs had been arranged in seemingly endless rows to accommodate the guests. I was seated near an elderly English couple and soon found myself overhearing their audibly muttered remarks about those guests who were unfortunate enough to arrive later than themselves. The man, much more than his wife, seemed to possess a fund of information, perhaps "gossip" would be a better term, but he reserved his most caustic comment for the appearance of black-white couples, of which there were a few. Each such pair would be referred to as a tragedy, and it occurred to me that any white person with a black spouse automatically became "black" as far as he was concerned. He was probably airing a general view, and I was left wondering what success could be hoped for in the improvement of international relationships, when there remained such arid areas of nonacceptance and intolerance at this level.

When all the guests had arrived, the Governor took his place before the concourse and the ceremony began. I shall long remember the impressive simplicity and dignity of the proceedings, probably enhanced by the prevailing consciousness of sharing in a terminal act, like a death. There was pomp and circumstance represented by the many military uniforms present, including the Governor's; there was the military band, which waited in sparkling silence for the unobtrusive signal to add their contribution to the occasion; and the Union Jack, which flapped in colorful gaiety against a background of changing green. And there was present a sadness overlaying the pomp, like mist on lush grass, translucent yet persistent.

On the Queen's behalf the Governor presented the citations and medals to those honored, black and white, after which the guests mingled, strolled and chatted together on the lawns. I noticed, however, that, like molecular particles which had been agitated out of a prescribed form and pattern then allowed to resume shape, the groups were soon either all white or all black. Whatever contact occurred was brief and painfully superficial, and this in spite of the easy friendliness and earnest efforts of the Governor's wife, who moved from group to group, sometimes carrying with her someone who seemed to be even temporarily unattached.

The old order changeth. Would this last investiture herald other changes in this historic building, sitting so snug and secure among its lawns, cultivated shrubs and ageless trees? Eventually an African will occupy the house and lawns. Would such occupation be followed by the same tatty depreciation which I observed upcountry wherever the European incumbent was succeeded by an African?

*

Early the next morning my friend telephoned. He would be busy all day and unable to see me because of the celebrations that night and the following day.

"What celebrations?" I asked. He then realized that though he had often intended to tell me about them, time and again something else had claimed our attention. However, he explained that today the fast of Ramadan ended, and as was customary, there would be general feasting, dancing and processions through the town, and he thought it would be worth my while to see as much of it as I could.

"On Sunday," he continued, "there will be a big open-air ceremony at Cline Town to mark the end of Ramadan for this year. Try to see it if you can. You'll get an idea of what our religion means to us, at least I hope so. I'll not be able to see you before sometime on Monday, so you'll have to be your own guide until then."

"I'm leaving for Liberia early Monday morning," I reminded him.

"Okay. I'll see you Monday." He rang off.

He had said that the celebrations would begin at night, but long before the sun slipped away behind the treetops the drumbeats could be heard from several parts of the town. After dinner I walked down to the cotton tree and was soon part of the crowd, forced to the edge of the road, in which a surging mass of singing, dancing, exuberant people, the Kabala procession multiplied several hundred times, were gathered.

It seemed to me that tonight every African was Muslim. This was an occasion for a good time and the religious origins or im-

155

plications did not matter a great deal. Europeans were everywhere in the crowd, wide-eyed and eager, or casual and amused, depending on whether and how often they had seen it all before. I liked all of it, the noisy singing, the drumming and the dancing—especially the dancing. One group of drummers formed a tight circle in the crowd, improvising their complicated rhythms with agile fingers, while young men and women, each in turn, would jump into the center of the circle and execute a spontaneous dance of intricate footwork and sinuous grace as the crowd clapped in time to the music and in encouragement to the dancers. Sometimes two dancers would jump into the ring simultaneously, perspiring freely as each tried to outdo the other, twisting their bodies in indescribably fluid movements in spite of the tiny space, the heat and the jostling onlookers.

Memory came flooding in on me. I had seen this before in different places and in different circumstances. Christmas in British Guiana, with the masqueraders and drums and the dancing men outbidding each other as they "jallayed" in much the same way. Carnival time in Trinidad, with the same again, slightly different, but much the same. And with memory came the tingling, the urge to participate, the trembling in the legs as they received the message of memory, those nearly dead echoes which needed this kind of revivification to be even vaguely heard.

Now the crowd shifted, swayed and moved along, taking me with it, excited and unresistant, happy in the anonymity of a black face among black faces; for who could isolate me, pick me out, say to me, "Who are you, what are you doing here?" I was a piece—a transient piece—of the night and of Africa, sharing for tonight an identity I had never before known with understanding.

Later there was the confusion of halted automobiles, nervous drivers, excited revelers and earnest, hard-worked but ineffective police. And drink, yes, that prerequisite to enjoyment. Soon there were shouts of anger above the sounds of revelling, and the tinkle of broken glass above the ripple of drumbeats, and cries of pain, and oaths, and the scuffling. But inexorably the crowd pushed forward, and I with it, my arms close across my chest, till I found myself freed in the sudden outlet of a side street, and walked away until I was far enough away to breathe easily once more. Strangely,

156

with the distance, the sense of involvement and identity fell away. This was Africa, and I was a stranger here.

*

Sunday morning was bright and clear and found me refreshed, dressed, breakfasted and ready to go. The hotel receptionist directed me on how to reach Cline Town and I set out, hoping to find a taxi near the City Hotel. No luck. Everybody in Freetown seemed to be on the road, and every vehicle seemed in use, most of them full to overflowing with men, women and children. I followed in the general direction of the hurrying pedestrians, somewhat envious of their long, flowing robes, mostly white, in which they appeared cool and comfortable in spite of the heat.

The route to Cline Town was very much like what I had always imagined a pilgrimage to be—hundreds of hurrying, long-robed figures, men, women and children, hooting automobiles, cyclists with their robes spread behind them like multicolored pillions—and others like myself, curious sightseers, black and white, all impatiently eager to see . . . what? There was something festive rather than religious in the air. The houses and shops which lined the route were crowded with people, every window, door and balcony seemed full of faces, people watching, smiling, joking aloud to each other, already in the mood for whatever was to come.

At Cline Town the main thoroughfare was joined by a narrow, dusty road which led off left between several large, handsome bungalows. At this junction numerous perspiring policemen were directing the automobiles and trucks to parking places while vainly trying to keep the road clear to other traffic. As the cars and trucks disgorged their occupants into the already-thick stream of people, police tried to urge them forward along the side street, now thickly lined on both sides by people who seemed disinclined to move. Adding to the general hubbub were several men with large collection boxes slung around their necks who harangued or wheedled the onlookers into reluctant charity, in contrast to the large numbers of beggars who hawked their disabilities with a kind of casual

157

assurance. Today was everyone's day and the spirit of giving was in the air.

I slowly forced my way along this crowded pathway; the going became easier as the road widened. Now along its grassy, tree-shaded verge, veiled women and small children sat grouped together on attractively woven prayer mats, all dressed in their gayest colors, as if for a picnic. Young and old women, fat and thin women; women with round, fleshy faces and bulging arms, thin-faced, handsome Mandingo women in beautiful gauze head-dresses and hands and feet dyed blue-black with Indigo—ugly women, beautiful women. I had seen nothing like them on my hinterland travels. If some of these beauties had been at Kabala, well . . . And I saw shy women, lowering their eyes as I looked at them; bold women, casually locking glances with me, their teeth fleetingly white behind slightly parted lips. I was getting a good long look at what African women could be like, and I was liking most of what I saw.

A short distance farther along, the pathway sloped gently downward at one side into a wide, grassy bowl-like amphitheatre, in which were already gathered thousands of men, each sitting cross-legged on his prayer mat, each adding his colorful costume and fez to the magic kaleidoscope, which seemed to repeat itself in varying shades and patterns as far as the eye could reach. Near the lip of the amphitheatre, farthest from the roadway, was set up a small, shaded dais with microphone and loudspeaker system; from this the chief *imman* would lead the faithful in prayer; near to this dais and slightly behind it was a wide platform with chairs for, I supposed, certain important visitors. The warm, bright air was filled with the buzzing of thousands of whispered conversations and con-trolled laughter. I wanted to find a point of vantage. Overlooking the roadway and concourse were bungalows set high on steep wooden or concrete pillars, with wide verandas now crowded with onlookers, mostly European. I called up to one of these groups and asked to be allowed to join them. They promptly agreed, and soon I had a clear, unrestricted view of everything.

Soon the cry went up: "H.E. has arrived. H.E.'s here." And threading its way slowly through the crowds was an open touring car, in the rear seat of which sat the Governor and his wife, lightly,

158

coolly, informally dressed, bowing and smiling to the people on both sides, who set up a resounding cheer which attested to the popularity of them both. The car stopped at the edge of the concourse, and a way was cleared for them through to the platform, where other dignitaries had apparently been awaiting their arrival, for soon they were seated, and, with them the Prime Minister and several others. Someone (I could not from that distance see who it was) mounted the small dais and immediately the crowd was hushed to complete silence. Everyone stood, then he began to intone the familiar prayers, pausing occasionally for the murmured response which rose from the assembly in sonorous waves. Now they knelt, each on his little prayer mat, and time and again they all bent forward until their foreheads touched the green earth. From where I stood it seemed as if a strong but gentle breeze had started at the roadway and blown across their ranks so that the fabulous human mosaic rippled forward and backward in easy undulations. Whenever the *imman* spoke, his voice re-echoed tinnily over the assembly, but it seemed to have little to do with the real progress of the service, as everyone was already well versed and fully familiar with all its parts. This was something each one performed each day and every day until it was part of living, not to be confused or forgotten. I was seeing the evidence of a vital religion, something completely different from anything I had ever before witnessed. These people did not need a Billy Graham to exhort them to religious fervor; they had not assembled here to be preached at, stimulated or encouraged to greater religious effort. They were here, voluntarily, to spend an hour or so in communal worship, celebrating something which was as immediate to them as birth and death.

Then it was over and the concourse broke up into hundreds of groups—families, relatives, friends, neighbors—greeting each other with the overspill of an annual experience shared again, the end of the rigors of fasting, the promise of feasting, the forgetting of tomorrow and its multitude of shortages. The magic carpet split itself up, the pieces forming and reforming smaller patterns, till they themselves broke in dispersal to become a thick slow-moving line along the narrow road.

159

*

That evening I dined with the Governor, his wife, and a few other persons invited to make up a little group for dinner; altogether about eleven persons, five couples and myself—odd man in.

They were all British, the men senior Government employees in various departments in Freetown, and, as is usual with such semiformal occasions, all cautious of speech and deportment in the presence of H.E., in spite of our host's easy and friendly example. While sipping pre-dinner aperitifs the conversation was vague, guarded and rather boring. The women, excepting Lady Dorman, seemed content to listen to their husbands and make the occasional indeterminate noise of approval whenever, from habit, they recognized the signal for intervention. Talk about the mass assembly that morning and the previous night's revelry soon wore thin, and, in some devious way, conversation got around to Sierra Leone and its future as an independent entity; and by the time dinner was announced it might be said that the "ice was broken" and people were speaking their piece. Sir Maurice took little part in the talking at this time, and Lady Dorman, with charming skill, intervened only to fill any hiatus which threatened to widen into general silence.

Some of the men surprised me. It is true that I had been in the country but a short while, had seen little of the land or the people; but even that little was not to be discounted out of hand. People had talked with me, frankly and freely in most cases. My black skin had something to do with it, I was sure, for it very likely presupposed an immediate sympathy and willingness to understand. However, I had seen and heard a few things, and here I was with men who were positioned close to the center of events. I asked questions and met only with half-answers and evasions. I was told that everything in Sierra Leone was proceeding according to plan, but no one would tell me whose plan was being operated. I was told that what might seem to me to be apathy and indifference was in fact a highly commendable reserve peculiar to the people of Sierra Leone, but no one would tell me how it was that Africans

160

in a predominantly illiterate country could be so amazingly reserved about something as emotionally loaded as freedom and independence. I was told that there was very little unemployment in the country, yet no one would explain why, on any day and every day, thousands of idle men and women could be seen sitting about the town, dejected and hopeless, without any prospect of honest employment. They sounded knowledgeable and authoritative, these men, but after what I had seen and heard, not very convincing, and even the way they spoke seemed to imply a certain personal distance from the things they said.

Listening to them I realized that they believed in the rightness of everything they said, without any pomposity or effort to convert me. They were simply right and knew it. When they spoke about leading the Africans gradually toward self-government and progress, there was no doubt about their firm belief that it was their responsibility and right to regulate both the pace and degree of progress, in spite of any attempts by Africans or others to interfere. They considered most African leadership outside Sierra Leone to be "reactionary," irresponsible, and very probably in the pay or control of Communists. They insisted that they knew and liked the Africans and really understood them.

"How much of this is reciprocated by the Africans?" I asked one of them, a handsome gray-haired man.

"All of it," he replied. "In Sierra Leone we operate in terms of equality and understanding. We are here only until there are qualified Africans ready to take our place, and these are being trained every day to do just that. In my department there are several very good boys who, in a few years' time, will be able to take over much of the responsibility."

I wondered how old those "boys" were. Since I had been in the country I had discovered that an African was a "boy," irrespective of his age, unless his social status or economic position insisted otherwise. Perhaps there was an honest intention to train Africans to take over all the administrative posts, but it seemed to me that, from my experiences in the short time I was in the country, the process was likely to be very protracted.

I had had occasion to visit some of the departments on some matter or other and discovered that, except at ministerial level, no

161

African was either willing or able to take any initiative or responsibility for decisions. I remember spending an entire day at the Department of Transport trying to clear up a certain matter which seemed very simple and straightforward to me, but which the African-in-charge insisted must await the decision of his superior, an Englishman. When I finally saw that gentleman and was moved to comment that I felt the African official could just have easily attended to it, he explained that it would have pleased him if that had been done, saying, "That is our main difficulty here, these fellows are afraid of responsibility. Probably it is our fault, because we have conditioned them over the years to wait for our final OK. Now it is proving a big drawback. They are very capable fellows, provided the operational sequence is laid out for them, but as soon as it is a matter for responsible decision, they shy from it."

Yet here I was being told that it was working well and smoothly. I could not help remembering that these men were all remaining at their posts after independence to keep their departments smoothly operative. From their manner as much as their words, I did not think they believed there were likely to be many changes in the near future which would affect their jobs. Then an idea struck me. These men were not really involved. They were here to do work which could not, as yet, be done by indigenous personnel, and that was all that mattered. They would probably have behaved similarly in Bristol, Brazil or Ruganda.

"How much real social life is there between black and white?" I asked.

"We all get along splendidly," he said, expansively. "None of the difficulties you find in other places. Black and white meet and mix socially without any bother at all."

"I don't know that I'd go that far." It was his wife speaking. Her voice was as gentle and assured as she expressed this disagreement with her husband's remark. It pleased and surprised me, coming as it did from "inside the camp," so to speak. "Now and again the groups meet vaguely at some special function, but apart from that I wouldn't say there was much real social intercourse. I mean there's hardly any entertaining done across the two groups."

Although she spoke quietly I think that everybody heard her. Her husband made some vague reply which did nothing to detract

162

from the obvious truth of her remark. Did I detect the fleeting reflection of a smile on the Governor's face?

"That used to be true some time ago" someone else intervened, "but there's a lot more mixing now. Quite a number of the chaps are going out to Britain to qualify and returning, so there's much more that's common between us nowadays."

A military-looking gentleman said, "You writer chaps set too much store by such things, you know. After all, the Africans would very likely prefer to be with their own people. Nothing to do with prejudice or anything like that, you know."

I did know, but I wanted to see how far some of them were prepared to go to preserve the myth of social integration.

I thought of a European schoolmistress I had met on a short visit to the colony's international school. She had carefully explained that, as soon as the European children entered their teens it was advisable for them to be sent back to Europe, lest they mature too quickly, and added that the educational facilities in Sierra Leone were unsuitable for European children beyond primary level. I think I rather shocked her by suggesting that the best results might be achieved if everybody worked hard to provide the best possible educational levels for all the children, black and white.

Like that schoolmistress, most of these persons here at the dinner table, thought of themselves as part of a group, distinct and separate from the "other group," but paying lip service to whatever tenuous bridges occasionally materialized between them. Yet there was no denying that these were intelligent, cultured, charming people.

*

After dinner we sat on the wide patio underneath a tall, spreading tree in which electric lights were cleverly concealed to provide illumination without conflict with the pleasant, natural surroundings. Large bats and tiny yellow moths flitted noiselessly among the branches, and as I sat there looking up beyond the pale green of the lower lighted branches to the faintly discernible silhouettes of the gently waving top, I remembered how, long ago as a small boy in British Guiana, I would slip outdoors at night and sit quietly

163

beneath the tall, fruit-heavy sapodilla trees, waiting until the marauding bats touched the topmost fruit, sun-ripe and bursting with goodness, and sent them crashing through the leaves to land unimpaired upon the thick cushion of dry glass I had earlier heaped under the tree.

It was not a dull dinner party by any means. Some of the guests had quaintly amusing stories to tell, and were very witty in a well-bred, restrained sort of way, which allowed for laughter without too much gaiety. Soon after ten o'clock, as if by prearrangement, wives looked at husbands, who obediently fidgeted apologetically and rose. I was about to follow but Sir Maurice laid a detaining hand on my shoulder and said, "Not you, we've not talked yet."

The formalities of departure were quickly concluded, and with replenished glasses, Sir Maurice, his wife and I sat down with the one guest who, like our host, had said very little during the earlier part of the evening.

"How was the trip upcountry?" Sir Maurice asked.

I told him of the places I had visited, people I had met, and something of the impressions I had gained from things seen and heard.

"Do you feel the same bewilderment about our approach to independence—or rather its approach to us?" he asked.

I confessed that, though I had heard a great deal in apparent defense of the situation, I still felt that I would favor the words "lethargy" or "apathy" in preference to the word "reserve," which had been used at official level to describe the general attitude to approaching independence.

"Tell me in plain English," he prompted.

"I get the feeling," I said, "that very few people, either in the colony or the protectorate, feel personally involved in either the spirit or the political fact of independence. The very fact that it was necessary for you to go on trek to 'sell' the idea to the Africans illustrates my point."

"May it not also illustrate the desire and intention of Her Majesty's Government to keep the people directly informed on what their new status will mean to them?" This from the other guest, whom I shall call Mr. Bixby. "If the entire scheme had, throughout its development, the understanding of all sections of the population, irrespective of whether they were willing to support it, or otherwise, there should have been no need for Sir Maurice to tell them about it at this rather late date. But I could not help observing that, in spite of Sir Maurice's efforts and those of his wife, there seemed to be very little interest in, let alone enthusiasm for, such an important event."

"You must not be too easily led astray by the seemingly obvious," Mr. Bixby defended. "I am very closely involved with several aspects of independence, and some of the preparations for it, and I know that the African at all levels is keenly enthusiastic. Personally I am sure that they are approaching it in the best possible spirit."

Sir Maurice's face lit up with a smile. I had the sudden idea that he had deliberately invited me to meet with the other guests that I might learn something of the perplexities of government; they were men who, in order to do their job well, were compelled by circumstances to take a line most favorable to themselves.

"Perhaps that's true," the Governor said. "From the moment it was decided that Sierra Leone would become independent, my business was to work to bring it about under the most favorable conditions. The present situation may not be ideal, but it provides an atmosphere in which everyone can work together without distracting or inhibiting frictions. It cannot be denied that there is a certain diffidence, shall we say, which is regrettable at a time when everyone should be enthused and stimulated, but it is preferable to a state of bitterness, agitation and unrest. Perhaps we who have administered the country have not ourselves always been fully aware of the wider field of our responsibilities, and have not, as a result, planned as carefully as we might for this impending event. But too-lengthy reflection on past omissions can be of little help now. The British Government is committed, fully committed, to the policy of granting independence to its colonies as soon as events indicate that such a step can be undertaken to achieve the best interests of the people of those territories. But political independence is only part of the foundation on which must be built the more complicated structure of economic viability and progressive social institutions.

"With independence there must be belief in its rightness and

165

responsibility for its effective operation. My trip in the hinterland was more than for the purpose of 'selling' independence. Each time I go I try to learn a little more of the people and their ways, and I try to arrange things so that they are able to learn something about me. The time is past when in Africa one governed from a distance —even the distance between this house and the cotton tree."

"But, Sir Maurice, how can you be sure that the policies you speak of are necessarily the best for the people?" I asked. "For as long as they were subject to decisions from Whitehall they had no choice, but will they not now be likely to think differently about what is best for themselves?"

"There will necessarily be changes," he agreed, "but I do not think we need anticipate anything so terribly drastic. You must bear in mind that much of the country's affairs have for years been in the hands of the Africans."

I spoke of the large number of unemployed I had seen, especially in Freetown, and the problem of its increasing as more and more youths left school. What would happen if subversive elements got in among them and stirred them up?

"We must, and quickly, find employment for our people," he agreed (saying "our people," something I had not heard from any of the other Europeans), "not in order to block the possibility of Communist agitation, but because people who are employed are in a better position to think and behave responsibly, and set about the job of general improvement in standards of living. Our plans for employment, as with other plans for the country's development, won't be based on fear. It is, however, in keeping with wisdom to take careful note of what has happened and is happening in other African territories that we might deliberately avoid the risk of serious error."

"I have spoken with some young men, Sir Maurice," I said, "and learned that they are eager to avail themselves of scholarships and other opportunities for study offered by Communist countries. Will any attempt be made to either stop them or restrict those opportunities? And do you see any danger in such a trend?"

"That is nothing very new," he replied, "and I would be very loath to deny anyone an opportunity for educational advancement.

166

Our task here is to bestir ourselves and provide openings which they can fill when they are trained, because there is no doubt that we'll need every trained one of them."

Conversation switched, I don't recall when or how, to life in the West Indies, with which both Sir Maurice and his wife were very familiar; he had been at one time colonial secretary of Trinidad. In this Lady Dorman joined freely, recalling many happy anecdotes of the times spent there. I felt completely at ease with these two charming people, whose easy manner betrayed little of the heavy responsibilities they bore every day.

For me the significant point of the whole evening was the Governor's oblique remark about other African States and the changing tide of events which kept many of them in a state of ferment. Did he, I wondered, imagine, or hope that Sierra Leone would escape the turbulence from those neighboring vortices? Did not the excessive popular apathy indicate in itself the very unrest against which this kindly, energetic man worked so conscientiously? If, as the Lebanese tradesman hinted, independence would be seen by the young unemployed of the protectorate as a magic formula for changing "have nots" into "haves," was it unlikely that the more numerous unemployed of Freetown would entertain the same extreme hopes?

It occurred to me that Independence Day would see a large number of visitors from neighboring African States and even farther afield; some of these persons might readily assess the local situation and recognize the possibilities for political agitation. Somehow, as I thought of Sir Maurice's hopes, my own fears increased, probably out of all reasonable proportion with the behind-the-scenes realities. In my heart I wished him every good fortune, and said so as I took my leave.

There was a message for me at my hotel. My friend wished to tell me that there had been some error in my air reservation—the plane would leave on Tuesday morning, not Monday, as I had thought. I therefore had an extra day in which to cool my heels and look around Freetown.

*

Early next morning the houseboys assigned to my room seemed to be suddenly very much in evidence, fetching newspapers, clean towels, etc., in and out of my room until the truth dawned upon me—they had heard that I would be leaving that day and wanted to remind me to show some tangible appreciation of their services— this in spite of the fact that the hotel management forbade tipping.

I called them together, explained that I would be staying another day, then tipped them anyway. It was funny to note that, in spite of the management's interdict, they expected and readily accepted whatever tips they could get. Their menial bowing and scraping still irritated me, and I could not believe that it was merely "put on" deliberately to present a kind of stereotype which would play upon European sympathies and stimulate further tipping, as someone suggested to me. These young men fell into the pose much too easily, indicating a long-established process of conditioning and acceptance. Perhaps it would take a long, long time to educate them away from it, or then again, something dramatic could occur to produce a more immediate change.

I spent the morning down among the crowded streets in the trading section of town, among the noisy idlers and patient market mammies, who sat on very low stools in front of the fruit and vegetables they hoped to sell. The number of vendors was truly amazing, each one selling the same kind of fruit or vegetables, not by vigilant competition, but merely sitting beside the displayed wares, as if content in the vain hope that someone would eventually buy something.

Everywhere were groups of youngsters, apparently of school age, but possibly older (it was difficult to assess their age, as they all wore short trousers), laughing and scuffling with each other, or merely sitting around and making fun of the vendors and passers-by. God, what criminal waste! I thought of the youngsters I had taught in Britain, and their anxieties about employment and the other responsibilities which awaited them on leaving school. For these young Africans the situation must have been vastly different, as

168

they approached their final schoolday without hope of employment, or the vaguest idea of what life held in store for them.

Remembering what the Lebanese trader in Kabala had said, I took a more careful account of the trading section, and it was true that all the smaller shops and a few of the larger ones were owned by Lebanese and Indians, whose wares were mostly tinned food-stuff, cloth, and the cheaper variety of domestic appliances. These goods were all readily saleable and presented little or no problems of deterioration. Some youths could be seen sitting outside these shops, as if hopeful of earning some pence by doing an occasional errand. The contrast between the prosperous Lebanese and Indians and the poverty-stricken Africans was very striking. The haves and the have-nots.

Wandering around I could not help noticing how dirty the trading section of town was—not merely because of the scattered garbage by the numerous shops and vendors' stalls—but the stinking decayed matter which cluttered the open drains along the side of the roads, and accommodated enormous swarms of flies. I had been told that every Sierra Leonean I met was a miracle of survival. Everything around me seemed to support that remark.

Later that evening my friend and I dined at the hotel and then visited the large new cinema a short distance from the cotton tree. Within the same building was a modernistic bar, managed by a tall, bosomy redhead with a thick Scots accent; a gaudy jukebox provided music which was too loud to encourage ordinary conversation. Here we sat after seeing the film. The other patrons were invariably European men with African women; sometimes a group of three or four young Lebanese men entered, quickly downed their drinks and left.

"Once upon a time the Lebanese men found wives among the African women, but nowadays they go home and marry their own women," my friend said.

I found myself thinking of the bosomy redhead and the strange patterns of human behavior. Men would come in, order a drink for themselves, invite her to join them in a drink, and chat with her awhile across the wide expanse of shiny counter. She would sip her drink, smile pleasantly and listen, until the next customer appeared to repeat the entire performance.

169

"I come in here quite often, but I've never seen her even tipsy," my friend remarked, noticing my preoccupation. "I figure she gives nothing away, at least not so's anyone can notice. That way she keeps everybody hopeful and happy. What's more, she's doing very good business with the bar."

Yes, it takes all kinds, and Africa is no exception. I sat with my friend until it was closing time, drinking and reviewing the pleasant time we had had together. I still did not fully understand his motives, but there was no doubt he loved his country and was deeply concerned about its future.

"You'll be hearing about me," he said, cryptically, as we parted.

170

Part Three

LIBERIA

In the lounge at Lungi Airport I got into conversation with an American student on his way to Liberia. The usual thing—he had come in two hours ago from Abidjan, on the Ivory Coast, expecting a stopover of no more than an hour before continuing on to Monrovia, but two hours had passed and the plane still sat quietly on the tarmac and we could see no sign of readiness for the takeoff.

Out of this irritating situation, and our gripes about it, we talked a little about ourselves and our reasons for being there. Chuck Randell was a graduate of Columbia University, in political science, hiking through Africa, studying at firsthand the development of political awareness and responsibility among African leadership; that's how he put it. When he learned that I had worked at City College, New York, it seemed to give us a point of common reference and we got on like a house on fire.

"What's it like back there?" he said, inclining his head in the direction of Freetown. "Things must be really jumping with independence around the corner. I rode in with a bunch of European guys—Germans, Frenchmen, Czechs, you know—like business representatives or salesmen. Figure they are all trying to get in on the ground floor when the boom starts."

Everything about him suggested an enthusiasm for living and knowing. About five feet ten inches of tough-looking muscle and large bones in a creased suit of tan linen, a wide, strong, pleasant face, and the inevitable crew-cut, which left each blond stub shiny, erect and somewhat pugnacious.

"Yes," I agreed, "I expect things will warm up, come independence." Things had to, there was no other direction in which they could possibly move except up.

"You know, Africa's great," he went on, "Boy, I've been in some places! Those guys know how to live. Christ, we've got such a lot to learn! You know something, before getting to Africa I had it worked out about Africans—you know, they were kind of like American Negroes but without the American living standards.

173

But, boy, some of those African guys I've met! They're *alive!*" The word took on special significance from the way he exploded it.

'What other parts of Africa have you visited?" I asked him.

"I've bummed through Egypt and Ethiopia and stayed awhile in Kenya and Tanganyika. Boy, that Tanganyika is some country, you know. I've seen a little of Nigeria and the Cameroons, spent a week in Ghana. Things are moving in Ghana; the country's like one big W.P.A. project with everything happening at once. Funny thing, I went around to their parliament building, you know, to take a look. Right in front of it is Nkrumah's statue. Whoever made it should have fixed him up with the national dress, you know. Lots more impressive than shirt and slacks."

I liked this chap. His enthusiasm was most infectious, although it required some effort to adjust to his rapid-fire staccato manner of speaking.

"Hope to stay around Liberia for a week or two, then back home —Akron, Ohio. Ever been there? Got to put in time on my Ph.D., but I'd like to come back to Africa, you know, to work with the people some place."

"Like a missionary?"

"Hell, no! Like an ordinary guy. Teacher or adviser, or something like that. Do you know lots of those guys just live off the land without knowing what the land can do? I mean, anything grows, so nobody worries much about soil biology or things like that. But they can learn. You should hear some of those guys talk—especially some of the French guys. Do you know, some of those guys know more about philosophy and classical literature than I'd ever heard about?" He laughed in wonder, in retrospective pleasure about things seen and heard. "How long are you fixing to stay in Liberia?" he asked.

I explained about my visit to Guinea and Sierra Leone and said I hoped to do about the same thing in Liberia.

"Guess I've seen more of Africa than you have," he said laughing.

Just then our flight was announced and soon we were airborne en route to Monrovia, following the irregular Sierra Leone coastline, with its multiple network of swampy estuaries. From the air there was nothing recognizable as a line of demarcation between Sierra

174

Leone and Liberia, no break in the panorama of flat coastal areas with a proliferation of lagoons and creeks. Ahead, the beaches of Liberia gleamed pink and enticing, edged by the rolling white-crested breakers, but from six thousand feet up it did not seem as if modern progress had ventured very far inland.

"Gee! Looking down there it makes you feel you can really go places and do things," my companion enthused. "It's like being personally involved in history and knowing that you are able to make things happen, to change events in a big way. I've been reading about what they've done in Brazil, you know, the new capital and all that. What's to stop these people from doing the same thing here?"

"You ought to join President Kennedy's Peace Corps," I suggested. "That would give you an opportunity to do things, and, with the President backing you, you can't miss."

He did not laugh at that. His face became serious, suddenly mature. "Could be," he said. "Yeah, I've been reading about that. I'll check as soon as I get home. Don't like the name, though, 'Peace Corps' sounds a bit odd, you know, as if it's against something or other. I'd like to team up with something which does things, you know, like clearing land, or building, or teaching folks how to improve their stocks, things like that."

We landed at Payne Airfield and hastily promised to get together some time in town before we became separated in the melee of chasing baggage and the formalities of customs and immigration clearance. I had a room at the Ducor Palace Hotel, and on the way there by taxi was very impressed by the building projects all along the route, most of them earmarked for government offices and ministries. Everywhere along the wide asphalt-surfaced streets huge American cars whizzed to and fro, sometimes driven by gleeful youngsters who seemed intent on proving how fast they could drive the shiny juggernauts.

We drove through the clean streets in the center of Monrovia, past the graceful old-colonial mansions and up to Mamba Point and the half-completed glass and ferroconcrete magnificence of the Ducor Palace Hotel, which dominated the entire skyline. European and African workmen swarmed everywhere, as if in a race to complete the building by some imminent deadline.

175

After the sticky heat outdoors the cool, air-conditioned interior of the hotel was most welcome, and though it was a severe shock to discover that my room would cost about eighteen dollars a day, it would have required more courage than I possessed to leave and begin searching for alternative accommodations, especially as the desk clerk hinted that I hadn't much time to make up my mind— there was a long waiting list of eager applicants. Eighteen dollars a day is a hell of a lot of money, I think, for a room, meals extra, but it was wonderfully comfortable, pleasing in design, complete in equipment, and opened onto a balcony which provided an excellent view of the town and the blue Atlantic. I luxuriated in a warm bath, then checked the many addresses of persons to whom I had letters of introduction.

From the balcony I could hear all around the various noises of construction: power drills cutting away at the rock behind the hotel, where they were building a new swimming pool; the frequent noise of blasting from a nearby stone quarry; the tap-tap of the stone-crackers, men and women who sat under makeshift sun-shades and laboriously reduced large rocks into small fragments; the noisy, grinding whir of cement-mixers, all part of a continuing activity which seemed the more remarkable because of the heat in which the workers labored. Below me a group of young men were carefully planting grass seedlings in the prepared earth along the sloping approach to the main door of the hotel where already several young cocoanut palms were swaying in the fitful breeze, nearly recovered from the ordeal of being transplanted a few months ago. All this was very encouraging, in keeping with my expectation of a country free and independent for more than a hundred and forty years. It would be fun wandering around here, among these industrious, energetic people.

*

That evening I dined in the hotel, and was glad I had taken pains to dress myself carefully. The other diners, all Europeans except one (who, I learned later, was a visiting diplomat from one of the newly independent French-speaking States), were well-dressed

176

in summer lightweights and brightly patterned dresses, cut to expose as much as possible of their very attractive suntans. Conversation was in German, French, American and English. The Germans seemed to be the more numerous. The food was truly excellent; even now I can still taste the wonderful hors d'oeuvre of fried prawns and wedges of chilled avocado. But when the check came and I realized how much the meal cost, I resolved to find some other eating place quickly. The room was expensive enough, but the food!

After dinner I took a stroll around the town. It was pleasant to walk downhill into the cool, refreshing breeze, along the wide, well-lighted avenues, bordered on each side by an interesting mixture of old-colonial-style buildings and sparkling new bungalows and business premises, all suggesting comfortable living. Now the clangor of construction had given place to potted jazz music from open windows and passing cars, injecting a certain lightheartedness into the evening, flickering neon advertisements, laughter and the continuous blare of automobile horns.

Suddenly feeling tired, I headed back toward the hotel, which, from its hilltop roost, dominated the skyline. I saw young soldiers at ease on guard duty in front of the executive mansion, groups of young Africans in front of a cinema's gaudy facade, high-stepping young girls in short dresses for the young men's appreciative whistles, and heard the intermittent wail of a police car's siren. Where was I? I paused beside a group of young men. The billboard advertised the film "Baby Doll." The subject was woman, the speech a kind of hybrid American, some accent-clipped Brooklyn, some long-drawn-out Texas, the attitudes Harlem. Each addressed the other as "Man," as in British Guiana, where name-calling indicated formality. Music belching through an open window of the night club adjoining the cinema, and the youths snapped fingers and flexed knees without any break in their conversation. Cool cats! What I needed was sleep.

While preparing for bed I switched on the radio. Pop music, or pop music interrupted by announcements or advertisements in a careful American-accented voice, each word clearly and slowly separated from its neighbor, as is the case with someone learning a new language. Pop music, most of it devoted to monotonous reitera-

177

tion of teenage love. I remembered the Liberian consul in Sierra Leone telling me something about Liberia's own cultural forms. I must look around very carefully.

*

Early the next morning I telephoned some of the people to whom I had letters of introduction. Lucky me! The first one had had a letter from Paris from a mutual friend and was expecting my call. "First things first," he said. He had made tentative arrangements for me to visit President Tubman.

"He's read your first book," he told me, " and would like to see you. I promised to take you to the executive mansion as soon as you arrived. I'll call for you just before ten and take you there."

This was sheer luck. I remembered having sent an autographed copy of *To Sir, with Love* to President Tubman soon after its publication in England, but had entertained little hope that his crowded itinerary would allow time for reading it, or that having read it he would remember either it or me. I was excited at the thought of meeting this man, who had become something of a legend and a mystery.

My friend must have been an important official, because the soldiers on guard duty at the mansion snapped smartly to attention when our car drew up. He led me up a thickly carpeted staircase (this was more of an effort than it sounds, because the thick carpet was protected throughout its length by a thick, resistant, plastic covering which felt so strange underfoot that twice I stumbled and would have fallen but for his steadying hand), along a similarly carpeted corridor and into a large reception room. It was already crowded with men and women, black and white, sitting singly or in groups.

We were lucky to find empty chairs, and I looked around to take stock of my surroundings. All the Europeans seemed to be businessmen, if one were allowed to judge by the smartly cut suits and expensive-looking briefcases. One group of American men and women I guessed were missionaries, as in conversation they occasionally referred to "Brother" or "Sister" John or Mary, and spoke

178

of tours of duty. Some of the Africans were well dressed, distinguished-looking men; others wore the wide, loose native garment of coarse striped cloth. There were several women present, some very smartly dressed and made-up, but everybody seemed preoccupied with the doorway of the reception room, and glanced anxiously toward it at the least sound of movement from the corridor.

"Gosh, are all these people seeking audience with the President?" I asked.

"Oh, yes," he replied. "Each one of them. And what's more, he'll do his best to see them all. Excuse me."

He left the room for a few minutes. It was quite amusing to observe the way in which everyone remarked upon his leaving and return, with glances in which was a mixture of hope and apprehension.

"I'd forgotten to tell the President's adjutant that we're here. He'll call us as soon as the Old Man is ready to see us."

"But what about all these people here?" I asked. If they too had appointments with the President, I could see little prospect of meeting him for some days hence.

"Oh, there's no definite sequence with the Old Man. He selects whom he will see, and that's that."

"What about the adjutant? Does he list the applicants in a way to determine priority?"

A uniformed official entered and called a name. Someone followed him out.

"No, everyone has direct access to the Old Man. There's no screening of any sort. It might take time, sometimes as much as a week or more, but he gets around to it. This room is like this every day except Saturday and Sunday, crowded with people, high and low, rich and poor. Some come to discuss industrial or other business ventures. Those Europeans near the door, for instance, I'm sure they're here to put through some business project or other. The missionaries may be after permission to acquire land for a church or school, or something like that. Those gentlemen over there," he pointed to the group of influential-looking, well-dressed Africans, "they're cabinet ministers. I suppose the Old Man has fixed a cabinet meeting for some time this morning."

179

"But how is it that cabinet ministers are waiting here with the rest of us?"

"Why not?" he replied. "They've got to wait until the Old Man is ready for them. He may have fixed a cabinet meeting for eleven o'clock this morning, but if something else turns up they have to wait. Perhaps he's held up settling somebody's domestic problem, but to him that would be as important as a matter of State."

I could not easily grasp this. "But how can he cope with it all? Surely his adjutant or someone else can relieve him of some of the less-important cases?"

"To him each case is important and he deals with them all—no middlemen. And the people love it. Any man or woman with a problem knows where to appeal as a last resort." He smiled. "Sometimes even as a first resort."

"Im wondering," I whispered.

"Wondering what?"

"Wondering why a President should adopt such measures. Is it that he loves his people and wishes to maintain personal contact with all of them at all times? Could it be that he might find such an arrangement profitable to himself in that he could discover all kinds of useful bits of information? Is it possible that he trusts none of those nearest to him and considers it safest to insulate himself with popular contact?"

"No one can stop you wondering," he replied, "but I'd advise you to do so to yourself. A lot of us remember the days before the Old Man took office. Then nobody could even see the President, at least none of the common people, so, whatever the reasons or motives, nobody has any grumble these days. If someone is in difficulty and needs financial help—or any other help, for that matter—all he needs to do is have a talk with the Old Man."

"I would imagine that places a considerable burden on the President," I replied, "for it must happen that very often matters of state must claim his attention over the problems of individuals, no matter who they are, or how important their problems might seem to themselves. If each day it is necessary for him to devote a lot of time and energy to the personal problems of so many people as these assembled here, you'll soon be in the market for another President."

180

"You just don't know the Old Man," he said, smiling. "He's as strong as a bull."

"Could you tell me something about these people here?" I asked.

"Guess I could, about some of them," he replied. "Better still, I'll introduce you to some of the ministers. Couldn't have picked a better time, with them all here."

He led me over to the group of cabinet ministers and introduced me to the Hon. McKinley A. de Shield, Postmaster General, the Hon. Charles D. Sherman, Secretary of the Treasury, the Hon. Harrison Grigsby, Secretary of National Defense, the Hon. Jacob Milton, Secretary of the Interior, the Hon. Dr. Nathaniel N. Massaquoi, Secretary of Public Instruction, the Hon. Joseph W. Garber, Attorney General.

Strangely enough, with the exception of one man, the Secretary of the Interior, I did not have the feeling of being with Africans. These men, in their smartly tailored suits, narrow, high-fashion shoes, grooming, speech and mannerisms, reminded me of affluent American Negroes; they were handsome men, who evidently lived well and carried with them a casual assurance of their own power and influence. For the most part they acknowledged the introduction perfunctorily, as is sometimes the case with men too immersed in very important matters to spare much attention to small fry.

The Minister of the Interior, however, invited me to sit awhile beside him, inquired into my reason for visiting Liberia and the probable extent of my itinerary. He seemed surprised to learn that I was not African, but told me of another Guianese, a dentist, who was fast building up a great reputation in the country. When I told him that I hoped to travel into the interior, he immediately promised to place such facilities as I would need at my disposal.

Unlike most of his colleagues, he was slim and very dark, with a thin face and very prominent nose, on which rested heavy horn-rimmed spectacles. As he spoke, gold filling glinted in his teeth, and he had the easy, relaxed air of a man accustomed to talking with people informally. His speech was not elegant, and I would hazard a guess that he could not boast high academic honors, yet I liked his simplicity, and he seemed sincere in his expression of interest and wish to help.

Afterward I was introduced to some of the women; some dressed rather extravagantly, I thought, but understandably one wore one's best for an interview with the head of state. Next I met three elderly men dressed in their narrow-striped national robes and cloth skull-caps. These introductions were carried out in a dialect, so I could only bow in acknowledgment of whatever it was they said.

Back in our places, I was asked, "What did you think of them, the ministers?"

"I was intrigued by the Minister of the Interior," I replied.

"Don't be fooled by his speech," I was told. "He's a very important man and wields a great deal of influence. Ever hear of Ghana's Krobo Edusei? Well, he occupies about the same role here. He knows the people of the interior, speaks their languages and has their confidence. He's very useful to the President."

Time was slipping by, every chair in the room was occupied, and I overheard a remark that an adjoining waiting room was equally crowded.

"I think it unlikely the President will be able to see me," I suggested, "so I'll call it a day and attend to some other things."

My companion seemed shocked at this and literally stammered his protests. "You can't do that. You're supposed to wait until the Old Man sends for you. He knows you're here and might call you at any moment."

"But we've been here nearly two hours," I argued. "And I'm sure all these other persons have much more pressing business than mine. I'm here only to pay a courtesy call."

"No matter," he replied. "The Old Man knows you are here and it would be very discourteous for you to leave now. Don't worry about the others. Some of them come here day after day until they see him. For instance, that gentleman over there"—he pointed to a neatly dressed, handsome man—"has recently been appointed to an important post in one of the ministries and he's here to say 'Thank you' to the President, so he's waiting for the opportunity."

"But could he not write a letter of thanks?"

"Perhaps, but it's customary to say it in person."

That set me wondering. How many more paid officials were similarly sitting, waiting, waiting? And what about the jobs they were supposed to be doing? The ministers were also waiting, so perhaps they had left the running of their departments in the hands of competent staffs.

At this moment two other well-dressed men entered the room, carrying neat briefcases; they joined the group of ministers and there was general handshaking and laughter. (It suddenly struck me that the handshaking I had seen in Liberia was quite different from any I had before encountered. On releasing each other's hand, thumbs and middle fingers were pressed and withdrawn with a loud, snapping sound.)

"Who are they?" I asked.

"The younger one is the Hon. J. Rudolph Grimes, Secretary of State, and the other is Dr. Edwin M. Barclay, Director of Public Health."

Whenever my companion mentioned a personality, he gave the full name, complete with initials, in very much the American manner. Now, as the great men exchanged pleasantries, he told me a little about them, but in that little I was surprised to discover how closely interrelated they were, either directly or through marriage.

"Now the whole cabinet's here," he whispered.

Again the uniformed official entered and called names. This time the group of missionaries collected their pamphlets and followed him.

Midday now, and my patience was worn very thin. Conversation even among the ministers had subsided, and each person seemed occupied with his own thoughts while keeping an eye and ear on the door. Suddenly there was a simultaneous struggling to stand up, as into the room stepped a short, sturdy, bespectacled figure, looking cool in short-sleeved shirt and neatly creased slacks of Shantung silk; his slim brown shoes were brightly polished, and in his left hand was a large cigar.

"The Old Man," my companion said, urgently nudging me to stand.

So this was the President. As I looked at the man some of the things I had been wondering about were immediately explained. There was no doubt about his self-assurance. He stood in the middle of the room, looked about him, spread his arms in an expansive gesture and said, "Ladies and gentlemen, I must apologize for keeping you waiting, but in spite of all my efforts I cannot

183

see any more of you this morning, as I must now attend some urgent discussions with my cabinet." (At this, their cue, the ministers began collecting their briefcases.) "Where's Braithwaite?"

I stepped forward, and he extended his hand to enclose mine in a surprisingly powerful grip.

"Sorry, I cannot see you now, young man," he continued, "As you can see I just couldn't make it. But get Mr. Baker, here, to bring you around at six this evening. I'll try to give you a few minutes then."

With that he turned and went out, followed closely by his ministers, and leaving behind, like an echo of his presence, the strong aroma of his cigar.

"Let's go," my companion said, and we joined the moving line down the stairs and out into the sunshine. Now I was able to appreciate the large number of people who had been waiting inside. Mr. Baker led me to a restaurant nearby with the bold sign "Heinz and Maria Bar." It was cool inside, air-conditioned and elegantly clean.

Over our meal I asked about the people who had been waiting to see the President. Why so many women?

"The Old Man is like everybody's father or uncle," he explained. "Many of those women go to ask his help in resolving their marital problems: errant or neglectful husbands, marriages on the rocks, things like that. Very often it only requires a word from him to bring things into line, as no man would deliberately incur the Old Man's displeasure. Sometimes a man has lost his job, so his wife appeals to the President. I saw at least two men there this morning who I know wish to ask the President to reinstate them in their jobs."

"Would he?" I asked.

"Perhaps. It all depends. Nowadays it is very rare for someone to be sacked from a job, especially a government job, because no head of a department would like to receive one of the Old Man's green slips."

"What are they?"

"It's like this—suppose you are employed at one of the ministries and you're regularly late, or careless, or something like that, so that finally the chief clerk becomes exasperated and fires

184

you. You or your wife might then get an audience with the Old Man and beg to be reinstated. You might even claim that you were wrongfully sacked, and, with a wife and children to support, it would not be too difficult to present a very touching situation which might move the Old Man to sympathy and persuade him to give you a green memorandum to your boss suggesting that you be given another chance. Such a memo would, in fact, be a directive, and you can see that nobody would wish to receive one of them."

"But does that not open the way to all sorts of abuses?" I asked.

"Perhaps," he replied, "but it might also be said that it prevents abuses. If the Old Man did not occasionally intervene in this way, there's no telling what would happen. Before the Old Man took office you could lose your job or be given a job according to someone's whim or how well you could grease certain well-placed palms. Things are very different now. Perhaps you would like to see something of the town? After we've eaten I must drop in at my office for a little while, but I'll pick you up at your hotel around three o'clock and show you around before it's time to meet the Old Man again."

*

Mr. Baker called for me soon after three o'clock and we set out on a tour of the town, beginning with the hotel itself, which, I learned, was constructed directly over the town's huge new reservoir. Here the road started, between the landmarks of the Monrovia lighthouse and the life-size bronze statue of Liberia's first President, J.J. Roberts. From here one had a clear view of Mamba Point and the elegant red-roofed villas and bungalows of the embassy and legation officials of foreign governments, which nestled against the sloping hillside, surrounded by low stone walls and cultivated shrubbery, while the blue sea provided an exciting, restless background. Hardly any grass to be seen anywhere, except for a coarse, broad-leafed variety carefully tended in front of the hotel.

From the hill we dropped down along the broad main avenue toward Government Square, where most of the ministries were

185

located, passing the executive mansion and its adjoining garden, which, I was told, was the special interest of the President's wife, and the place where she annually conducted a Christmas party for the children of the city. Hotels, banks and imposing residences, bright with clean paint and oozing prosperity.

Now and then my companion would point to a building and say, "That's the President's."

At first I became somewhat confused, thinking that he was referring to State residences, then he explained that they were buildings owned by the President and now rented by him to the State as temporary accommodations for one government office or another. It seemed that the Old Man was a very important land-owner, among other things.

Further along the scene changed. We drove through busy Camp Johnson Street, flanked on both sides with shops of every description, and rendered somewhat down-at-heel and dingy by the sleazy apartments which surmounted them, festooned with strings of drying laundry. Our progress was slow because of the casual crowd of shoppers and idlers, and together with the heat there was the overpowering stench of drying fish.

At the end of Camp Johnson Street the road widened and turned up toward Camp Johnson Point, past the low buildings of the University of Liberia, which, in the shade of overhanging mango and palm trees, looked more like a quiet residential hotel than a seat of learning. Farther on I could see the domed mass of the Capitol Building, which I was told had cost more than two million dollars. As we drove I was getting a quick brief on the important places of Monrovia, but much of their importance seemed to be related to their structural cost. Not many details were forthcoming about their purpose or productiveness.

I was shown the site for the new law courts, and that of the new executive mansion, where a huge skeletal structure was gradually taking shape. If the old mansion cost two million dollars, this mammoth new structure would probably cost several times that amount.

"Where does the money come from for all this?" I asked.

"We're a rich country," was all the answer I got.

Farther out we drove into Sinkor, an area being developed

as an important residential section of the city. I gasped in admiration and wonder at the beautiful ultramodern bungalows and two- or three-storied houses, each one sheltered and fondled by palms or other shady trees. There was plenty of space between the buildings, so that one could see them individually and admire not only the house, but its personal setting also. The churches too were of modernistic design, contributing to the atmosphere of comfort and wealth.

"Nice, eh?" he said. "All owned by Liberians, but many of them rented out to Europeans and Americans. Many of our ministers and other high government officials live here. You know something, some of these new houses were designed and built by two of our own architects. That's one over there." He pointed to a new, low-lying bungalow in which elegant lines were combined with a tasteful use of glass, wood and concrete to a degree that one felt that the building was designed right there, on the spot, to harmonize and conform with the trees which surrounded it and the earth from which it rose like a beautiful, natural growth.

"Wonderful," I agreed.

"Those two boys studied in Europe, and we're very proud of them. Won't be long before they'll take over some of the big contracts which are going to foreign contractors."

Standing in front of the houses were big, shiny American cars, resplendent and very imposing.

"Let's go visit a friend of mine," my companion suggested, and without waiting for my reply, he swung into a wide entranceway and onto a charming villa.

In reply to our ring, the door was opened by a handsome young woman, who smiled in welcome and invited us into a large well-appointed room. After the introductions she invited us to take some refreshment with her, then left us for a few moments. Much of the furniture was beautiful and evidently expensive, and all the fabric-covered units, even the cushions, were further protected by the same kind of thick plastic covering which permitted me to appreciate the beauty and costliness of the piece, but greatly reduced the comfort which such elegance promised.

This was the home of an important government official, to whom my companion was rather vaguely related. Soon Mrs. Brown, our hostess, returned, followed by a houseboy, who carried a tray laden with drinks and a bucket of crushed ice, which he set on a small table. Then he quietly departed. Mrs. Brown was an excellent hostess and interesting conversationalist, with a very fine wit and easy good humor. It was obvious that she was accustomed to her role of charming hostess. She apologized for her husband's absence—he was attending to some urgent matter of State.

While chatting with her a small, chubby child entered the room. She laughingly presented him as her eighth and was quite amused at my amazement, for neither her smooth face nor girlish figure suggested motherhood, let alone eight children, three of whom were at school somewhere in Europe. Presently the houseboy returned with a pitcher containing the milk and the pulp of green cocoanuts. This she served with brandy and ice, a most refreshing mixture, and as I drank I remembered that this was also a favorite drink in Guinea.

*

After this pleasant interlude we turned back toward town to be on time for my appointment with the President. We were directed to a waiting room one floor above the reception room, where we had waited during the morning. Although we arrived on time, several men were already there, including the new appointee, who wished to express his thanks to the President. Much of the conversation I overheard related to concern about the price of latex, the raw material from which rubber products are manufactured, and I readily concluded that the men were rubber-planters. When I said this to Mr. Baker, he corrected me, and explained that most of the men were state officials, but each of them operated rubber plantations or farms, which provided a considerable source of revenue to them.

Apart from rubber, the conversations were about recently purchased American or German cars, trips abroad, and the prospects of "getting in on the ground floor" of new industrial projects. Apparently the President had requested some of them to see him that evening, for there was quite a bit of speculation about what he would say and do. Mr. Baker told me who some of the men

188

were, and again I learned of the concentric rings of relationship operating within the Government. I tried to discuss this with my companion but he parried every lead I made, leaving me with the suspicion that he too was involved in the pattern.

"How is it that these men are public servants and rubber-planters at the same time? Either of those interests would require full-time attention, it seems to me."

"Oh, they need not clash," he replied. "Our office hours are from eight or eight-thirty in the morning to two-thirty in the afternoon, with a short lunch interval. That leaves lots of time to do something else. Most of the wealthy planters leave town on Friday afternoon and spend the weekend upcountry on their farms, where they have nice houses with all modern conveniences."

"Do they operate cooperatives?" I asked.

"No, they grow the rubber trees and sell the latex to the Firestone Company, which operates its own large plantations but buys the produce of the farmers."

Other gentlemen arrived, and gradually the waiting room filled up. By seven-fifteen I was becoming increasingly irritable at the prospect of another long wait, and impatient with my companion's attempts at reassurance. As was the case during the morning, a few persons were called into an inner room, while the rest of us waited and hoped. At seven-thirty or thereabouts, the President entered the room, looking refreshed and cool, and as before he apologized for the long delay but regretted that he could see no one else. As he spoke he caught sight of someone he recognized, and, addressing him by name, advised him not to worry about certain attacks made upon him by others.

"Nobody can harm you while I'm President," he promised, at which the old man beamed and cried his thanks.

We had all stood when the President entered the room, and now he shook hands in dismissal. When he came to me he again graciously apologized for whatever inconvenience I had been caused through waiting, and asked how long I would be in Liberia and what my plans were. I told him I wished to visit as much of the interior as possible and hoped to spend about two or three weeks in the country. Turning to my companion, he said, "Baker, see to it that our visitor is given every facility while he's with us. If he

189

needs transport, arrange it through one of the departments. If anyone queries it, tell them to refer to me." With that he wished me a pleasant visit and withdrew.

I was delighted, but my friend was positively enraptured, and kept repeating, "See what I mean? He'd been thinking about you all the time. Suppose you had left before he appeared, eh? What then? Tomorrow we'll go to one of the ministries and get you fixed up with a car and chauffeur."

"Oh, I won't need a chauffeur," I protested.

"Yes, you will," he insisted. "Especially in the interior. You'll need someone with you who knows the people and their customs. In any case, it means a job for somebody, so why not?"

I couldn't argue on any of those points.

On the way to my hotel I asked, "Do you know what the President meant by his remark to that elderly man?"

"Yes, he works in one of the ministries—been there for years but some of the younger men have been making things difficult for him, that's why he was at the mansion to see the President. But the Old Man already knew about it, as you saw for yourself. Nobody knows how he knows or who tells him things, but there's very little which happens anywhere about which he doesn't know."

Maybe this was the reason why the President saw anybody, anytime. It might be tiring and sometimes inconvenient for him, but if he thus was able to keep his finger firmly on the country's pulse, it was probably worth it.

*

Early the next morning I went with Mr. Baker to one of the ministries, and with the President's name as our magic talisman, I received authorization for a car and driver from the largest taxi service in town. The driver proved to be an eager young man who claimed to know his way about the hinterland as well as he knew Monrovia. I liked the look of him and arranged for him to call for me at the hotel at six o'clock the next morning for our trip up-country. I explained to the owner of the taxi service that I ex-

190

pected to be in the hinterland three or four days, traveling most of the time, and asked that the car be checked for road-worthiness and made fully dependable. My plans for an early start were due to the lesson I had learned in Sierra Leone. I wanted to see all I could, yet be as comfortable as possible.

After these arrangements were completed, Mr. Baker left me to return to his duties, and I wandered around. Down by the waterside, where the Lebanese and other business houses crowded each other, the street was clogged with vehicular and pedestrian traffic in spite of the herculean efforts of two whistle-blowing policemen to keep the traffic moving.

Though there were many idlers sitting around, I could feel the dynamism, the thrust, the movement, expressed in everything the people did—their carriage, their strong laughter, even the attitude of the idlers, who looked as though in a moment they could move to productive effort. Passing one shop I saw a comfortable-looking pair of sandals, which I imagined would be fine for upcountry, so I went in to inquire about the price. A young African was sweeping the floor, while behind the counter, at some distance from the doorway, a Lebanese man sat reading a newspaper.

"What you want?" The Liberian leaned against the broom, which he held as a prop, and placed himself in front of me, barring my progress beyond him.

"I'm interested in some sandals I saw in the show-window," I replied.

"Twelve dollars," he said, in a flat, decisive voice.

I felt both affronted and irritated by his casual impoliteness, and the fact that he did not even ask which pair of sandals I meant.

"What do you mean, twelve dollars!" I countered. "You don't even know which pair I want."

"Anything in that window, twelve dollars," he insisted.

Any moment now I would say something rude to him, so I pushed past him and walked over toward the Lebanese, who had put away his paper and was approaching us.

"Tell me something, please," I said to him. "To whom does this shop belong?—to him or to you?"

"I own it," he replied with a smile, "but he behaves as if it is his."

191

"In that case you should insist that he be a little more polite to customers," I told him.

"I insist. Always I insist, but it make no difference," he replied.

"Then why don't you fire him?" I could not understand his attitude.

"So I fire him, and tomorrow I employ another one just like him, only I don't know the other one. Better I keep this one that I know. Did you want something? Shoes, shirt, perhaps?"

I explained about the sandals, but unfortunately a pair in my size was not available. The young Liberian grinned at me as I left. Perhaps, as someone had told me, Africans do not respect Africans, and he thought me an African, even a Liberian. As my irritation subsided I realized that I was being treated as one of them and not liking all of it. I would have to learn to forget myself sufficiently to realize that it was, in its own way, a kind of compliment that the young man felt he could be casual with me. Perhaps one day he would understand a little more about human dignity and be able to be more tactful and courteous.

I climbed a steep incline to another roadway and was attracted by a group of men and women standing before a two-storied building from which there was a great deal of coming and going. Someone told me that it was a courthouse, and that the court was now in session. Yes, anyone could go in and sit. I went up two flights of stairs and entered a narrow, elongated room, at the far end of which a man sat behind a high desk on a raised platform; in his right hand he held a gavel, which he occasionally banged on the top of the desk before making some remark or other. At floor level, before him, two other men sat at a desk facing each other; near them was the dock—a raised platform railed on three sides. Behind this platform were several wooden benches, on which sat a score or more persons, probably interested observers.

My entry seemed to have attracted some attention, for everyone turned to look at me, their expressions temporarily frozen like the "stills" from a movie. I had the feeling that I had somehow committed a breach of protocol, and, in an attempt to correct this, walked toward the judge (for such he was) and apologized for blundering into his courtroom, excusing myself by the fact that

192

I was a stranger and merely wanted to see what was going on. With a smile, the judge, an apparently very young man, accepted my apology and invited me to take a seat nearby and see "How we dispense justice here."

The case seemed simple enough. Someone had been found in possession of an article which was not his, but denied stealing it. The owner of the article had seen the accused in the immediate vicinity of the article shortly before its disappearance and presumed theft. It was interesting and rather entertaining to watch the main protagonists in this case, who were not the accuser and accused, but their lawyers, who indulged in such objections and counter-objections that the judge was finally moved to ask, "Who's objecting about what this time?"

The proceedings may have been of serious concern to the man in the dock, for he stood in jeopardy of his freedom, but to me and probably others present, it was like a small comic scene from a Gilbert and Sullivan operetta, a kind of parody on jurisprudence, with the judge's gavel a recurrent punctuation. There was an informality similar to that of American courts, but the little dignity was further lessened by the judge's occasional humorous asides to the lawyers, one of whom would have looked all the better for a shave and a clean shirt, and by the conduct of the lawyers themselves. Neither of them seemed to fully understand even the unnecessarily long words he used, as these were often incorrectly used and badly juxtaposed.

I wondered where these men were trained, and how many poor souls were similarly dependent on their unskilled direction. Before the case ended, I took advantage of a lull in the proceedings to thank the judge for his courtesy in permitting me to visit with him, then hurried away. If time and opportunity permitted I'd try to visit the high court on my return from the hinterland.

I needed a map of Liberia in order to plan my itinerary but could not obtain one at the book shop. I went to the HQ of the Ministry of the Interior and drew a blank there, also. Someone suggested that I try the office of the International Cooperation Administration. I went there and was given four excellent maps of Liberia. Odd, that!

193

*

Back at my hotel I planned my route, prepared my gear and paid my hotel bill so that I would be free to move in the early morning. I went to bed early and was up, ready and waiting at six. At seven o'clock the car had not appeared and I was by now quite angry and worried, in my mind running through the hundred and one unpleasant things which might have delayed the chauffeur.

He arrived at seven-thirty, bright-eyed and cheerful and genuinely surprised at my cold greeting. I told him he was one and a half hours late and asked if he did not realize it. Didn't he notice the time? His reply was simple and completely disarming; he could not read, nor write, nor tell time.

So simple a thing, but it shocked me. I have encountered illiteracy in many ways and thought that none of its forms would surprise me. But I had never linked it with so everyday a thing as reading the face of a clock. It really shook me. Then when we were rolling smoothly along the highway, out of Monrovia, I had a sudden thought, and asked him how fast we were traveling. The speedometer showed sixty m.p.h. He looked at it and merely said, "Not fast."

The sweep of the needle across the dial told him whether his speed was fast or slow; the numbers were meaningless.

The wheels sang their special song of hurried flirtation with the wide, smooth road as we raced through Monrovia and out along the highway to points east, north and south. As we approached the Capitol Building someone stood in the roadway and waved us to a stop. It was a policeman requiring a lift to the new Police Academy, seven or eight miles along the route, and I agreed that he should ride with us.

As we drove along he told me about the Academy and its aims to develop a cadre of efficient police officers as part of the Government's new plan for improvement of its law-enforcement departments. He said that one of the greatest problems besetting the Academy was the low standard of education among those recruited for officer training.

194

"It is not that they are illiterate," he said. "They can read and write quite well, most of them, but they find it difficult to comprehend things, to readily assess any given situation, to use any initiative or imagination. Perhaps this is in itself a reflection of our general educational system, which does everything except teach the young people to think. Our big problem is that we cannot yet afford to be merely an educational institution—we have to produce police officers."

"Whom do you mean by 'we'? The Government or the Academy faculty?" I asked.

"Both. The Government pays the bills and makes facilities available to us. At the Academy we have a training and administration staff of American officers and instructors, pretty much the same as with the Army, together with a handful of Liberian old-timers like myself who assist with basic training. The place is directly on your route, so if you'd like to drop in for a moment, it would be my pleasure to show you around."

The Academy was a collection of single- and two-storied buildings widely dispersed over a stretch of land which had been cleared and leveled to a pleasing conformity; the installations were all brand new and painted in attractive pastel shades of gray, yellow, red and white; there were residential quarters, administration buildings, stores, etc., and plenty of room for drilling and other outdoor activities. He took me into the Main Administration Building, and, walking down a corridor, we passed an open door to a room, in which I glimpsed a young police cadet standing stiffly to attention before a desk, behind which sat two officers. The odd thing about this tableau was that both officers were leaning backward in their chairs, with their feet on the table before them.

My friend escorted me through the building, which was furnished and equipped with as much concern for taste as for efficiency. Evidently a great deal of careful thought and practical planning had gone into producing this establishment. It was not long before, as I expected, my friend gave the President full credit for the idea and its execution.

Because my time was limited, I could see only a little of the whole, but it was enough for me to realize that part of the challenge which these Africans had to face was the need to hurdle decades in their rush to catch up with the times. Much of what I saw bore the unmistakable stamp of the present, but the young men with whom I spoke, though evidently of no high educational attainment, were putting their best feet forward and doing quite well at it, I was told.

My driver proved to be a very entertaining fellow and an excellent chauffeur. His small hands rested lightly on the wheel, seeming to caress it into the curves in perfect harmony with the action of feet on clutch and brake. He wore dark glasses against the glare of the bright sun, but his mobile features were accustomed to laughter and generally remained relaxed in a kind of half-smile, the sort of thing one sees on the face of sleeping infants. He maintained a lively chatter as we drove along which at first I found very difficult to understand; there seemed to be no end to his words—or so it sounded to me. "Friend" was "fren," "man" was "ma," "time" was "ti," and so on, but by listening attentively to him, I soon got the hang of it and from then on I realized how very knowledgeable he was about all sorts of things.

We rushed through roadside villages of snug little bungalows of wood or cement blocks, with here and there a tiny hut of primitive thatchwork, the old and the new tightly sandwiched together beside the wide modern highway. We were driving through open country, green and rich-looking, rolling softly in a way reminiscent of the Seine valley around Normandy. At Kakata we suddenly encountered the strange sight of two ultramodern buildings, one on each side of the roadway. The larger one, The Cuckoo's Nest, was a gaily painted two-storied weekend rendezvous, with bar and restaurant on the ground floor and facilities for weekend accommodations and dancing on the upper floor. Kenneth, my driver, told me that only the "Big Shots" used the place; they alone could afford it. The other building, equally ultramodernistic in design and color, was tucked neatly under some large trees; it was the home of the resident manager of The Cuckoo's Nest.

"Who owns this layout?" I asked Kenneth.

"I think it belongs to the Old Man's daughter," he replied. "Perhaps it belongs to the Old Man and his daughter runs it, something like that. I'm not sure."

About a hundred yards beyond The Nest was the wide, imposing gateway leading to the President's Montserrado country residence and farm. Immediately inside the gateway was a gatehouse, a large bungalow-type structure with a wide patio, on which lounged several men and women, possibly off-duty guards; beside the gate were two guards in dark blue uniforms, pistols on their hips. Ken told me that the uniformed men were part of the President's personal bodyguard.

"The Old Man's farm is really something to see," Ken said. "I drove one of the Old Man's guests in there some time ago. Wonderful, you know, smooth macadam roads, everything nice, and his house . . ." He smacked his lips loudly to express the ultimate in perfection.

In talking with Ken, as with other Liberians I had met so far, their love for the President was unmistakable. They spoke of his possessions with pride, as if somehow they shared in everything he owned. They also spoke of him with the same deep affection one had for a very familiar relative, who was approachable at all times, helpful at all times. Even the younger men, I realized upon reflection, though critical of governmental policies and the attitude of certain ministers, exhibited the same deep regard for the President.

At Kakata the macadam-surfaced road ended, and now we trailed a thick cloud of red dust behind us from the laterite road, which, however, led wide and smooth ahead of us. Here and there we passed powerful grading machines at work to keep the roads a level, all-weather network throughout the country. At one place Italian engineers were building a wide by-pass through a low hillside, using an interesting collection of heaving tractors, graders, rollers and other equipment. The engineers in charge were European, but the hands operating all this equipment were African. The fairytale of the seven-league boots had a lot of meaning here, for I felt sure that some of these drivers were handling equipment which was the most up-to-date in the world—in the evenings they would return to their small, unlighted huts to rest.

Ken kept the speedometer hovering around seventy miles an hour—"Not too fast," he claimed. Just that much faster than "Not fast."

We passed Salala, Repula, rode through the bustling townships of Totota and Gbanka, and on through the thicker forest growth from Kpein to Gahnpa. Here and there we made a short stop along the open country to relieve ourselves, or at a village for water. These villages were the tidiest I had so far encountered in Africa. Whether wooden or thatch huts, the grounds were always neatly swept and free from the ugly collection of garbage which had been a familiar sight in other places.

Women were forever sweeping; the children seemed clean and healthy; but I noticed that the water supply, the creeks and river-shallows still supplied the needs for both drinking and washing. However, the general cleanliness was a start in the right direction and must surely have required a tremendous amount of health education to achieve this degree of popular cooperation.

At Gahnpa we turned south towards Tapeta. Now the road was somewhat narrower as it cut through thicker forest regions filled with tall trees, some of them already dead and waiting for the high wind which would blow them over to rot among their fellows or to straddle the roadway until removed by the villagers. Our progress was twice halted by these obstructions, which, Ken told me, could be even more frequent during the rainy season.

Sometime in the early afternoon we stopped by a roadside fruitstall, where oranges, bananas, mangoes and papayas were displayed, although no attendant was in sight. Ken sounded his horn, and from a pretty creeper-covered bungalow emerged a smiling, thick-set fellow followed by a brood of young children, capering and squealing around him. We bought some fruit and quite naturally fell into conversation. He worked as a customs official on the border between Liberia and Guinea, and told a few interesting stories about his experiences on the job. In his own time he operated a small farm—a few acres of rubber trees— together with land on which he produced all the green vegetables, fruit and chickens he needed, with lots to spare.

"I live off the land," he told me, "and it provides more than enough for me and my dependents." This with a nod toward the children.

"How many children have you?" I asked him.

"Eighteen, net," was his amazing reply.

He invited me into his bungalow for a drink, and I assumed that the invitation included my driver, but Mr. Dunbar, for that was his name, indicated otherwise, and, indoors, told me that it was "not done" for drivers to sit with officials and their guests. Later he showed me around his "yard," the tree-crowded area around his house, where oil-palms, mango trees, orange trees and others, wrestled with each other for head-room in the sun. There were two women, both well advanced in pregnancy, working quietly together at some needlework (it seemed to be repairs to the children's clothes). They shyly extended hands in acknowledgment of the introductions, then half-hid their blushing faces behind their work when he said, "I forgot to mention two more in the oven."

He told me that his father, a famous African chief, had had over forty wives and fathered nearly one hundred children; he had no ambitions to equal his father's record, but he intended to get the most out of life.

"I'm thinking of getting married around December," he said.

Immediately I looked at the two women, and he must have read the unspoken question, for he observed, "Not one of those —a new one." He explained that there would be no problem of friction between the women; there was plenty of room for all of them and their children, and enough food and clothing to meet their needs. Anyone who wished to leave was free to do so, but so far no one wanted to leave. The children were from various women, who, if they chose, brought the children and left them in his care. He loved all of them, but his special delight was a pert, chubby-cheeked little girl of about four, who seemed to know that she occupied the favorite position in her father's heart. Some of his older children were away at boarding schools run by missionary organizations. He was a Baptist.

Again I looked at him and the children, so he explained that he was a Baptist by religious persuasion, but an African and a Dunbar by birth and natural inclination; in his heart there was no conflict between the two. He attended church and fulfilled his obligations, but his private life was his own business, especially as he claimed that none of the women ever complained. It was refreshing being with him; everything about him suggested an intense love of life, yet with a strong sense of responsibility.

199

We talked about Monrovia, government, national development, education, other African States, and many other things. I found him quite well informed.

"Here in this backwater I do not think of those things to any great extent," he confessed. "I am primarily concerned with providing for my children and these women. I've a good job, thanks to the Old Man, and I can live quite well. I try to educate myself by reading anything I can, and listening to the radio, and I'll see to it that my children get more education than I did—especially the boys. The girls, well, they'll learn to read and write, I suppose, but fifteen, sixteen, seventeen, perhaps, some young rubber-cutter comes along and the next thing you know they've gone to live with him. After all, it's life."

Before I left he showed me a whisky bottle, into which was crammed a weird collection of cuttings from the roots and bark of trees, rendering the alcohol somewhat cloudy in appearance.

"This is the stuff to keep you young," he said, wagging his finger suggestively. "With a drink of this each day I'll still be laying them when I'm a hundred."

I tasted the bitter, throat-searing brew, and was prepared to accept that it was capable of all the qualities he enumerated. It also required a cast-iron stomach. I left him after promising to share a meal with him on the way back, as there was no alternative route to the north of the country.

*

While I had been chatting with Mr. Dunbar, Ken had had a sound sleep in the car, which he had run under some shady trees, so now he was quite refreshed with sleep and fruit. He did not seem to mind the least bit about being left outside, so I said nothing about it. We were now running into the high forest region, the road a red gully between the thick leafy growth which often met overhead to shut out the sun and close us in a gloomy corridor, pierced occasionally by shafts of bright sunlight. Apart from an occasional magpie and heavy-headed bill bird, there was

200

no sign of wild animal life. No monkeys or squirrels, nothing. I asked Ken about this.

"We used to have monkeys around here, once upon a time," he said, "but the people ate so many of them the others disappeared into the bush—gone to the Ivory Coast and Guinea, I suppose. Only things left are snakes."

We raced through Tapeta, turning southeast to Tchiehn, the farthest point of the highway. We would spend the night there and retrace our steps next day. The road from Tapeta to Tchiehn widened considerably. At the Cestos River we crossed a new, excellent modern bridge, designed in graceful lines of ferro-concrete and steel. Ken explained that it was one of the unification bridges, part of the President's scheme to link the people of the coastal regions with those of the hinterland, that there might be easier and more frequent communication between them. He called it the President's "Unification Policy."

I was deeply impressed by the bridge, because it seemed to be built with an idea to future development in vehicular traffic. Here in the hinterland more and more I got the feeling of growth and thrusting movement. The towns through which we passed were bustling with activity, and, oddly enough, there were very few thatch huts to be seen. In what one might call "the bush" I saw villages of neat wooden or concrete cottages, with roofs of unpainted, corrugated, galvanized iron which glittered in the bright sunshine.

I had letters of introduction from the Minister of the Interior to his resident Commissioners requesting that they give me such assistance as I might require when in their territories; so I sought the District Commissioner at Tchiehn to introduce myself. He was away, but his chief clerk readily made me welcome and arranged accommodations for me. Ken assured me that he had relatives in Tchiehn and would prefer to stay with them.

In the future I shall be very hesitant about using the term "bush" with reference to the African hinterland, because I so frequently encountered the same kind of modern living conditions one might only expect of cities and major towns. In the Rest House, where a room was placed at my disposal, there were bath, shower and toilet facilities, electric lighting and refrigeration, a very comfortable bed and easychairs.

After a meal, the chief clerk showed me something of the D.C.'s compound, the administration building, residential quarters, and the central courtroom, or barrier, where the D.C. held court and dealt summarily with simple cases. As we walked around he told me something of the many and varied problems inherent in the commission.

"The D.C. has to be father, brother and boss at the same time. He must be sympathetic, approachable, fair and friendly, but when he gives an order there must be no doubt that he intends it to be obeyed. It's the only way to deal with these people."

He made it sound as if both he and the D.C. were somehow different people from those of whom he was speaking. "Is your D.C. a sort of justice of the peace, or has he some special training in dispensing the law?" I asked.

"Well, I suppose you can say his commission covers all that. In dealing with most cases it is usually a simple and straightforward matter of deciding who's right or wrong, who's guilty or innocent, or what piece of property belongs to whom. Sometimes it's not so simple as that, and then it might be necessary to use what you might call 'trial by ordeal.' "

Into my mind flashed visions of the frightening ordeals I had read about in histories dealing with the Middle Ages of European development. Somehow that sort of thing seemed very remote from this quiet compound, with its modern bungalows and the regular whirr of the electric power generator.

"What kind of ordeal?" I asked.

"The usual kind," he replied. "Hot coals, broken glass, sharp knives, things like that. Doesn't take long to sort out the guilty party."

He made it sound supremely matter-of-fact, as if I ought to know and understand. I should have let the matter lie there, but my amazement forced me into indiscretion.

"But can you really accept that sort of thing as decisive?" I asked. "Surely the very thought of stepping on hot coals would be enough to frighten anyone into confessing to an act of which he might well be innocent. . . ."

202

He looked at me with what seemed to be a mixture of doubt and pity, as if he was not quite sure whether I was merely putting on an act. Then he said, "No innocent person ever needs to confess. If he's innocent, he's safe."

"Then why do you need to resort to law at all?" I persisted.

"I suppose one must move with the times," was all he said.

Time and again I was discovering that behind all the indications and examples of encroachment from outside, especially from Europe and America, there was a hard nucleus of essentially African thinking which cocked a defiant snoot at change; a moment ago he was talking of "these people," as if from a great distance of better educational and social opportunity, yet now he was fully identified with them in this presentation of primitive justice.

We walked out of the compound and the main road toward the village. The sun had set, but a pleasant twilight persisted, softening the harsh outlines. Here and there, between the houses, groups of women were gathered around blazing fires on which huge gasoline drums emitted thick clouds of steam.

"What are they cooking?" I asked him.

"Palm Oil," he replied. "They boil the kernels until all the oil is extracted from the pulp, then when it cools they drain off the oil. Old-fashioned, perhaps, but effective."

We passed groups of young men and boys sitting together in friendly conversation by the side of the road. Any woman or girl I saw always seemed to be busy at something or other; only the men had time to chat. He led me down a side street to a bar, a dilapidated one-room structure, so arranged that there was yet ample space for some roughly made tables and chairs near a narrow counter, behind which there was barely room for the large resplendent refrigerator and the even-larger barman. A curtained aperture beside the refrigerator led into another room, or storehouse, for the barman dodged into it quite regularly to restock the refrigerator. On the counter was a record-player, which bawled pop music into the room, making conversation difficult, but the half-a-dozen-or-so men sitting with their drinks seemed undisturbed by it.

My companion waved greetings to them and introduced me to

the barman, who, it seemed, was the proprietor and a local chief. He insisted that we have a drink with him, but didn't seem to notice that we were all shouting at each other over the noise of the music.

Gradually it became quite dark in the bar and a lantern was brought in. Then I realized that the refrigerator must be either gas- or oil-fueled. The lantern seemed to make little impression on the gloom, instead it attracted a large number of flying insects. Someone suggested that it would be better sitting outside, so we each took a chair and moved out, reforming ourselves into one group.

I was introduced to everyone, and they went through the now-familiar routine of surprise and interest on discovering that I was not African. They wanted to know what I was doing in Africa, in Liberia, and then came the flood of questions, about everything in the wide world, it seemed to me. They were surprisingly uninformed: Where was British Guiana? What kind of people lived there? Were the West Indies somewhere in India? And questions like that. What was it like living in England and France? They'd heard tales about black people in the U.S.A. and Britain, ugly tales of indignity and maltreatment. "Always the nasty things get noised abroad," I thought.

When I tried asking questions there were few answers, and the little said was guarded. So I let it slide, and we talked about things like the palm-oil crop, and the new Unification Bridge, on which several of them had worked.

Presently the chief clerk said he wanted to return to the compound, as he had some matters to attend to. I wanted to stay awhile longer with the group, so he left me. As I had vaguely suspected, he represented authority, and with his departure the men spoke more freely. Life was not easy and their complaints were numerous, but they assured me that things would soon be put right when the Old Man returned.

I learned that the President visited each district periodically, and those were occasions when every man or woman had an opportunity to be heard. Anyone could say his piece without fear, and complaint could be made against the district commissioner himself.

204

To hear them tell it, the President dealt justly with each complaint, and was no respecter of personalities or positions. They told me of instances when he had commanded officials to refund monies which had been unjustly levied and of officials publicly reprimanded. They believed in what the President said and did, and all insisted that the President was a man of his word.

What was so amazing about all this was the feeling of identity each one of them had with the President. I got the feeling that to each one of them, William V. S. Tubman was more than the head of State; he was father and friend, and so sure were they of the relationship that the many irritations of local officialdom were bravely to be borne, together with the everyday insufficiencies of food, clothing and shelter, until his next visit.

"I'd like to be a writer, like you," someone said. "I've got plenty of things in my head I'd like to write about—things about Africa. I've got a book in my house, with a map, a big map of Africa, with colors—with red for places that belong to the British, and green for places that belong to the French, and other colors for other places in Europe. I don't think there's any color for America. Maybe they haven't got any place, at least not yet. Liberia is yellow, because we're a republic, I suppose. Other places want to be like us, become republics. I've been hearing about the Congo, they want to be a republic. I'd like to write a book about Africa, telling about what will happen when all the countries become republics like us. Sometimes we listen to the radio from Sierra Leone, and we hear about those other places in Africa. Sierra Leone will be a republic soon, won't it?"

"Not a republic," I replied, "but independent."

"Not the same thing?"

"No, not the same thing."

"Anyway," he went on, "when they all become republics we'll tell those countries in Europe to keep out. I'll put it all in my book. We'll tell them that if they touch one African republic they touch them all. We'll tell them, 'Look, man, you interfere with one of us, we all get mad at you, because we're all Africans.'

"It's funny, though, about some Africans. Two, three years ago me and my good friend traveled way up to Gahnpa, where is French

Guinea. We stay there nearly three weeks and one day we meet this man with three women. They were selling stuff, you know, skins and things carved from ivory and black wood, and other things, handbags, sandals. But those three women, tall and straight, and they look at you as if you're only big as a mouse. Jesus Christ, those women had black stuff on their hands and feet from dyeing cloth and stuff, but you only had to look at them. Man, I wanted a piece off one of them something terrible. So I get near to her. But you know what happen? That woman looked at me like I was small, small, and she says, 'I'm a Mandingo woman.' Just like that!"

As he recounted this misadventure, so clear was the imagery he presented that we all laughed heartily.

"So what did you do?" someone asked.

"Nothing. What could I do? But the funny thing is, she was an African, wasn't she? 'I'm a Mandingo woman,' she said, as if she was a queen or something."

"You want to write that down in a book, Joe?" someone asked.

"No, but I'd like to write something else in my book. I'd like to say that an African is an African, whether he is Mandingo or Kru or Mande or Vai."

"Keep thinking about it," I said. He was the first Liberian I had met who spoke of wanting to write. "If you want to do it sincerely enough, you'll do it, one day."

"Not me, good friend," he said, shaking his head negatively. "Never. I never went to school, so I cannot read or write. But it's all up here, here in my head."

We talked and drank, while the moon rose overhead, cool and friendly with her retinue of stars. I could hardly believe that it was really me, here, now, sitting with these pleasant men, simple men who were accustomed to measuring distances by the number of days required to travel from A to B; for them any discussion of affairs outside Tchiehn, outside Liberia, was an adventure into the unknown, so vast was the picture conjured up by the word "Africa." Another thing, my black skin made me immediately welcome, my willingness to be friendly and sympathetic made me acceptable. For the time being Paris seemed a million miles away.

206

The next morning Ken and I made an early start. He seemed in very fine fettle and had a parcel of food someone had prepared for him. As we passed through the village he honked his horn outside a tiny hut and a stout, smiling young woman rushed out to wave excitedly at us. Ken acknowledged it, a wide smile on his face.

A few miles along the road from Tchiehn we met a land-rover from the Department of Health Education in Monrovia; the two young men in it were health educators, whose job it was to visit each village and hamlet in the area and confer with the residents on ways and means of improving their local health conditions. Now I understood why the villages through which we had passed all looked so clean and free from garbage. Although the young men were living rough while on trek, sleeping wherever night overtook them and eating where and when they could, they were full of enthusiasm for the job they were doing. For me it was another example of progress without fanfare.

We stopped for a brief visit with Mr. Dunbar, then proceeded toward Gahnpa and Sanokole. Here and there we passed village schools, most of which seemed to be operated by one or another of the American missionary organizations, probably the same kind of mission school to which Mr. Dunbar owed his education and where some of his children were being taught.

There seems to be no limit to the vast fund of good will in the world, irrespective of the labels under which it operates. What is surprising is that so little of it is effectively used. Time and again I saw plenty of evidence of the life and work of American men and women dedicated to service for a religious principle, but, in my view, achieving very little in terms of positive results because they quite unselfishly tried to do everything for the African, believing that he was fundamentally incapable of doing anything for himself, by himself. "Childlike faith" was a term often used in reference to African converts.

I stopped to visit one of these schools—a simple, neat, wooden structure on the edge of a smooth, green playground. It must have required many months of patient backbreaking labor to produce this patch of orderliness where everything grew unchecked. The children, all boys, were romping with a small football. One of them, a skinny youth, did wonderful feats of control with his bare right foot and the ball. They were all dressed in a simple kind of uniform, shirt and shorts of cotton material, and seemed happy and well cared for.

Inside the schoolhouse were the usual paraphernalia—desks, benches and blackboards. I spoke with one teacher, a thin, pale American man of about thirty-eight, earnest, sincere, and probably very good at his work. He was completing his second field tour and would soon be returning to the U.S.A. for a vacation and posting to another field station. His task was to teach his young charges reading and writing and the elements of healthy living. There was religious instruction, but it seemed to be complementary to the other pursuits and not an end in itself.

As I talked with him, it occurred to me that whether or not they realized it, he and others like himself were responsible for setting many young minds on the arduous road to inquiry and discovery. He was providing the key which would unlock the first of an unending recurrence of doors to the varied storehouses of knowledge and information. Would there ever come a time when those self-same inquiring minds would wish to pursue discovery and experience among people unlike this missionary, whom they probably loved and trusted? Was there any way in which he could now prepare them to meet the new and sometimes disturbing challenges which might lie ahead?

*

Approaching Sanniquellie we were diverted around a big road building project. An American company had set up its construction and maintenance depot, and the African air was vibrant with the loud sounds of modern man at work. Several types of heavy cranes and bulldozers were snatching huge mouthfuls from the red hillside, while others were leveling and pounding the earth into smooth conformity. We did not stop to inquire about the project, but continued on to Sanniquellie.

208

This was an eye-opener! The town center was a crowded, untidy agglomeration of shops and small dwelling houses, most of them uglier than the huts they must have superseded, because they were designed in the style of huts and only succeeded in looking uncompromisingly solid, like individual prison cells. The central street cut its way callously through these buildings and became wider where the administration section spread itself in a pleasant tree-shaded meadow with soft rough-cut lawns. Here the buildings were smart, freshly painted bungalows and two-storied buildings, and I had the feeling that this was the new pattern of development and that eventually the ugly slumlike conditions in the center of town would give way to improved structures like these.

We called on the District Commissioner and were courteously received. After a most refreshing wash he showed me around; beginning with the new centralized school in the heart of town; a series of well-designed single-storied buildings set in a pleasing grassy campus. Although only about a year old, it was already achieving an enviable reputation as a progressive coeducational institution.

I was told of the extensive assistance Liberia had received in furthering her educational programs from the United States International Cooperation Administration, which, as the need indicated, provided everything, including school buildings, equipment and specialists in teacher-training, and advice on administration and plans for reducing illiteracy. UNESCO was also playing an important part in Liberia's planned educational programs. I was told, with pride, that the modern, new two-storied building in which the D.C. lived recently served as the meetingplace for top-level talks between President Tubman and Guinea's President Sékou Touré. Its many modern facilities included air-conditioning. From the many things I was shown, it was evident that Sanniquellie was being developed as an important center, in keeping with the President's plan to unify all Liberia into a progressive, viable entity.

All the persons I met were officials of one sort or another. All were eager to sing the President's praises, to give him credit for every positive idea, every success or achievement in the drive toward progress. It was like a Litany, well-rehearsed and familiar, yet so naturally expressed that I was easily persuaded of their sin-

209

cerity. However, whenever I veered my questioning to matters of Liberia's relationship to other African States, there was little response, and that little expressed in the vaguest of terms.

After making sincere approving noises about the house where the two Presidents met, I asked about the extent of cooperation between the two countries and was told, "We get along as good neighbors should."

"Was there much movement between Guinea and Liberia?"

"Yes, the people have always been in touch, to and fro."

"Any likelihood of ideological interaction resulting from such movement?" I was trying to surprise them into some kind of spontaneous response.

"Not much chance of that. The movement was predominantly among traders of one kind or another who were mainly interested in buying and selling, mostly diamonds. Besides, Liberia would not be fruitful ground for new ideologies."

Careful and a wee bit smug. "What about other African States—Ghana, Sierra Leone, the Congo?" I asked.

"Liberia is on the friendliest of terms with everyone. As for the Congo, Liberia has taken the lead in most of the resolutions relating to the crisis-ridden country."

I was then given an example of the President's stature. Recently, it seemed, Tshombe of Katanga had cabled President Tubman, suggesting his interest in visiting Liberia, but the President had quickly replied, advising Tshombe that such a visit would not meet with public approval, and Tshombe's personal safety could not, in the circumstances, be guaranteed.

So it went. No one seemed willing to express a personal opinion which was not quite obviously "in line," so I allowed myself to be shown and told about all the nice things. Perhaps they were not very keen to speak freely with a stranger, especially a stranger who wrote things down.

*

In the late afternoon I left for Gbanka, where I planned to spend the night before shooting north to Zorzor, Voinjama, and Kolahun. We arrived late in the evening, yet, with typical unquestioning hos-

210

pitality, the District Commissioner quickly made arrangements for our accommodation, and in a way which assured me of a sincere welcome. This was something I encountered throughout Africa, this predisposition to friendliness. Before leaving for my African trip I remember having chatted about it with a European colleague. We got on the subject of aid to Africa, and I think I expressed the view that Africans might not wish always to be on the receiving end—they too might like to be givers.

"What in the world could those people from the bush give to advanced Europe?" he asked in amazement.

Now each day I was finding the answer to his question. Africans and other so-called backward people could teach the rest of the world a few lessons in friendliness, now, before they too discarded as useless and old-fashioned these simple and encouraging reminders of man's kinship with man.

Early the next morning, after breakfast, I wandered on foot around the village. Near the administration compound, in front of a low building, several score of schoolchildren were gathered in a rough semi-circle about a flagpole, from which fluttered the single star and stripes of the Liberian flag. When I caught sight of them, their arms were raised in salute, and I could hear a murmur of sound as they repeated something, probably their daily oath of allegiance. "Very much in the American manner," I thought.

I waited until the ceremony was over, then approached and asked to see the headmaster.

He was a short, slightly built African. I explained that I was visiting the village and had myself been a schoolmaster in England. He welcomed me and showed me around his school, which catered to children of both sexes from about eight to sixteen years of age. I noticed that most of the children carried several textbooks and was told that the children had to buy the books they needed.

Listening to scraps of conversation between the children, I found it very difficult trying to understand them. Their intonation was American-inflected, but the words were deprived of their endings and sounded strange and un-English. The headmaster introduced me to the members of his staff, two of whom were Americans, one black and one white. For them this stint was both a challenge and an experience in living, but they were candidly critical of the setup,

211

deprecating the fact that the curriculum and textbooks were "too American."

One of them told me, "Most of these kids learn to read and write, after a fashion, but few are able to apprehend quickly what they read. You see, they have not grown up with the habit of reading, so it is mainly a schoolhouse chore. If you listen to them you'll know what I mean. Books are things they like to own—as if they could become literate merely by association with the books —but there is very little interest in inquiry, or appreciation of the pleasure to be had from reading.

"This does not mean that they lack ambition. They all want to be doctors and lawyers and scientists, something big, but such ambition is not related to serious study and application. They all hope to go to college, preferably in the U.S.A., and seem to imagine that by some strange process the mere fact of being in an American college will transform them into brilliant people."

"Part of the trouble is an insufficiency of schools," his colleague suggested. "Right now, in this school, we have to cope with a wide range of age and ability in each class, and one has to be content with the little positive result achieved. With more school space it would be possible to grade your children and teach more effectively."

"Perhaps," the other agreed, "but even with what schools there are, much more could be done by better planning, especially at primary level. Better methods. Teach the infant to think while teaching him to read and write. Make books meaningful to him. In my view somebody will soon have to begin to think of producing educated Africans instead of half-educated quasi-Americans."

They said they were both enjoying their stay in Liberia.

"What are your impressions, so far?" I asked.

The black one replied, "You quickly discover that a black skin does not make one African. I'd never before realized how American I was, not black American, just American. So many things I once took for granted now appear terribly significant, probably because I'm forced to do without them—newspapers, radio, novels, conversation, friends. Guess if I remained here long enough I would either forget about them or find substitutes. You know, you see something funny or read something and want to talk about it,

212

and it's not easy to communicate the whole thing if there is no point of common reference, no understanding of the nuance which springs from an appreciation of mutually familiar circumstances. Guess these fellows feel the same way when they are in the U.S.A., even if they too are in a predominantly black group."

"And you?" I asked his white countryman.

"I came over here to teach, that's all. It so happens that the people here are black. That doesn't matter one way or another. Sometimes I'm irritated, pleased, frustrated, pleasant, sad, what have you, but it's all part of the business of teaching. It would be the same wherever I was, but it is the thing I want most to do."

It was time for school to commence, so I left them, and shortly afterward Ken and I were on our way north. Near Belefuanai we stopped to refuel at a small filling station. Chatting with the attendant was a young officer in the blue uniform of the President's personal guard. He came over to us and spoke to the driver, who turned to me and said, "The officer wants us to take him back to Gbanka."

"Nothing doing," I replied. "Tell him we're headed in the opposite direction."

At this the officer—he wore a lieutenant's metal chevrons on his shoulder—came over to my side of the car, his right hand resting lightly on the pistol holstered at his hip. "I've got to get to Gbanka."

It was like something out of a cheap cops-and-robbers film, the right hand vaguely implying some kind of threat. My temper is not always dependable and suddenly I was angry. "You'll just have to do what you would have done if we had not come along," I replied.

"I can commandeer this car." (I think the word he used was 'commandeer,' although I got his meaning more from his manner than from the words he used.) He flicked open the holster but made no attempt to withdraw the pistol.

I turned from him and said to Ken, "Just what the hell does this fellow think he's doing?"

Poor Ken was quite agitated. Perhaps he better understood the situation and knew, from experience, what might happen. He opened the door, walked around to the officer and whispered to

213

him. Whatever Ken said must have impressed him because, without another glance at me, he walked off to lean sullenly against the petrol pump.

The attendant had been observing this interplay intently from a safe distance. Now he hurried over and filled our tank, eyeing me slyly.

Once more on our way, I asked Ken what he had said to the officer.

"I told him that you were a big man from Europe, and that the Old Man himself had given you this car to do some special business. Those fellows can make a lot of trouble just because they are close to the Old Man. He had a gun."

Yes, he had a gun, and that meant power. Maybe it was well that Ken had acted so correctly and avoided an unpleasant situation. Men with guns are very prone to rely on them as the final argument.

*

Zorzor, Voinjama, Kolahun, all were spaced nearly equidistant along the continuous borders with Guinea and Sierra Leone, each a counterpart of the other, presenting an incongruous but encouraging juxtaposition of primitive and modern living, modernistic multi-storied buildings here and there rising alien and somewhat contemptuous above the small metal-lidded huts and shops.

On the road we passed the nameboards of training establishments, one for teachers, and the other for agricultural students, proof that lots of things were happening here in the interior which escaped attention in Monrovia. Anyway, I was eager to get back to the capital, among other things to arrange for my flight to Ghana. I suddenly realized that although I had traversed much of the country, I had not seen a single wild animal, not so much as a field mouse. Perhaps they had either been hunted to extinction or fled before the advance of the bulldozer.

*

Back at the hotel it was a treat to step out of my dusty clothes and soak myself in a warm bath. I had dinner in town and a good

214

night's sleep, and the next morning went to the Ministry of the Interior to thank the minister for the many courtesies I had received upcountry through his good offices.

The Minister of the Interior received me very graciously and expressed his gratification that I had had a pleasant and interesting trip. I had arrived as he was about to perform a small ceremony, and he invited me to witness it.

Soon afterward a senior member of his staff entered the room. The minister introduced us, then, from a small casket on his desk, he took an intricately engraved metal decoration suspended from a wide silk ribbon striped blue, white and red. This he placed over the head and around the neck of his colleague, saying that the decoration had been conferred on him by President Tito of Yugoslavia, but unfortunately he was ill and away from his office during the President's visit. It was one of several decorations which President Tito had conferred on staff members of the Ministry of the Interior.

Later that afternoon I went down to the Air France office and made a reservation for a flight to Accra, the capital of Ghana, on Sunday. I retired early that night and slept late into Saturday morning. I was not the only one. I met Chuck Randell at the restaurant doing justice to a large breakfast of ham, eggs and coffee. He had returned the evening before from upcountry.

"How was the trip?" I asked.

"Fine, fine." His enthusiasm seemed somehow watered down. "How was yours?"

I gave him a quick rundown on some of my impressions.

"I moved around quite a bit upcountry," he told me, "but I can't say that I liked a great deal of what I saw. Things are happening, of course, but there was not enough involvement of the people at the lower levels. At least that's the opinion I got while up there. You see, they're building roads. Okay. But it's always with a few bulldozers, a couple of white technicians and a handful of African laborers. At the same time hundreds of men are sitting around idle in the villages. I figure they could do the job just as well without the bulldozers and lots more local labor. It would kind of give the people a stake in what's going on. I figure it this way. Back home everybody wants to help Africa and they're pouring money over here. That's fine, but the money should be for things the Africans cannot do for themselves. Wherever you go you see guys blasting around in big American cars, going no place. Where the heck does all that money come from? I figure these people could do a heck of a lot more for themselves if American money was not so easily available."

His youthful face was taut with concern and serious reflection. "You know, pal, that idea about me putting in a bid for the Peace Corps thing is not so hot. I don't figure I'd fit in with it. Wherever I go the place is lousy with guys from home throwing their weight around. I guess the Africans put up with it because of the dollars. What the heck do you think a few guys like me could do here? Nothing. I figure we ought to get down to serious talking with the Africans, not only here, but in other places—you know, tell them they can get on with some things for themselves. Jeez, it's crazy! Guys upcountry won't walk a couple of hundred yards. They've got to drive, and all of them talking crazy bop talk."

"Sounds to me like chickens coming home to roost," I said.

"Christ, is that all that America stands for? Do you know that whenever these Africans want free education and training they point their noses Stateside, but those who can pay for it go to Europe. What the hell do we in the States think we're doing! I figure we'll have to change our whole attitude in dealing with them. I got to talking with a guy up at Bomi Hills, he'd done some training Stateside. You know what he said? He told me, 'You Americans need friends in Africa to support you against the Communists, and that kind of friendship costs money.' That's what that guy said."

"Only one man's opinion, Chuck."

"But if you look around you can see it's a pretty general attitude. Say, did you get up to Zorzor and Voinjama? Did you see the block buildings they're putting up? All that expensive stuff upcountry where simple building could do as well or better! And people sitting around all day on their asses waiting for work!"

We left the restaurant and wandered along in the bright warm sunshine. Near the President's mansion a body of about a hundred soldiers was drawn up for inspection; they looked very young and

216

inexperienced and aggressively self-conscious in their green khaki uniforms.

"Everything is like a mirror, a crazy distorting mirror, of America's influence here. Those guys look just like American dogfaces, but different. Perhaps this bunch is due for the Congo."

"Cheer up, Chuck, it could be worse."

He accompanied me to my hotel where we found Ken comfortably asleep on the back seat of the car. We drove out to the beach at Sinkor for a swim, and afterward I sent off some telegrams to Accra and Kumasi to inform some people to whom I had letters of introduction of the date and time of my arrival.

*

Next day I was at the airport at least half an hour before takeoff time. There was no attendant at the arrivals section, and when one finally arrived he brusquely told me I was too late to board the plane, which was sitting outside on the tarmac like a huge somnolent bird. After some argument he dealt with my ticket and I was passed through customs and immigration. The flight controller, however, refused to let me board the plane. He insisted that I should have been at the airport an hour before takeoff time, and reminded me that it was so stated on my ticket, in the small type.

His attitude was rude in the extreme, quite unlike anything I had ever previously experienced, so there was nothing to do but return to Monrovia. Luckily, Ken had driven me to the airport and had waited to see me leave; now he rushed up to help take my bags to the car.

The Liberian customs officer had observed the *contretemps* between me and the controller. He came up to me and said, "It often happens this way, if the passenger is black; but white people arrive only a few minutes before takeoff and they rush them through to the plane. These American bastards like to treat our people like dirt."

Because of his remark I took another look at the plane. It was a Pan-American Airways jet plane from Robertsfield Airdrome to

Accra—direct flight. Something else, the customs officer must have thought that I was a Liberian, hence the "our people."

"I'll make a protest when I get back to Monrovia," I told him.

"Save your breath, good friend," he replied. "Do you think they care? What will your protest do? Last week six people from Guinea were here about twenty minutes before takeoff and they wouldn't let them travel. Protests won't help. They run this airfield."

However, as soon as the Air France office opened on Monday I presented myself and made my complaint. The French staff was most helpful and arranged a flight for that very afternoon. About the other thing, they shrugged. "We get many complaints like this," one said, "but there is nothing we can do. Perhaps you might like to send a formal protest to P.A.A. headquarters in the U.S.A., but I'm not sure that would do any good. Maybe one of your ministers could help, or even bring it to the notice of the President."

"I'm not a Liberian, only visiting," I said.

They shrugged again.

I was more than an hour early on Monday. The clerk at the counter remembered me and carelessly remarked to a colleague, "If you're tough with them they learn in time, or walk."

I was very angry at this needless insolence, and told him I thought his conduct in the entire incident was unbusinesslike, bigoted and extremely stupid.

He ignored my outburst and merely remarked to his colleague, "This one is a talker."

218

Part Four
GHANA

My seat on the plane did not allow me any sight of the city of Accra before landing. My first sight of Ghana was the nearly deserted arrivals lounge and the charming, attractive air hostess in a smart white uniform who attached herself to me and led me quickly through customs and other formalities.

There was no one to meet me and I felt rather dismayed at the prospect of scouring the town in search of a hotel room. I mentioned my worry to her and she led me to the inquiries desk on the off chance that there was a message for me. No message, but the inquiries clerk remembered that someone had been there the day before inquiring for me. My name had been on the flight manifest but there was no information about me.

Next, with the names and addresses of two persons to whom I had letters of introduction, we tried telephoning, but without result. My air hostess then suggested that I book at the nearby hotel and try to contact my friends on Tuesday morning. That Monday was a holiday (Easter Monday) and those who could, usually went into the countryside, so it was very possible my friends were out of town for the day.

She found a porter to take my bags and walked across the courtyard to the hotel to ensure that I found a room. Her entire demeanor was courteous, helpful and very charming; in startling contrast to my most recent airport experience. I should like to pay this small tribute to her, and all those other hostesses of other countries who, through their cheerful and considerate conduct, contribute immeasurably to the comfort and pleasure of air travel.

I secured a room and, after a shower and change of clothing, went into the hotel lounge. It was a large all-purpose room, roughly sectioned-off into dining area and bar lounge. Along the front of the hotel was a wide covered veranda equipped with collapsible chairs and tables. Both the lounge and veranda were crowded with people of many nationalities. Indians, the women in colorful saris, bright-eyed but silent, while the menfolk kept up a continuous loud conversation in Hindustani; African men and women in their na-

221

tional dress; a group of six British Army sergeants sitting around a table loaded with beer bottles, applying themselves seriously to their drinking; a happy crowd of Lebanese drinking to someone's birthday anniversary; Germans, Frenchmen, Americans, Czechs; small children climbing up the slim steel pillars which supported the veranda roof; waiters hurrying to and fro laden with frosted bottles and tinkling nuggets of ice. Hurry, bustle, and some confusion.

In a corner of the lounge, a Mandingo peddler crouched on the floor, his knees drawn up to his chin, hands hidden within the folds of the striped robe, which nearly concealed him. Close by was a wide assortment of native craft and handwork exposed to tempt the tourist. As soon as anyone paused by his wares, his face would immediately pop into view, ready to go into his spiel.

There was an air of excitement about the place. I found a seat on the veranda, ordered a drink, and gave myself up to savoring the "ambience." Across the street huge bulldozers, tractors graders and other earth-moving machinery were creating a wild, clanking cacophony amid thick clouds of red dust, as they leveled and pounded the earth to extend the airport's runway facilities. Trucks laden with building material lumbered back and forth along the road. People, people, on foot, on bicycles, in cars, on trucks, hurrying people, as if every one of them were caught up in a collective race against time. New arrivals, passengers in transit, and locals taking advantage of the pleasure of being, even temporarily, involved in the atmosphere of travel to far-away places.

I hardly noticed the change to night, or that the noises now were concentrated around the veranda and lounge. The sky had become a black void in which the stars were pendulous and bright; large insects battered themselves vigorously against the light bulbs, then fell to their doom underfoot.

When dinner was announced I was one of the first to be seated. All the tables were set with places for four, and it was amusing to watch the way in which everyone tried to find an empty table. When this was no longer possible, the latecomers looked the guests over, deciding with whom it would be agreeable to sit during a meal.

I was finally joined by an English family of three—husband, wife, and eighteen-year-old son. After nodding to me in greeting, they

222

restricted their conversation to themselves, and I was able to gather that they owned a farm in Kenya and were on the way to Britain, combining a holiday with the boy's entry into an agricultural college. Now and then I looked at their faces, trying to make up my mind about the kind of opening gambit which could make our enforced propinquity more comfortable.

I could not help overhearing the mother's reminders to her son about keeping warm in Britain. She promised that they'd go shopping together in London. The boy, a husky fellow, more reddened than bronzed by the African sun, was somewhat embarrassed by her motherliness. He occasionally darted a glance in my direction, probably hoping that I either was not listening or could not understand. It was so funny I could not help smiling. The boy noticed and blushed; the mother looked at me and smiled; the father looked at me and said, "It's his first visit home since he was eight."

Just like that, as if they were as anxious as I to break the ice.

"It hasn't changed much," I replied, "only colder."

"He thinks I'm fussing," the mother said, "but it will be very different from Africa."

"I agree. I've only been in Africa a few months and my main preoccupation has been keeping cool."

"Aren't you an African?" the father asked.

I explained that this was my first visit. Soon we were chatting in the most friendly fashion about Britain, the boy's scholastic possibilties, and the things they planned to do on their holiday. They said nothing about life in Kenya, and I did not inquire, although I wished I might. I think we all enjoyed our meal.

*

Next morning I again tried telephoning my contacts, this time with some success—one of them promised to call for me in an hour. In the interval I took stock of my surroundings. The airdrome was set some distance off an arterial road, or so I judged from the heavy vehicular traffic moving to and fro. So British, I thought, easily recognizable by the way the traffic kept to the left; to change

223

it would be a major operation. One way or another the British left an indelible mark on Africa.

Across the road was a pleasant housing site of bright two-storied units, arranged on the side of a grassy knoll intersected with paved roads. A passerby told me it was one of the new "villages" for aged ex-servicemen and their families. Behind the village small sections of land were available to them for market gardens or for raising chickens. Soon after nine o'clock my friend Josh arrived in his car. We had some coffee while getting to know each other. He was a junior civil servant studying law in his spare time and saving to go to Trinity College, Dublin, for further study and qualification.

We drove into town along a smooth macadam road, past smart new drive-in petrol stations, under roadway arches gay with bunting in the colors of Ghana, past houses and bungalows hiding discreetly behind trimmed hedges, very much in the English fashion. There was an air of cleanliness, order, modernity and comfort here, and I was told this was one of the residential sections. We passed the roadway leading to the presidential quarters, indicated by flags and a sign prohibiting the sounding of horns. Farther along the road was green, tree-shaded parkland, a cool and inviting interlude before the huge fashionable hotels and towering blocks of offices.

We passed under an arch erected in memory of ex-servicemen who were shot during a protest march in the struggle for self-government, and outside the House of Representatives I saw the life-size statue of President Nkrumah—Josh referred to him as Osagyefo—in short-sleeved open-necked shirt and slacks. At the base of the statue was the inscription "Seek ye first political freedom and all other things shall be added unto you."

"Is the name 'Osagyefo' the African equivalent of 'President'?" I asked.

"No, it means Redeemer," Josh replied.

This was unlike any African town I had yet seen—with banks, shops of every kind, offices—but for the preponderance of black faces I might have been in the business section of any large European town. Our first stop was at a bank, Barclay's, because I needed to get some local currency. The staff was mainly African, but here and there I saw a European, English specialists, probably, men and women. My general impression was of quiet order and assurance. Clerks, supervisors, messengers, everyone seemed concerned with the job at hand. I was attended to with the same courtesy and dispatch as were the other clients, black and whites.

Afterward I was shown around the town. There were new buildings everywhere. Tall edifices of gleaming glass and stone, some colorfully painted, like the new Trade Union Building and the Co-op Building, the latter in pleasing harmony with the trees and grassy space carefully preserved around it.

"This is Ghana," Josh said, proud. "All this is Ghana, the Ghana we built in less than five years."

We drove through the crowded, busy, shopping center and parked, as I expressed a wish to see the street market. I had heard about the Ghanaian "market mammies," now I saw them—large, muscular women, looking as powerful and durable as bronze or ebony. I paused by a stall where two of them were chatting together in dialect and roaring with deep laughter, their broad, damp faces and sparkling teeth suggesting a love of life, a pleasurable satisfaction in living. One of them said something to me but I did not understand. My friend replied in the same dialect. Then the woman said, in English, "Don't only visit, come and live with us."

Her companion whispered to her in dialect; she laughed and replied, "I'd have to fatten him up a bit first."

I got her meaning and laughed, wondering what kind of giants their husbands must be.

As we walked, my companion said, "They're very powerful, those women, economically and politically. You'd be surprised at the amount of business they control, especially with local produce."

"And politically?"

"Most of them are party members, the Convention People's Party, you know. They're solidly behind the Osagyefo. And there's the National Council of Women."

"I'll agree with the 'solidly' bit."

He grinned, acknowledging the point. "That's very obvious whenever there's a procession or a visit from some foreign dignitary; they're always well represented. Anyone who tried to undermine the Osagyefo would have to reckon with them."

225

"Are they only active in the party?"

"Generally speaking, yes. But women as a whole are taking their place equally with men in every department of our national life. You saw them in the bank. They're in the civil service, the professions, industry, the Builders' Brigade, everywhere. However, they never make equality an issue."

This section of town was truly international. Among the tide of black faces could be seen Europeans and Asiatics, while the names on the stores were German, Indian, Pakistani, British, French, and many others. It was a stimulating experience, being in the crowd. The African women, for the most part, wore variations of the national costume: an ankle-length, wrap-around skirt, or *lappa,* and a close-fitting jacket which flared at the waist. Some of the younger women carried a stole of the same material slung elegantly over one shoulder. The market mammies wore colorful headkerchiefs, while the business girls and others went bareheaded, their hair modishly styled. Josh told me that because the lappa was a simple square of cloth, a woman could easily pack a dozen changes of clothing into a suitcase and have them uncreased and ready to wear.

It had now become, for me, terribly hot, and I envied his cool, neat appearance. We returned to the car and he remarked, "All this is Ghana. With a few notable exceptions, all this is new. Now I'll take you to see what remains of the Gold Coast."

After a few minutes' driving we entered a shabby slum section of littered streets and tumble-down buildings, a shocking sight after the elegance I had just left.

"All this will soon disappear," Josh said, with quiet emphasis. "These people are gradually being rehoused, and we'll be able to rebuild this place in keeping with our dignified standards."

We moved on. The more I saw, the more I marveled. I had not expected anything so advanced, so attractive. Men and machines working on a new highway, part of it already in use with a modern roundabout and road marking to help control the heavy traffic. Away from the center of town the planners were maintaining the close relationship between man and nature by preserving as many shady trees, flowering shrubs and grassy sections as possible near and between the bright new buildings. Several new streets, squares

226

and parks were named after the President. New buildings were rising everywhere—flats, offices, shops, schools, churches. One church, near the C.P.P. headquarters, was one of the most gracefully modernistic I'd ever seen.

"That's our cathedral," I was told.

I was taken into the C.P.P. headquarters, colorful outside in blending pastel shades, cool and even more colorful inside. The walls of the entrance hallway were covered by vigorous murals depicting Ghana's struggle toward independence, and a light, graceful stairway led upward to the offices of officials on the middle floors, and those of the party secretary on the upper floor, which provided a clear view of the surrounding area.

"The Osagyefo will soon be taking over the office of party secretary," Josh said. "By the way, how long do you expect to stay in Ghana?"

"Until the week-end. My flight to Paris is booked for Sunday next."

"Okay. I've arranged for some time off, so we can see as much as possible of Accra and run up to Kumasi for a couple of days. Let's have some lunch now, and later this afternoon I'll try to get you to meet some of our leaders."

We lunched at a fashionable new hotel some distance away from the crowded town center. The restaurant was a separate single-story building designed to take full advantage of light and air. Patrons could dine in the spacious dining hall or on the wide, shaded veranda. There was a delightful touch to the place. The waitresses, all African, wore uniforms—a bright replica of their national dress.

"This is something of an experiment," Josh said, "not only here, but in Africa generally. Previously there were no waitresses. Men served as waiters, houseboys, gardeners, etc., while the women remained at home. I have an idea that it was a kind of conspiracy to emasculate the African. Anyway, as women are moving into everything, they are now being trained to wait on tables. This is the first batch. When their training is complete, they will go out to staff other new hotels being built here and in other parts of the country."

"Is it a private venture or governmental?"

227

"Governmental. This hotel is part of a government-sponsored scheme, and many others are on the way."

"Do the girls like the idea of waiting on tables?"

"Judging by the way they're rushing to get in, they like it. It is well-paid, dignified work. No tipping is allowed, so they can feel the same pride of service as any other worker."

The girls were handsome and well formed, with a certain shyness, which added to their attractiveness. Perhaps after a year or two they'd be as tough and blasé as waitresses the world over, unless . . .

"As with most other jobs, I expect many of these will leave to be married?" I asked.

Josh considered that for a while, then replied, "Perhaps, but there will always be others. Plenty of others."

Remembering other countries, I asked, "Is this a polygamous society?"

"Oh, yes. Now and then somebody or other starts talking about a 'one-man, one-wife' law, but that always gets the women up in arms and it's soon forgotten."

"Would they not benefit by greater personal security?"

"Only a few. As things are, no child is considered a bastard, because if a man associates with a woman, she is, by local custom, his wife. A child born to her is her child, and has its place as a member of her family. Fathers acknowledge their children and support them as they are able. Some men prefer to have one wife, but most of us have two or more."

He'd included himself. More than one wife—working days and studying nights. I took another, more respectful, look at him, to better evaluate his talents.

"In Europe I've attended many meetings where the rights of women were discussed. I had imagined that, in a polygamous society the status of a woman is, to say the least, very low."

"That's typical of the outsider," Josh replied. "They always know more about us than we do of ourselves. In fact, any attempt to change the present arrangement is always met by vigorous opposition from the women themselves. Let's face it, women outnumber men in this country, and the way things are, everyone is served."

228

He appreciated the double-entrendre in his remark and laughed heartily with me.

The meal was excellent, but pervading everything was the consciousness of Africa, of Ghana. These Africans were relaxed in the consciousness of dignity with purpose; one could nearly reach out and grasp a handful of the energetic spirit.

Afterward we drove around, looking at the continuous building, building—there seemed to be lots of work and no idlers in sight.

I was taken to the headquarters of the Builders' Brigade, a kind of civilian army of workers, where youths of both sexes received training as engineers, carpenters, cobblers, blacksmiths, anything and everything designed to fit them for a useful life in their society. They all wore khaki uniforms and were supervised by a corps of tough, smart ex-servicemen who seemed to take great pride in their responsibilities. I sat awhile with a group of them and exchanged wartime stories while my companion made some telephone calls. When he returned, he told me a short interview had been arranged with the Minister of Defense.

*

The minister, the Hon. Dr. Graft Dickson, a slim, well-tailored African, received me very courteously and, after formally welcoming me to Ghana, chatted with me about my visit and promised to extend to me any help I might wish. He told me that his home was in Ashanti, and invited me to visit him, but this was not possible, as my stay was not long enough.

"I've a surprise for you," Josh promised when we'd left the minister.

Now we drove toward a headland where a high, turreted building was in process of repair and extension. Workmen swarmed everywhere.

"This is Christianborg Castle. An integral part of the history of our struggles," Josh said. "It was once the residence of the Governor. Now we are reconditioning and extending it as accommodations for important guests of state."

No visitors were allowed in the precincts while work was in

progress, so I had to content myself with the little we could see from the road. All this was a source of obvious pride to my companion. Even when he spoke of the castle dungeons and his forbears, who were imprisoned or perished there, he seemed to derive added stature and satisfaction from the telling, and the knowledge that his roots ran deep in the very earth itself.

We drove along the coast road, the tires singing in counterpoint to the crash of the huge breakers on the rocks; fishermen with circular seine nets waded waist-deep in a shallow, flooded area on the other side of the road. Farther along we passed the farms where girls of the Builders' Brigade were clearing the ground and tending rows of vegetables. At intervals along the road were signs indicating sites reserved for Government, with warnings against anyone else attempting to build on them.

"Where are we heading?" I asked.

"Wait and you'll see. It won't be long now."

The road now swung inland in a straight line across flatland too sterile to support more than separated tufts of tough, withered grass. In the distance I could see the tops of tall derricks, and soon we drove onto a flat plateau where an army of workmen was engaged in a wide variety of tasks. We parked and followed a concrete pathway which was crisscrossed by inset rails, to a wide concrete apron from which several docks projected into the sea. On these docks were the tall new derricks and cranes which I had glimpsed as we approached along the road.

"This is Tema Docks," Josh said, with as much pride as if he had singlehandedly built it himself. "Not long ago all this was wasteland, with only a tiny fishing village to give it any identity. Look at it now!"

I looked. It was a massive feat of engineering. The length of the docks suggested that they were designed to accommodate ships of any draught. Running to and from each dock was a network of railway lines, which led off to a central marshaling yard some distance away. Storage and other sheds were in various stages of completion, together with many types of installations and services necessary to the effective operation of a busy port.

"When completed, it will be the premier port of Ghana," Josh told me. "But this is only part of it. Let's go."

230

We drove out of the port section, along a wide, newly paved road, to another building site. In Britain I had seen the building of entirely new towns, complete with schools, shops, churches, pubs, etc. This was a similar project.

"This will be Tema Town," my companion said. "A new town to accommodate the workers and businesses which are indivisible from port life and would otherwise spring up unplanned and unlovely. We've tried to anticipate as far ahead as possible the nature and extent of development likely to occur."

There were smart new office buildings, shops, schools, and housing units for one, two, or more persons, with adequate garage space for car-owners, and plenty of playground facilities for children as well as adults. The designers seemed to have considered everything, including the color scheme, which was as pleasing as the careful landscaping. Some workmen, digging a deep ditch to contain a sewer pipe, were singing as they worked—a resonant, rumbling sound, strange, new, yet immediately familiar.

Looking at all this I remembered a remark by a Ghanaian visitor to Monrovia. He had said that "Ghana was capable of imagination and hard work." That seemed to be borne out here.

*

That evening we did a spot of pub-crawling, starting with hotel bars after dinner and winding up at a dance hall soon after midnight. I enjoyed the music immensely, the compulsive, teasing, seductive "high-life," and danced until the perspiration streamed off me. In the dance hall I noticed an appreciable number of Europeans, some of them with African partners. They all seemed relaxed and thoroughly enjoying themselves. For the first time since I arrived in Africa I saw Africans and Europeans mixing socially in an atmosphere of ease and relaxation. The women were very exciting, probably because of the naturally sinuous way in which they responded to the music, their bodies half-hinting all kinds of pleasures.

I woke around three o'clock in the afternoon, showered and went down to the lounge, where I had to make do with beer and a reluctant cheese sandwich. I had brought my scratch pad, and hurried to write down all I could remember of the events of the previous day.

Now, as I edit and reshape my report, I try as far as is possible to confine myself to the facts. In reproducing conversations I have always tried to repeat what I heard, as far as my habit of making notes each night makes this possible. None of this report is contrived or created for effect. Sometimes, however, I find it advisable, even necessary, to use my own words, the better to relate the whole scene, or create a kind of sequence where in fact conversation had been an interlacing, excitable exchange which often overlapped as we eagerly intruded on each other. Now I wrote until nearly six o'clock, when Josh arrived.

First he took me on a short trip to see the University of Ghana, and then to the house of a friend, where several men and women were gathered to meet me, I was told. We drank and talked, mostly about literature, especially about what they referred to as "Negro literature." Here I jumped in with both feet, because I do not subscribe to the idea of so-called Negro literature any more than I do to "white" literature. I said that I wrote as I felt, that I wanted to write, had to write and wanted to write about life—all life—refusing to restrict my interests by considerations of the thin capsule which could not restrict any thinking, or loving, or feeling.

There was talk of the "African presence," as if it were some special kind of spiritual essence peculiar to Africa. I made the observation that my enforced separation from Africa may have diluted to invisibility whatever claim to the essence should have justifiably been mine because of my color. They argued against me, but in sophisticated, friendly fashion. I enjoyed being with them, and was often amazed by their wide appreciation of contemporary European literature and thought. They occasionally spoke rather scathingly of Britain and the British, but never forgot to mention their association, however limited, with British institutions, especially the universities.

Naturally we got around to politics. Some of them were party members. For my benefit it was explained that they followed a Socialist ideology and were not Communists. Someone said, "It's odd, but there's socialism in Britain as in many other European countries, but no Briton or American can accept socialism for Africa. If we show any inclination to follow our own political course, we're immediately called Communists."

"Perhaps it's not merely your political ideology, but . . ." I was interrupted by a handsome girl, who was clever, witty and conscious of her obvious attractiveness.

"I know what you're going to say: we're friendly with the Communists."

I was going to say no such thing, but I let her carry on.

"We're an independent state, and we've got to have the courage to independently run our country and choose our friends. Why should we let anyone tell us who our friends should be?"

"There's no such thing as friendship, internationally speaking"— one young man said—"only associations, which are subject to being bent, twisted, broken and mended, as situations dictate. Internationally speaking, a country, especially an African country, should be prepared to take full advantage of friendly associations while the situations are favorable. At the moment Africa is riding high and everyone is eager to wipe our noses, but who knows?— tomorrow it might be South America or China or Lapland. Then, to hell with Africa!"

This was greeted with general approval.

"Like those nice, shiny aircraft on the airdrome?" someone asked.

"Yes, like those. Did you see those big Ilyushin planes on the tarmac when you arrived?" he asked me. "Gift from Russia—six of them. That's what I call friendship."

"Nothing for nothing and very little for sixpence," I replied, paraphrasing an old Guianese saying.

"I'm all for accepting all they have to give," another said, "but meanwhile we must learn to do things for ourselves, just in case the supply is suddenly cut off."

"We're not the ones who need to worry," the girl said. "It's those new states which are supposed to be independent but are content to sit up and beg from their old masters like performing dogs. Some of them would even fight against us if de Gaulle or MacMillan told them to. Sons of bitches."

I was surprised by her vehemence, and language, but I did not

233

show it. It was probably intended to shock me, anyway. We talked about the Osagyefo, the party, neighboring African States, the Congo, Angola, space travel—anything. They spoke freely and intelligently. Before I left them I learned of several Guianese residing and working in Ghana, all doing very well.

*

As planned, Josh and I set out for Kumasi early on Thursday morning, following the smooth-paved road out of town and out into the green countryside, through sudden villages and hamlets where I glimpsed uniformed children at play, old men chatting together and wives busy at household chores, their tiny infants securely slung on their backs. Often, on the edge of a village could be seen a few modern houses, to where the wealthy retreated from the bustle of Accra, Josh said. The road curved snakily up a steep hill, on top of which was perched the Osagyefo's new house, under construction. Looking backward across the steep slope, Accra could be seen in the distance, indistinct, like a postcard picture of Bethlehem at Christmas.

We stopped at a village, as it suddenly occurred to Josh that he should telephone his wife at Kumasi to let her know he was on his way. This was significant to me—telecommunication between villages and towns and individual dwellings.

There was an air of prosperity about the towns and villages through which we passed—shops, stores, filling stations, all well stocked and clean—and the people seemed cheerful and neat, especially the children, fat, cheerful, and noisily healthy. But the hospitality took on a somewhat menacing note. Here and there Josh decided to stop on one pretext or another—water for the radiator, or to see a relative—and someone was sure to offer us a drink: "At least one beer, only one, just to please us," they'd insist; or "a little whisky, perhaps." They made the "perhaps" sound like "of course." I stuck to iced beer, but Josh refused to hurt his friends and relatives and drank the whisky. However, this seemed in no way to interfere with his driving, and soon after noon we reached Kumasi.

234

I had thought it would be a village, or small town, at best, in the depths of the countryside. What I saw as we drove slowly in were bright new houses and bungalows, stores, cinemas, blocks of flats —in short—Accra reproduced, only newer, perhaps cleaner, if that were possible. It was fantastic. New buildings in every phase of construction!

"That's the general hospital," Josh said, pointing to a huge, beautiful white building surrounded by lawns and shrubbery. And so it went! It was difficult to keep in mind that this was Africa, in the bush.

We lunched at a government hotel and then drove to one of the Rest Houses, where I would spend the night—a neat, well-equipped bungalow with bath, toilet, electricity, refrigerator, a small lounge and two comfortable-looking beds. The uniformed attendant took charge of my bag, and Josh and I set out to meet some of the town's notables.

First I was taken to meet the Mayor of Kumasi, the Hon. James Owusu, a short, thick-set, pugnacious-looking man, who welcomed me warmly to Kumasi in sharp, clipped English. He invited me to attend a ceremony that evening at the Kumasi Zoo, where he was making a presentation to an Indian *mahout* who had brought a young elephant from India to the Kumasi Zoo and stayed long enough to see it settled down comfortably.

"If you can stay until tomorrow afternoon," the Mayor told me, "I'm opening an exhibition at our central library. Russian books. You know any Russian? Come if you can. Pleased to have you."

When we left him, Josh said, "He's the most influential man in Kumasi. If anything is to be done, he gives the say-so."

If Accra surprised me, Kumasi went one better. I was not quite prepared for the wide-paved streets, large modern buildings, and obvious effective functioning I saw everywhere. We visited the Department of Health, and there I ran into an old London university colleague, Ohene Darko, a health-education specialist, with whom I had shared many an amusing episode during our days together in London.

The Kumasi Cultural Center is situated in a pleasant park. Here an attempt is being made to preserve the old and historic and

235

at the same time give impetus to the new and progressive. In one corner of the park is a life-size reproduction of the house of a Ghanaian chieftain as it existed centuries ago, complete with courtyard and a Tree of Truth. Artistically woven royal clothing, beds, stools and the chief's bath were all there, excellently preserved, as were a set of "talking drums," which were played for me by a young assistant to the curator.

Some short distance from the chief's home was an exhibition hall, an elegant structure of stone and glass, which now housed a one-man exhibition of carvings in bronze and wood by a local doctor. The general idea, as Josh put it, was to make Kumasi as big and as important as Accra, and was part of an over-all development plan to prevent too much migration toward the coastal strip. The same depth and extent of development was going on at the coastal towns of Takoradi, Cape Coast, Salt Pond, Sekondi, and others. Now, through the Volta Dam and other projects, it was hoped to transform the northern territories into an important industrial district.

On Josh's advice I returned to the Rest House for a nap. He went off to see his wife, and promised to call for me at seven that evening.

The presentation ceremony was a simple affair, attended by a handful of persons. The Mayor made a short speech and, in the name of the people of Kumasi, presented to the *mahout* a beautiful robe of *kente* cloth, that distinctive interweave of gold and blue which is peculiar to Ghana. Afterward I became part of a group in a local bar, returning to my quarters around midnight. The attendant had thoughtfully prepared me a bath of cool water, and it was heaven to lie full length in it.

*

Early next morning I was awakened by the attendant. He had brought me a cup of tea. I could not help smiling as I recalled the many stories I had read of this most British of institutions in the most unlikely of places. Near the bed I noticed a small radio, and,

236

more from curiosity than expectation, I turned the switch. Coincidence can play strange tricks. From the radio came a few crackles of static . . . then a clear voice saying, "This is London calling in the Overseas Service of the B.B.C. Here is the news."

I nearly dropped my tea, placed it carefully on a side table, and howled with laughter. The amazing juxtaposition of tea and B.B.C. was too much! Good Lord! That brash young woman the other night had said something about "ridding ourselves of everything that could remind us of colonialism." How was she going to achieve that? Tea and the B.B.C.! No, my girl. If the truth be told, you'll wind up loving them to death, without even realizing it. Those British! Those goddamned crafty, farsighted British! Tea and B.B.C.! What a combination!

Josh called for me at around ten o'clock and we went to the zoo to take a look at the gift elephant. Although only a few months old the ponderous animal was colossal, yet rather pathetic and lonely. Josh was as interested in the animals as I was and confessed that it was about the only way he had of seeing wild animals, or, at least, anything as wild as these.

We spent the morning cruising around some distance beyond Kumasi—green, rich country, people everywhere. Even where the forest growth was thickest one would come upon neat little bungalows surrounded by a space cleared of trees and producing lush green vegetables. The villages were clean and orderly, probably the result of the Health Department's active program. Whenever possible I stopped to chat with the locals, and found them to be charming, friendly people.

We arrived at the Russian Book Exhibition on time, but the affair did not get underway until about an hour later, much to my irritation, as we planned to return to Accra as soon as possible to avoid having to drive too far into the night. I was introduced to the visiting Russians, and would hazard a guess that they too were less than pleased at the African's casual attitude to time.

When finally all was ready, the Mayor read a short speech, the Russian representative replied, and the Exhibition was declared open. There was no time for me to examine any of the large number of books and periodicals displayed, so Josh and I, after farewells all round, were on our way, non-stop to Accra.

*

Next morning I went to the Air France office and checked my flight reservation—past experience was still a sharp reminder. I met Josh as arranged. He seemed very pleased with himself, and before I could ask the reason, he thrust a copy of a local newspaper, *The Evening News,* into my hand. I read it all. Apparently the Osagyefo had broadcast to his people very early in the morning. It was a forthright and telling message indicative of his intention to "promote greater efficiency in the machinery of the Government and tighten up party discipline."

In the speech the President expressed his determination to make war on ostentatious living, vain pride, haughtiness in high places, and a contemptuous attitude toward the masses. He said, among other things:

> I have stated over and over again that members of the Convention People's Party must not use their party membership or official position for personal gain or for the amassing of wealth. Such tendencies directly contradict our party constitution, which makes it clear that the aims and objects of the party among other things are the building of a Socialist pattern of society in which free development of each is the condition for the free development of all—a pattern of society consonant with African situations, circumstances and conditions.
>
> I have explained very clearly this Socialist structure and have on many occasions elaborated the Five sectors into which our economy may be divided.
>
> These sectors are: first, the state sector, in which all enterprises are entirely State-owned; second, joint State-owned private sector, which will incorporate enterprises owned jointly by Government and foreign private capital; third, the cooperative sector, in which all enterprises will be undertaken by cooperative organizations affiliated with the National Cooperative Council; fourth, the private-enterprise sector, which will incorporate those industries which are open freely to foreign private enterprise; and fifth, the workers'-enterprise sector.
>
> I have had occasions to emphasize the part which private

238

enterprise will continue to play in our economic and industrial life. A different situation arises with Ghanaian businessmen who attempt to combine business with political life.

Being a party member of the Assembly—and much more, being a ministerial secretary or a minister—means that the persons who take up these positions owe a duty to those who have elected them, or who have given them their positions with confidence.

To be able to maintain this confidence, therefore, they should not enter into any type of industrial or commercial undertaking. Any party member of Parliament who wishes to be a businessman can do so, but he should give up his seat in Parliament.

In other words, no minister, ministerial secretary or party member of Parliament should own a business or be involved in anyone else's business, Ghanaian or foreign.

In spite of my constant clarifications and explanations of our aims and objectives, some party members in Parliament pursue a conduct in direct contradiction of our party aims.

They are tending, by virtue of their functions and positions, to become a social group aiming to become a new ruling class of self-seekers and careerists.

This tendency is working to alienate the support of the masses and to bring the National Assembly into isolation.

I am aware that the evil of patronage finds a good deal of place in our society. I consider that it is entirely wrong for persons placed in positions of eminence or authority to use the influence of office in patronizing others, in many cases wrong persons, for immoral favors.

I am seeing to it that this evil shall be uprooted no matter who is gored. The same thing goes for nepotism, which is, so to speak, a twin brother of the evil of patronage.

At this point, I would like to make a little divergence and touch upon civil service red tape. It amazes me that up to the present, many civil servants do not realize that we are living in a revolutionary era. This Ghana, which has lost so much time serving colonial masters, cannot afford to be tied down to archaic snail-pace methods of work which obstruct expeditious progress.

We have lost so much time that we need to do in ten years what has taken others a hundred years to accomplish.

Civil servants, therefore, must develop a new orientation, a sense of mission and urgency to enable them to eliminate all

239

tendencies toward red tape-ism, bureaucracy and waste. Civil servants must use their initiative to make the civil service an effective instrument in the rapid depelopment of Ghana.

Let me now come back to the party. It is most important to remember that the strength of the Convention People's Party derives from the masses of the people.

These men and women include those whom I have constantly referred to as the unknown warriors—dedicated men and women who served the party loyally and selflessly without hoping for reward.

It is therefore natural for the masses to feel some resentment when they see comrades whom they have put into power and given the mandate to serve the country on their behalf, begin to forget themselves and indulge in ostentatious living.

High party officials, ministers, ministerial secretaries, chairmen of statutory boards and corporations must forever bear this in mind. Some of us very easily forget that we ourselves have risen from amongst the masses.

We must avoid any conduct that will breed antagonism and uneasy relations. Let us always keep in mind the fact that constant examination and correction are necessary for maintaining the solidarity of the party.

The aim of all corrections, however, must be to build and not to destroy. The central committee proposes to issue instructions shortly on the duties and rights of party members.

Finally, I wish to state that in considering remedial measures, I have found it necessary to direct that a limit be imposed on property acquisition by ministers, party officials and ministerial secretaries in order to enable them to conform to the modest and simple way of life demanded by the ideals and principles of the Convention People's Party.

Countrymen: Our mission to Ghana and to Africa and the unique personality of our party as a vanguard of the African Liberation Movement, impose upon us increasing responsibility, not only to set our own house in order, but also to set very high standards from which all who seek to emulate us shall draw devotion and inspiration in their own struggles.

I wish you all good luck and a good week-end.

"Well, what do you think?" Josh asked me. He had sat smoking as I read.

240

"In my opinion, any leader who makes statements and demands such as these, must himself be free of any taint or suggestion of complicity in similar pursuits," I replied.

"Right. No one can point a finger of accusation at the Osagyefo."

"Cannot or dare not?" I asked.

"Cannot! The Osagyefo has no personal fortune or financial interests, because his needs are provided for by the party. But personally, he lives very simply and neither smokes nor drinks. As you rightly said, only a man who himself leads an exemplary life would dare make such a broadcast."

"What do you expect the reaction to be among the officials at whom this is aimed?"

"Something in the nature of a 'thunderbolt in the great hall.' Some big heads are likely to roll. Man, I could name names. The Osagyefo has not made a single unfounded claim. Lots of officials have been blatantly misusing their position in every conceivable way, and it's high time some action was taken. The rank-and-file of the party has begun to grumble, and the matter has been raised at several study groups recently."

"Study groups?"

"Oh yes it's part of our party structure, so that activists and others can keep abreast of Socialist thought and information."

I'd heard the same thing in Guinea.

"Let's walk down to the market and listen to what people are saying about this broadcast," he suggested. On our way he asked, "I wonder what the international press is going to make of it. They're sure to see something ulterior behind it, some weakening of the Osagyefo's personal or political influence. It's as if they deliberately refuse to see the truth."

"Do you mind if I ask you a straight question?"

"Of course not—go ahead."

"Time and again in his broadcast the President made reference to Ghana's mission in the 'vanguard of the African Liberation Movement.' Does this not seem to be an expression of hope or ambition to leadership beyond the national scene?"

"It does not. It merely emphasizes our responsibility to the cause of freedom—beyond our own requirements. It indicates of identification with all people engaged in the struggle for freedom. We in Ghana believe that the eventual salvation of individual African States can only come from the unity of the whole African continent. Without it the imperialists would still have plenty of opportunity to perpetuate economic dependence and racial discrimination among us."

This was familiar ground to him, and he spoke with the assurance of the believer. "But, even as Ghana has found her own way and is plotting her own course toward economic development and eventual solvency, other African States, especially the newly independent ones, may wish to engineer their own destinies, and might resent your attempts at either preaching or teaching them, no matter how plausible or acceptable your doctrines might appear to be.

"It is not a Ghanaian doctrine. It is a simple truism, obvious to any but those who wish to enslave us. Recently the Osagyefo stated that the idea of the desirability of a Union of African States, or republics, was, in principle, acceptable to all leaders and political movements in Africa. Gradually there will be a development forward to examine ways and means. It is inevitable."

We were now among the market crowds. Here and there I caught the word "Osagyefo," but most of the conversations were in the national language or some associated dialect. From Josh's pleased appearance I guessed that whatever he overheard mainly pleased him.

Later he said, "The reaction will set in later, probably next week, after the big boys have had an opportunity to digest the broadcast and evaluate their own positions."

"Suppose they got together and decide to resist?" I asked.

He seemed amused at the very idea. "Resist whom? The Osagyefo was not speaking on behalf of President Nkrumah, he was speaking on behalf of more than four and a half million people, and he was speaking on behalf of the Government and the party. They would resist at their peril."

He left me at my hotel after we had agreed to make a big night of it, my last night in Ghana. The newsboys were doing a brisk trade among the guests in the hotel lounge and veranda, and there was undoubtedly a great deal of interest in the broadcast. I retired

242

to my room to write, as I wanted to make some verbatim extracts from the broadcast.

*

That night I'll long remember. First we went to a small party, where I ate large helpings of local food and met several Guianese, who were now working in Ghana. Some of them were boyhood friends of mine, and it was wonderful to have a reunion so far from home, but in such pleasant circumstances.

Afterward we again did the rounds. I drank very little, but something deep within me seemed to have opened up to absorb all it could of the people, the sounds, the color, of Ghana. In just a week I had seen very little, yet enough to convince me of the enormous potential which can emerge from a willingness to work and a belief in one's destiny. There was much I did not understand, but judging on the evidence of things seen and heard, there was a great deal I could and did admire. Before parting, Josh and I drank a small toast to what had been for me a wonderful, wonderful experience—a kind of homecoming.